C000024784

Boating with Buster

DEAR PETER AND KIRSTEN,

Boating
with
Buster

THE LIFE AND TIMES OF A BARGE BEAGLE

WITH BEST WISHES,

[signature]

Alison Alderton

Copyright © 2018 Alison Alderton

The moral right of the author has been asserted.

Apart from any fair dealing for the purposes of research or private study, or criticism or review, as permitted under the Copyright, Designs and Patents Act 1988, this publication may only be reproduced, stored or transmitted, in any form or by any means, with the prior permission in writing of the publishers, or in the case of reprographic reproduction in accordance with the terms of licences issued by the Copyright Licensing Agency. Enquiries concerning reproduction outside those terms should be sent to the publishers.

Matador
9 Priory Business Park,
Wistow Road, Kibworth Beauchamp,
Leicestershire. LE8 0RX
Tel: 0116 279 2299
Email: books@troubador.co.uk
Web: www.troubador.co.uk/matador
Twitter: @matadorbooks

ISBN 978 1789014 389

British Library Cataloguing in Publication Data.
A catalogue record for this book is available from the British Library.

Printed and bound by CPI Group (UK) Ltd, Croydon, CR0 4YY
Typeset in 12pt Gill Sans by Troubador Publishing Ltd, Leicester, UK

Matador is an imprint of Troubador Publishing Ltd

This book is dedicated to the memory of

Buster

And is for all those whose hearts he touched

Contents

Foreword

WENDY HALL

I was five years old when I had my first encounter with a Beagle; my father came home with a two-year-old dog called Buster. Being the middle child of five girls, my dog became my best friend; we would go everywhere together. Living in the country, he was never on a lead. He would trot alongside me when I was on my bicycle and, when playing with other children, if one of them pointed a toy gun or even a stick at me, Buster would knock them over and take it away; never aggressively, just determined.

Together with my husband, Doug, we have had our own Beagles since 1966. We got our first 'show' Beagles in 1968, two sisters whom we had a successful show career with. Our greatest achievement was in 2002 when Champion Cliffmere Quadrant won Best of Breed at Crufts. Doug and I are International Championship show judges and have judged Beagles and Dachshunds in Australia, South Africa, Japan and Europe. We have been Beagle Welfare Officers. Doug is currently President of the Beagle Association, serving on the committee for 30 years as Chairman and Vice Chairman. Currently I'm Chairman of Eastern Counties Dachshund Association. Our whole lives revolve around our dogs.

The first point of contact with someone who wants a Beagle puppy is usually on the telephone. I will spend up to an hour talking to potential owners about the pros and cons of Beagles, which was how Alison first contacted me. She was not put off by my frank conversation. A hound is not for everyone; they are hard work. It takes dedication and determination to train a Beagle and they are the most wilful of hounds. I shall always remember the grin on Roger's face when he held in his arms this six-week-old bundle of trouble. I knew it was the right home for the puppy; they were asking the right questions, wanted to know as much as possible about the breed. Alison and Roger, her husband, took their own Buster home with them when he was ten weeks old and so started this little hound's adventure.

I must admit I had some reservations when, some months later, Alison phoned to say they had bought a barge and were going to take Buster with them. I had visions of this puppy continually falling into the water but I was told he had a life jacket, which made me feel better. Buster became a celebrity in the boating world; his adventures of crossing seas and waterways are well documented. I would receive updates from Alison about his exploits; he always made us smile.

When old age and illness crept into Buster's life, Alison and Roger tailored their lifestyle to fit in with their best friend's needs, always putting Buster first. Thanks to this book, Buster's adventures can be enjoyed by all.

Wendy & Doug Hall
Cliffmere Beagles
Lincolnshire

Foreword

BRIAN CASSELLS OBE

When someone writes of the exploits of their pet, it's useful to be able to say, "Oh yes, I remember them," and this time I can really say I do remember Buster the Beagle! He and I met on the southern shores of Lough Ree, one of the large lakes on the River Shannon, when Alison, Roger, Buster and their barge, *Lily*, lived in Dunrovin, an idyllic nest for any waterway lover.

Personally, I'm a cat lover but I have been custodian for just over a year for my daughter's black Labrador, Olive, so I can empathise with any who have parallel interests: boating and pets. It's obvious how Buster became well known on *Lily*'s waterway circuit; when spotted, he ran forwards to greet me with a constantly wagging tail. I'm tempted to say Alison was easily recognised when Buster was around but you know what I mean, his wagging form had appeared in so many waterway publications; as a pair they were easily identifiable.

I don't know if this is fact or fiction but I can visualise Alison sitting at her computer desk whilst Buster was curled up contentedly at her feet, listening to the click of the keyboard. Alison is a gifted writer. When I asked her to contribute a piece for the *IWAI Waterways* book, she painted a word picture of Dunrovin and the gardens that conveyed the reader into that mystical place where even the birdsong could be visualised in the background. I've followed the exploits of *Lily* and her crew over many years, pottering about on the English canals, even tasting the salty brine before her baptism on the mighty River Shannon, then being transported to Europe where *Lily* began an even more adventurous career on the waterways of Holland before braving the Baltic and now resting in Denmark.

Knowing Alison's gift as a talented writer endowed with a pleasant, affable personality, I look forward to her latest project, her long-overdue description of the many navigational adventures undertaken. Of course, there have been lots of canine waterway stories already written by numerous authors but I know this tale will be different because few writers have that special ability to paint a story with words quite like Alison Alderton.

Alison, it is my delight to be associated with your new book. Knowing your ability to depict pictures with your writing, it will be a success.

Brian Cassells OBE
Author and IWAI Past President
Ireland

Prologue

ALL DOGS CAN SWIM

"I'm going in." The words were clear, loud, to the point.

Knocking the engine into neutral, I turned and saw the soles of my husband's boots disappear as he dived into the swirling grey waters of the river.

I waited.

And waited some more.

Turning back to the controls, it slowly dawned on me this was the first time I had been alone on our 48 foot (15m) long replica Dutch barge. I became aware of the background murmur of the Beta engine and the increasing breeze rustling through the tall trees on the furthest bank. The barge weighed in at a hefty twenty tons and I was alone on her in the middle of the river. Slowly we were drifting; it felt as if too much time had passed. A sinking feeling was beginning to develop in the pit of my stomach. How long should I wait?

Moments before, the sound of barking dogs seemed deafening; the black-and-white Collie charging up and down the towpath incessantly yapping now nowhere in sight, the owners having beaten a hasty retreat with the dog doing what Collies do best – circling and bringing up the rear in an attempt to bind its flock together. Buster, our ship's dog, stood his ground. His reply to the teasing Collie was to raise his hackles, curl his top lip and growl before letting out the unmistakable, reverberating cry which only a hound possesses. Buster's cry stopped the dog in its tracks but not for long. The Collie was persistent and back it came, bolshie, tormenting, thinking it was safe on dry land. Buster let out a bark so deep and powerful it raised him off his feet, causing him to momentarily jump on the spot. Landing heavily, he teetered on the edge of the steel deck before speeding off after the Collie. They ran parallel, the Collie on the bank, Buster on the barge. He circumnavigated the boat successfully on the first occasion but, on the second, he forgot the beautifully curving stern, running straight on to hit the water at speed with all the grace of a bouncing bomb. The enormous thud as his body made contact with the surface sent out a spray of water so elaborate it could compete with any water feature found at a stately home. Roger had followed him just moments later, neither of us aware whether our beloved Beagle could swim or not.

Suddenly, Roger broke through the water's surface and disturbed my thoughts. I let out a long, deep breath, only then realising I had been holding it for all this time, and relief washed over me. Shaking the water from his head, Roger trod water, gathering his thoughts. Turning towards the boat, he raised a hand and I knew he was alright. Straining to see beyond him, I stood on tiptoes and there, six or so yards beyond, was the familiar tan-and-white head of Buster, his long, floppy ears floating weightlessly on the water. I put the engine in reverse and slowly moved closer to them.

Approaching, I could hear Roger encouraging Buster to swim towards him. I reverted back to neutral, not wanting to get too close, aware of the prop spinning beneath.

"Come on, boy," Roger called.

Buster looked at his master, then promptly turned away and headed towards the bank, the Collie dog still on his mind. He swam well and made the bank long before my husband. The breeze was blowing the barge towards the bank so I gingerly let her drift slowly in. Constantly checking the depth gauge, I picked a spot by a tree which I could easily fasten to and let the elements invisibly push me to safety. Glancing back, I saw Buster could not get ashore, the man-made bank preventing him from doing so. Now he was struggling, he reached up and slipped, moved along and tried again. Helpless in the boat, it was a painful sight for me to watch. Then, from out of nowhere, a blur of fast-moving colour caught my eye; a man was running along the towpath to help. He stopped and, leaning down, attempted to lend a hand but, as he reached out to grab my dog's collar, Buster snapped at him. Under no circumstances was he about to allow a stranger, let alone the owner of a Collie, to aid and assist him. Roger was soon swimming up behind Buster and, in one swift movement, boosted him up onto the bankside. The man backed off as Buster launched himself into one of his fiercest howls.

A moment of madness followed as Buster ran to and fro along the bank, picking up the scent of the Collie whilst Roger struggled out of the water, his heavily saturated clothes a dead weight dragging on his body, making movement difficult. Buster suddenly stopped, realised he was soaking wet and shook himself hard, spraying us all in river water. Then, with his head to one side, he dropped his upper body onto the ground. Bottom in the air, tail held high, he shuffled around and around in small circles, grumbling under his breath, first one way, then the other, perhaps clearing water from his ears. With the barge safely moored, I was reunited with my husband and together we watched our mad Beagle in exhausted bewilderment.

"Why on earth did you jump in?" the man asked Roger. "Don't you know all dogs can swim?"

Roger and I looked at each other and instinctively knew what the other was thinking: boating with Buster was never going to be dull …

Section One

ENGLAND

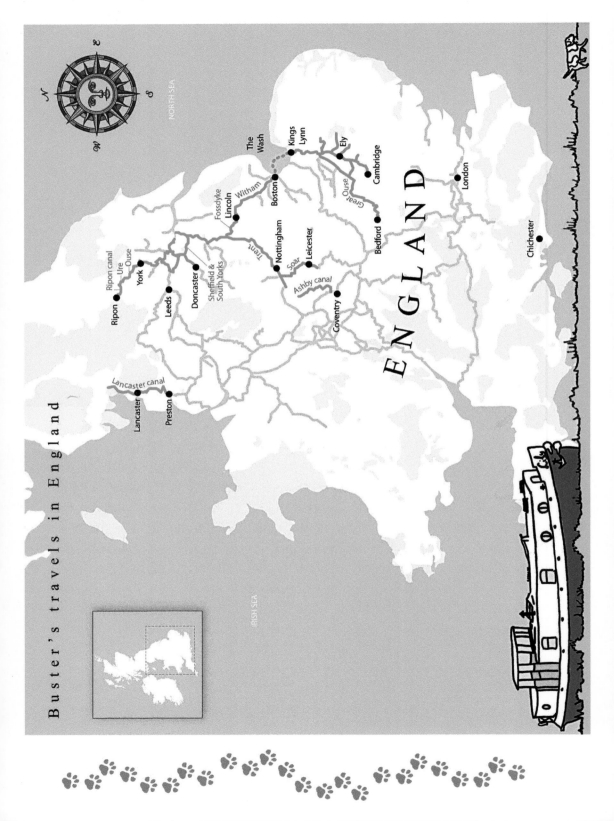

Buster's travels in England

ENGLAND

NORTH SEA

IRISH SEA

The Wash

Kings Lynn

Ely

Cambridge

London

Chichester

Boston

Witham

Lincoln

Fossdyke

Great Ouse

Bedford

Nottingham

Leicester

Soar

Trent

Ashby canal

Coventry

Sheffield & South Yorks

Doncaster

Leeds

York

Ouse

Ure

Ripon canal

Ripon

Lancaster canal

Lancaster

Preston

Chapter One

"A BEAGLE, ARE YOU MAD?"

The Beagle is courageous – a hunter – and can be as stubborn as the day is long. But this is not because he is defiant; rather, that he has been bred to be tenacious when working a scent.

Elizabeth I reputedly had her own pack of Beagles, which she used to hunt hare. These dogs were smaller than the breed as we know it today and were known as 'Pocket Beagles' because they fitted snugly into the huntsmen's large, pocketed overcoats or saddlebags, making them easy to transport. Packs were also referred to as 'Singing Beagles' because of the way they bayed and called to one another.

One of England's most famous ships was named after this plucky little hound. The name suited her well, as she battled through ferocious storms and seas to enable her crew to carry out hydrographical surveys of Patagonia and Tierra del Fuego. Later, under the command of Robert FitzRoy, the HMS *Beagle* made the journey again, this time joined by a young naturalist, Charles Darwin. For five years, the ship explored and charted the seas and coastlines whilst Darwin collected samples from ashore, writing a series of diaries that were later published as *The Voyage of the Beagle*.

3

I had always had a fondness for Beagles. When walking to school as a child, it was necessary to cross a main road and to help was Mrs Thorn, the 'Lollipop Lady'. Her house sat adjacent to the crossing point and, through the iron gates of the driveway each morning and evening, sat her faithful, beloved Beagle. I could not recall whether the animal was a dog or bitch; I did not even remember his or her name but that bold, handsome little hound, which appeared to have eight legs when trotting briskly at Mrs Thorn's side, made an impact on me. When, many years later, I wanted a dog of my own, the memory of this one was foremost in my mind.

Once my husband, Roger, and I had decided that our lives were incomplete without a dog, we did a lot of research, concluding that the Beagle ticked all the boxes. The breed had a short, easy-to-care-for coat, an even temperament and great stamina and was a good size. Best of all, Beagles did not have an overpowering doggy odour: they smelt wonderful – warm and sweet. With walking and boating featuring greatly in our lives, all the Beagle's attributes appeared, on paper, to be a perfect fit. But when mentioning to others that we were considering a Beagle, most raised their eyebrows, shook their heads or even asked if we were mad. These reactions intrigued me. Surely these cute-looking dogs could not be the cause for such concern? I had concluded that they could be wilful but had not been prepared for these negative reactions. However, the more that others tried to put me off, the more determined I became. It was a Beagle I wanted, and it was a Beagle I would have.

The Beagle Association put us in touch with a suitable breeder in Lincolnshire. Doug and Wendy Hall of Cliffmere Beagles were well thought of on the circuit, winning many awards and judging top shows. Wendy spent time discussing the breed and our lifestyles with us – it was as important to her as us that a Beagle was the perfect match for our way of life. Visiting them and the litter of six-week-old puppies, I knew in my mind exactly what I wanted. Roger and I even had a name in mind – Monty – taken from Montmorency, the inquisitive, mischievous Fox Terrier in Jerome K. Jerome's novel, *Three Men in a Boat*. Our new dog would be a boy in the traditional tricolours of a Beagle – black, tan and white – the black forming the shape of a saddle across the middle of his back.

On arrival at Cliffmere, we found the kitchen floor covered in cute, wriggling puppies, a mixture of tricolours and bicolours. Only two tricolours remained, a dog and a bitch. Admiring the tricolours already spoken for, I began to wish we had left home earlier. A plump, bicoloured puppy boldly sauntered up to the baby gate, promptly sat down and gave me a look capable of melting the hardest of hearts. As I leant over to touch him, he became mesmerised by my hand. Stretching further, I tried to brush it across his head. Following the movement, he fell onto his back and there he lay, all four legs wriggling in the air. I liked him, he was a joker, and Wendy noticed the connection. When she took the two tricolours from the room to come and play, she scooped up this little chap too.

The tricoloured boy was the runt of the litter and, although extremely small, was very sweet and appeared bold for such a little thing. The bitch was pretty; extremely affectionate towards Roger, returning to him several times, allowing herself to be petted but ignoring me. Once Wendy placed the bicoloured puppy on the floor, he strode directly over, walked around me and promptly stuck his head up my trouser leg. His warm, wet nose tickled my skin; I could feel the heat from his breath. Retracting his head, he chewed my laces before investigating the rest of the room. Noticing the open door to the garden, he made his escape, followed by Wendy, who quickly retrieved him. Again, he came over to me, this time sticking his head up my other trouser leg before running across the room to Roger. He leapt onto Roger's legs, blasted in on the game with the other two puppies, demanding attention, and got plenty. He was going to be our dog but he could not possibly be Monty – the name did not suit him at all.

Four weeks later, we returned to collect our puppy. I sat in the back of the car, nursing our new bundle; he was warm, soft and comforting. I loved him instantly. A few miles up the road, he began to fidget and look uneasy, then was sick all over me, the towel he was wrapped in and the car seat.

Our new puppy was six weeks old when we first met him

It was not a good start to our lives together but, with the mess cleaned up, he settled down to sleep for the remainder of the journey. The car sickness was problematic. Every evening after work, Roger and I drove a few miles to familiarise our puppy with the motion of a vehicle. Placing him in the car, I whispered in his ear, "I wonder what adventures await the puppy today?" We would almost manage to get back to the house without incident, thinking we had cracked it, when he would throw up. It was a frustrating exercise but perseverance paid off and, eventually, he became an excellent traveller. The car became a safe place for him, his 'time machine' in which he would fall asleep and wake up somewhere else. He never knew where it would take him but he could be sure it would be somewhere exciting.

For a while, we were undecided what to call our new puppy. One of the largest in the litter of twelve, he was chunky; instead of walking around things, he blasted his way through them. With these characteristics in mind, the name Buster was chosen; a far cry from Montmorency and Buster's pedigree name of Cliffmere Union. As with all pets, he had other affectionate names but the shortened version of Buster – Buzz – was most frequently used. He also developed a voice in which he spoke to us. By this I mean the voice we gave him when Roger and I imagined him replying to us, not his natural barking voice. To us, Buster's 'human' voice had a slight intonation of boredom. Nothing fazed him; he was a know-it-all.

Buster had a tan-and-white coat. The rich tan colour fell over his face and around his eyes and long, soft ears. His back was also this luscious colour but his chest, underside and legs were as white as snow, as was his muzzle and the wide blaze down the centre of his forehead. Thick, stubby, ginger eyelashes surrounded his deep brown eyes. At the bottom of his back, right in the very centre, was a white patch which, when viewed from a certain angle, resembled the shape of Australia. On the back of

At home, a crate provided our new puppy with a safe place and was a good training tool

his white neck was a small, circular, tan patch. It stood alone, as if stamped on at the end of a production line, declaring, 'That's it, you're done.' Buster sometimes developed a frown, which gave the impression he had maybe stayed up late, reading a good book. He was a handsome Beagle and rather aloof. He would often look down or sideways at me as if he knew better and, on many occasions, he most probably did.

Roger and I vowed that, once we had a dog, our lives would be devoted to him, and so they were. Buster became our priority; we wanted what was best for him to enable a full and rewarding life. Everything we did was done with him in mind and so, as parents would with a child, we enrolled him in school.

"A Beagle, and this is your first dog. Are you mad?" I looked at the dog trainer in shock. Why would I be mad choosing a Beagle … there was plenty to like about the breed. "What d'you mean?" I was almost frightened to ask, fearful of her response. Did she know something I did not, or had I missed something vital when reading up on the breed?

"Totally untrainable, that's what they are. You'll certainly have your work cut out with this one." She nodded towards Buster, who suddenly seemed small and frail, unlike the bold, boisterous pup he was at home. I looked across the wide-open space of the church hall towards Roger for moral support but he just raised his eyebrows and shrugged his shoulders. "Look at the way he's sitting," the trainer scoffed. As Buster was half hidden behind my legs, I stepped to the side to get a better view. He sat upright but was slouched over onto one hip, his head tilted to one side and facing slightly downwards. His long, floppy ears fell each side of his face, almost hiding his eyes and brushing the tip of his nose. He looked so cute I could not help but feel a big grin spread over my face. As I gazed at him affectionately, intoxicated by puppy love, I became aware the dog trainer was not thinking the same. To a chorus of tut, tut, tutting, she swiftly reached down and, placing her hands each side of Buster's chubby body, pushed up the slouching hip, repositioning him so that he was sitting upright and looking straight ahead. "It's bad for their hips, sitting like that," she said, and walked off to examine the next dog in the new puppy class, a fluffy Golden Retriever who was busy chewing his lead.

I looked down at Buster and his gaze met mine from beneath a deep frown. He let out a sigh, as if totally bored by the whole event, then slouched back down, this time onto the opposite hip. The action had not gone unnoticed and, once the dog trainer had stopped wrestling with the Golden Retriever's lead, she stomped back to us, reached down and again placed Buster in the position she wanted. No sooner had she turned her back on him than Buster did the same thing again. I swallowed a giggle and tried to look harshly at my puppy, who was now grinning back at me from his recumbent position. Perhaps she was right and he would be untrainable but I did not want a dog who would do just as he was told. I wanted my dog to have personality, to be a character. Untrainable he may be but I did not care and, from the look on Roger's face, neither did he. We grinned broadly at each other. It had been a long time since we had had something to smile about.

After developing a fondness for rope toys at such a young age Buster was always going to be good at boating

Once the puppies had been inspected by the dog trainer, it was time to parade them around the church hall. Some walked nicely, others jumped up and tried to tempt their owners to play; one laid on his back and rolled about, refusing to move. The Retriever grabbed his lead and ran off with it in his mouth and Buster scrabbled under a stack of chairs and hid. When I eventually coaxed him out from his hiding place, he trotted alongside me nicely. This was going extremely well, I thought to myself, then he squatted and did a huge, stinky poo, wiping the smile from my face as quickly as he had placed it there.

Still receiving comments about the inadvisability of our choice of dog, we knew no different, and perhaps this was just as well. We were starting our new dog-owning life with one of the most notoriously difficult-to-train breeds, yet this meant nothing; it was all new to us anyway. As it turned out, owning a Beagle and going boating were very similar. There were three factors we took into consideration when boating: you never know what might happen, always expect the unexpected and never take anything for granted. These, we soon found, could also be applied to life with a Beagle.

Chapter Two

THE BOXGROVE YEARS

Boxgrove, nestling at the foot of the South Downs in West Sussex, was our home. The village was small and neat and had a church with the remains of an ancient priory; knapped, flint-fronted houses; a small shop; and surrounding farmlands criss-crossed with public footpaths. Most of the fields grew wheat, barley and rapeseed but, on occasion, we were blessed with the low-lying, soft blue flowers of linseed. As consumer demand changed, many fields were allocated to grow iceberg lettuce, and straight, uniform rows of salad leaf covered in billowing, white fleece appeared: protection, should the departing winter lavish a frosty, farewell kiss. Great reels of hose, taller than a man, occupied the pathways, the grinding and clanking as the winch retracted the gargantuan water sprayer alongside the neat rows blending with birdsong and becoming an everyday sound we grew oblivious to.

Buster became friends with a fun-filled, zest-for-life Golden Labrador named Beano. The two dogs frequently met on daily walks and would play fight, roll around and have a great time. Beano, however, was a bad influence for he had a penchant for lettuce and, without warning, would stop play, run as fast as he could along the neat rows of green orbs and, every now and then, chomp out the heart of a lettuce. He would shake his prize as hard as possible, sending crisp salad leaves flying in all directions, falling to earth in a confetti-like trail. Once this neat trick had been observed by Buster, he took to doing the same thing but without Beano's accuracy. In his usual Buster style, he just blasted in. Being shorter than Beano, he was unable to quickly thrust his head and neck downward when aiming for a lettuce, so ended up falling flat on his face, squashing more lettuce than he chomped. Beano never ate the lettuce but Buster would banquet on the ones he managed to grab, jealously guarding them. He never lost his taste for the crop and would sit at my feet whenever I prepared anything containing iceberg lettuce, optimistically waiting for a morsel, perhaps recalling the days when he and Beano ran in gay abandon across the lettuce fields.

Most of my day was taken up by long walks. I often felt the need to walk myself into exhaustion to avoid dwelling on unhappy thoughts. Roger and I had had our share of heartache, having undergone a programme of in vitro fertilisation (IVF) which was extremely emotional, not to mention costly, as well as ultimately unsuccessful in giving us the family we wanted. It was a time of false hopes, long drives to Harley Street, congestion charges, parking meters, being poked and prodded, anxious waits, bitter disappointments and darkness. The aftermath was life-shattering; unable to cope, I suffered a nervous breakdown and had to give up my job as a funeral arranger. I thought I had no future and later attempted to take my life.

Looking back at those times, it was as if they happened to someone else and I viewed it all as a bystander. Roger and I tried our best to move on but found ourselves becoming disheartened, fed up with our lives and false pretence, putting on brave faces and trying to fit into our place in society. Going over and over the same old ground, we felt constantly battered, our past weighing as heavy as fully

Buster brought comfort during a dark period of my life

laden trawler nets, hidden from the majority yet constantly dragging us down into the depths of despair. Physically tired and emotionally worn down, there seemed little to wake up for each morning. Taking on Buster slowly helped heal the wounds, motivating me to get up and go out. The unconditional love he showered on both of us gave living a whole new meaning. Yet, sometimes the dark shroud would still engulf me and, when it did, it was time to take to the hills.

Buster and I would be gone for hours, trekking to the top of the South Downs and immersing ourselves in the long views across the flat land to the sea. Halnaker Windmill was a favourite, from where we could look down on the village of Boxgrove, the church tower a speck rising above the trees. Up there, I felt free and believed that Buster did too as he happily snuffled around or sat with his nose pointed into the wind, taking in the scents wafting by. He had a fascination for views, sitting with me in silent contemplation. I would take along an apple which we would share. These were precious moments accompanied by the song of high-flying skylarks, the rustle of capricious breezes and the scent of warm corn and wild flowers. Sometimes, we would run down the hill together, the tall grasses whipping against my legs, laughing through breathlessness as my crazy hound jumped, frolicked and barked beside me. Buster was full of life; everything was new and exciting. His joy was infectious and gave me hope.

Beagles love nothing more than setting off alone to follow a scent; natural behaviour that was impossible to quench and why the Kennel Club's standard for the breed stated: 'The man with the lead in his hand and no dog in sight owns a Beagle.' As a preventative measure, most owners only allowed their dog off-lead in an enclosed space but our dog trainer was adamant: "If you don't do it now whilst he's a puppy, you never will." So, with her encouragement, we gathered the confidence to try Buster off-lead and, although there were times over the years when we watched, waited and waited some more for our Beagle's return, he frequently enjoyed a free, off-lead life.

Buster generally stayed close to my side when off-lead, sensing I needed his companionship. However, when Roger joined us, he became more adventurous and less concerned for my well-being. This often meant he became carried away when stumbling across a scent, sometimes disappearing in hot pursuit. Initially, one of us would chase after him but we soon realised this was futile as he moved so fast. The best thing to do was simply remain at the point where he went missing, or where eye contact had last been made, and wait. Nine times out of ten, Buster would return to that spot. After all, he would not be much use as a scent hound if he could not find his way back.

The Beagle's tail was known as a 'flag' because, whilst his nose remained firmly fixed to the ground, his tail waved in excitement, making it possible to read thoughts through action. At times, Buster's flag waved fast enough to rotate, becoming known as his 'helicopter tail', and sometimes it appeared he would be lifted bodily off the ground. Over the top of long grass or crops, his tail was a godsend and the only way of spotting him tracking a scent. Beagles had great stamina and waiting for one to return could be a long-drawn-out affair, as well as stressful

A windswept day on the South Downs

if there was a main road nearby. A Beagle did not stop once on a scent and became completely deaf to his owner's voice or any background noise, resulting in many falling victims to road accidents. Choosing safe walking locations was vital and, with open fields surrounding our home, we were fortunate.

The way to a Beagle's heart was through his stomach; constantly hungry, he was always on the lookout for the next meal. "Buster didn't go out for a walk but went out for a snack" became a common expression of mine as he was a lover of litter bins, picnic areas and the doorways of fast-food outlets. With his nose on the ground and his bottom in the air, he happily hunted out the merest of morsels and downed the most disgusting things, from manure to chewing gum. The advantage of this was that training with the aid of treats was successful and, wherever we went and whatever we wore, it was imperative to have a bag of doggy treats; the smellier the better, making our Beagle's return more reliable.

Roger and I took Buster to try out many water-based activities to prepare him for a life afloat. At this stage, we did not actually own a boat but had dreams of doing so. Being close to the seaside enabled strolls along the sands at Bognor Regis, where Buster would gallop without a care in the world, jumping groynes, chasing seagulls and dipping his paws in the foaming tide. On other occasions, we visited local waterways, such as the Chichester Canal and Portsmouth and Arundel Canal. These formed parts of 'London's Lost Route to the Sea', a series of waterways that provided shipping with an inland route between London and the Portsmouth Naval Docks, protecting them from the perils of the coast during the Napoleonic Wars. There were walks through quiet countryside to Chichester Harbour, where Buster had the opportunity to experience the hustle and bustle of Chichester Marina. Visiting the marina's modern sea locks, we watched the boats come and go or we walked down to the old locks where the fresh waters of the canal dripped through the cracks of the dilapidated gates to splash into the dark, briny waters of the harbour. Here, it was possible to look out across the mud flats, watch the wading birds foraging for food and taste the sea salt on our lips.

The Wey and Arun Canal formed the bulk of this so-called lost link of waterways. Over the years, sections had been slowly restored and put back into water. Loxwood, from where a trip boat operated, became a favourite place to enjoy a drink in the pub garden

Trip boat Zachariah Keppel on the Wey and Arun Canal

adjacent to the canal. Strolling along the towpath, we watched butterflies and bees busily hovering over the huge white blooms of the giant hogweed.

Familiarising Buster with water and wildfowl at Petworth Park

Roger would step onto the Canal Trust's work boat, taking Buster with him. This simple act and feeling the boat's slight movement was invaluable training for our dog. We tried to cover as much as possible – visits to canals, rivers and lakes, seaside promenades and piers and even short boat trips, and Buster loved every minute of it.

As well as training Buster, visits to the inland waterways enabled me to research and photograph them. I had been writing boating articles for years, a hobby alongside my day job, but, finding myself unemployed, this was developing. Training Buster and researching waterways went hand in hand and was gradually becoming a way of life. I dared to dream that this could become a freelance career.

Chapter Three

A FIRST TIME FOR EVERYTHING

In early spring, we hired a small, tug-style narrowboat in which to explore the Ashby Canal. Opened in 1804, its original purpose was to transport coal from mines at the northern end to the main canal system near Coventry. This canal was chosen purposely for Buster's first boating holiday as, being lock-free, it allowed plenty of time to keep tabs on our new-to-boating Beagle. Locks could be dangerous places, especially for a young dog, so we planned to slowly introduce these to Buster. To further enhance his safety, a smart, red, doggy life jacket was purchased, which he wore with pride.

The narrowboat had a large canvas covered area to the bow, known as a 'cratch', which came in handy for storing wellingtons and damp coats. It was also a great place to sit during warmer days and a safe area from where Buster could view his first 'real' encounter with canals. He had no qualms about stepping onto the boat and thoroughly enjoyed exploring the interior, snuffling into every nook and cranny.

Before Roger started the engine, I wanted to make sure Buster felt safe so sat up front with him, cuddling and gently talking to him. The last thing I wanted to do was frighten him; he had done so well already. Below decks, I had set up a special area, placing his travel crate containing his bed in a position where he could clearly

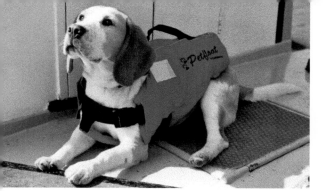

Buster wearing his new life jacket

see us. Inside his bed, I put a couple of his favourite toys. If Buzz became nervous, this would act as a safe place for him to retreat to or for me to place him.

Roger was more than capable of handling the narrowboat; he had spent much of his youth holidaying on them with his parents. This was ideal as I could concentrate on looking after Buster. When the engine sprang into life, Buster tilted his head to one side and listened intently but did not seem bothered by the noise or vibration. We slowly eased out of the mooring and onto the canal, the whole procedure taking just moments. I had not even heard Roger untie so the movement was as much a surprise to me as it must have been for Buster.

The entrance to the Ashby Canal was at Marston Junction, where it immediately entered countryside, an ideal doggy environment, and Buster was all too aware of the enticing scents. He quickly became confident, standing up on his back legs to lean over the side and breathe in the air. At first glance, the surroundings seemed barren as most of the vegetation associated with canals – such as lilies and irises – was slumbering, dormant beneath the water. However, there were rewards to be found in the hedgerows and along the banksides, the delicate snowy-white blossom of the blackthorn and the cheerful pale-yellow flowers of the primrose. Butterbur, one of the first flowering perennials, sent up clusters of flesh-coloured flowers on tall, tubular stalks above rounded leaves. It was believed the name Butterbur came from the practice of using the plant's large leaves to wrap butter. They looked similar to Buster's floppy ears, which were certainly large enough to wrap a pat of butter in.

Following the contours of the land, the canal lazily wound its way beneath numerous stone accommodation bridges. Mooring to take advantage of the pretty rural scene, we sat out to enjoy the early spring sunshine. I had purchased a tethering stake for Buster – a long, coiled metal spike, similar in appearance to a large corkscrew, onto which was attached a strong cable. Once screwed into the ground, the cable was attached to the dog's collar, allowing him freedom of movement. In theory, this should have allowed us to sit out on the towpath and

not worry about Buster running off or chasing bikes and people – typical behaviour for a young, boisterous pup.

Early spring on the Ashby Canal

Unfortunately, sensing freedom, Buster ran at speed along the towpath, reaching the end of the cable with a violent jerk, his chubby body and galloping legs flying from beneath him. There was a loud 'twang' as something gave way. Buster fell heavily and lay still; apparently injured. With hearts in mouths, we raced towards him, collapsing on the ground by his side, fearing the worst. Closer inspection revealed – much to our relief – that Buster was fine and he was up and sniffing around after a few seconds. Whilst the cable had held firm, the plastic catch on his collar had broken. Buster was certainly living up to his name.

As Roger guided the boat into Battlefield Moorings, the newly opened daffodils were taking a battering in the bitter breeze. We wasted no time discovering the jewel in the Ashby's crown – Bosworth Battlefield – where the deciding battle in the War of the Roses was fought on 22nd August 1485. Buster snuffled away, enjoying the walk despite the cold whilst we

Roger and Buster at Stoke Golding

became engrossed with interpretation boards recounting how Richard III, the Yorkist king, was defeated and slain by Henry of Richmond, who then became Henry VII.

Back on the boat, we stripped off layers of clothes and muddy wellingtons, glad to be back in the warm. The weak spring sunshine had warmed the cratch and, with the breeze whipping in from the bankside, I rolled up the offside covering to allow in more sun and light. We tucked into bowls of steaming tomato soap and crusty bread rolls.

"D'you think Buster could have some soup?" I asked Roger. "There's a little left and I'm sure it won't hurt him."

"Yeah, why not. Poor little mite, it'll do him good having something warm." I poured the small amount of soup left into Buster's bowl and he greedily lapped it up, looking at me with grateful appreciation.

"Buzzy, look at you!" All around his lips and chin, Buster had a bright orange stain. "You look as if you're in drag, a pantomime dame. Perhaps we should call you Widow Twankey?" With that, he went off and sulked.

A few minutes later, never one to hold a grudge, particularly where food was concerned, he returned. Passing me, he leapt up onto the gunnel, obviously thinking he could access land, but had chosen the wrong side of the boat. I was going to shout at him but thought better of it; my disturbance could break his concentration, cause him to topple into the water. Instead, I watched in astonishment as he balanced precariously on the narrow edge, as if a tightrope walker on a high trapeze. Instinct cut in, I rushed towards him and gathered him into my arms. Holding him firmly against my body, I lowered him down.

"Are you alright, Buzzy boy?" He nuzzled into my body. Buster seemed fine but the misadventure may have caused delayed shock because, a little while later, he threw up the remains of the tomato soup.

The way events were panning out, it was inevitable Buster would fall in sooner or later and this he did at Gopsall Wharf when we made a brief stop to take photographs for an article I was writing. Roger loosely tied Buster to the tiller, locking the retractable lead after giving him a couple of feet to move freely. Once we were off the boat, Buster decided to come along too, taking a leap

Buster liked to help with the ropes

onto the quayside. However, the length of lead was too short and he fell in the water between the narrowboat and the stone walls of the wharf. Roger was quick to go to his aid as there was little room and, in hindsight, the taut lead should not have been locked off. Roger reached down and grabbed the handle of Buster's life jacket, hauling him out to be left hanging dejectedly with water dripping from his paws. He was not amused. After enduring a thorough towelling off, he had a short stroll around before skulking off below deck. Cuddling up to the hot water bottle made for him, he soon drifted off to sleep, allowing us to continue our journey accompanied by the sound of his snoring. I would like to have said it was as musical as Handel's *Messiah*, which he reputedly composed whilst staying in the nearby Gopsall Park, but, unfortunately, I could not …

It was dark and eerie in Snarestone tunnel. Snuggled in the cratch, Buster huddled beneath my arm, the warmth of his body comforting. As Roger eased the narrowboat through the subterranean world, the tunnel light played tricks, formed silhouettes, creating shadows with mysterious shapes and patterns.

"Does it smell good, Buzzy?" Buster inhaled deeply, drawing in the scent of cold dampness. He was not scared; he was totally transfixed by the alien environment.

The Ashby abruptly ended at a small, winding hole, a quiet spot, over which loomed the solemn, Victorian, Gothic-style buildings of Snarestone Waterworks. The remaining route was infilled but easily recognisable and possible to explore on foot. Buster relished the off-water diversion, happily sending rabbits scurrying into the undergrowth.

At seven months old, our puppy was growing up with boating in his blood. He had found his sea – or perhaps I should say canal – legs. He had learnt to 'walk the plank' to reach dry land, as well as help with the ropes, all of which, to him, was a big game.

Chapter Four

BADGER DINGLE, PADDLE AND RAIL

One of my passions, other than boating, was architecture. A lover of the unusual, I was especially fond of follies and the era when romantic, landscaped grounds were not complete without a Doric temple, hermitage, sham castle or tower. For many years, I had supported organisations that acquired buildings such as these to use as holiday homes. By doing so, they preserved important pieces of architecture, whilst providing an income to help towards the restoration of other significant structures.

Roger and I had stayed in several of these special properties along with Buster. The Temple in Shropshire, near the charming town of Bridgnorth, was one of the most enchanting. It was approached along a shady, tree-lined carriageway leading to Badger Dingle, an area of woodland, sandstone cliffs and ravines landscaped by William Emes, a pupil of Capability Brown. Perched on a ledge overlooking a lake, level with the upper branches of the trees, the view was spectacular and allowed excellent birdwatching, particularly in the evenings when resident owls glided silently through the wooded valley.

The Temple was originally constructed as a tea house and a regular pastime during our stay was to sit on the veranda, sipping tea from bone china cups. Buster would lie at our feet or sit on the edge, transfixed by a small flotilla of ducks far below on the lake. It was so picture-perfect and sophisticated, it was easy to become carried away and imagine ourselves in a classic romantic novel but these moments never lasted long as the antics of our Beagle brought us crash-banging back to reality.

The grounds became Buster's adventure playground. He rampaged through undergrowth, rambled along ravines and, on one occasion, blundered through a black, muddy pool, the odour of which lingered on his fur for days. He had no fear or let-up, running and leaping into deep gullies and around great stone boulders. He would nose into shrubs and bushes, one day coming out with his muzzle covered in small ticks which Roger and I spent the afternoon removing with the aid of a bottle of gin – for Buster's wounds, not us. Buster hated the aroma of juniper from then on and, if anyone attempted to kiss him after downing a measure, would screw up his muzzle and turn his head away.

With the River Severn running through the county, we could not resist taking to the waters. Britain's longest river, covering 220 miles

The Temple in Badger Dingle

Buster on the veranda of the Temple

(354kms) from its source to the sea, passed through some of the country's most beautiful landscapes and was once a thriving trade route. Nowadays, the upper reaches were unnavigable to most craft, although evidence of the once-bustling wharves and inland ports remained to fascinate those with a passion for industrial heritage. The best way to explore was by canoe.

Having never set foot in one, we nervously booked a 10 mile (16km) downstream paddle from Bridgnorth to Arley, followed by a steam train ride back to the starting point on the lovingly restored Severn Valley Railway. The canoe company agreed that Buster could come along. By now, he had a good understanding of water and, with his own life jacket, I was confident he would not run into any problems. He wasted no time jumping into the canoe and giving it a good sniff. Roger and I were fitted with buoyancy aids; catching Buster's eye, I was sure he was laughing at me – I looked like the Michelin man. After

a short safety talk, our canoe was gently pushed onto the gloriously clear waters of the Severn for a practice session. Buster caused a few wobbles as he made himself comfortable but quickly settled, looking as if he had been canoeing all his life.

Soon, we were gliding through Bridgnorth. As we swept beneath the town's bridge, several people stopped to watch. I was sure it was Buster's presence that drew their attention. He looked grand in his bright red life jacket, inquisitively observing his surroundings. Occasionally, he glanced over the edge of the canoe, watching the waters ripple away, feeling the coolness on his face. Despite the canoe only drawing a few inches, it

Roger and Buster enjoying the downriver paddle.

rubbed against gravelly shoals in one section and rattled over rapids in another but, for the most part, it was a gentle, soothing trip. The picturesque hamlet of Hampton Loade was a popular watering hole, where we enjoyed refreshments and Buster ran freely in the adjacent meadow, before we relaunched to negotiate the final few miles.

Downstream from Hampton Loade, the banks became steeper, enclosed in several places by stunning, red sandstone cliffs. The total silence of the canoe allowed some up-close-and-personal encounters with the river's wild fowl, including some inquisitive mute swan cygnets. By this time, Buster was growing weary and did not pay them much attention; instead, he rolled into a tight ball for an afternoon nap as Roger and I paddled on to the pretty village of Upper Arley. Approaching the designated meeting place, I leant forwards and gently stroked Buster.

"Hey, Buzzy, it's time to wake up." He slowly stirred, stretched and yawned. Canoeing, it would seem, could be easily taken in a Beagle's stride.

Arley Station on the Severn Valley Railway

It was a short, uphill stroll to the nostalgic Arley Station and the Severn Valley Railway. The standard-gauge line ran steam-hauled passenger trains between Kidderminster and Bridgnorth.

The railway led to the decline of trade on the River Severn and, when faced with the huge giants of steam, it was easy to see why: their pulling power was unstoppable. This was Buster's first train ride and he behaved impeccably, probably due to tiredness from all the fresh air. Steam railways were one of Roger's interests and, over the years, Buster visited and rode on many more, becoming captivated by them. Should one of us gleefully sing out, "Choo choo, come on, Buzzy, come on, Buzzy, choo choo," he immediately knew there was a train nearby. Even in the car, this phrase would entice Buster from slumber to catch a fleeting glimpse of a locomotive.

Chapter Five

BROKEN BONES AT ANIMAL FARM

With my parents living close by, Buster spent a great deal of time with them. Their house – my childhood home – was a menagerie; a veritable 'animal farm' backing onto open fields with views to the South Downs. Chickens, geese, pheasants, peacocks, ducks, sheep, cats and a horse called this their home and Buster was thrust into their lives. Being exposed to many different creatures from an early age was of great benefit to him and the open fields allowed long walks. Dad would walk around the perimeter of the nearest field, staff in hand, followed by Minty the sheep, Buster and, sometimes, bringing up the rear, one of the cats. They were quite the local spectacle.

At harvest time, Dad often helped and occasionally went shooting on the land. Buster enjoyed tagging along, sitting at the side of the field as the combine harvester trawled up and down, throwing out billowing clouds of dust, leaving behind the evocative scent of warm straw as its great, rotating forks gathered up the ripe crop. Waiting until the last moment, foxes, rabbits and giant rats would run out in front of the harvester. Being quick on the trigger was paramount but usually the creature escaped with no more than a woof from Buster and a disappointed sigh from Dad.

Minty the sheep and Fee-Bee the horse having a friendly chat

Dad bottle-feeding a Texel lamb with Buster overseeing the proceedings

Boating with Buster

Fee-Bee, my sister's horse, was a fine chestnut mare – an Arab-Hanoverian cross – and Buster loved nothing more than walks across the fields with the two of them. With her Arabian characteristics, Fee-Bee was quite skittish and Shirley had to use all the skills gained working at the local racing yard to handle her. The animals came first at my parents' home which was always busy with people coming and going, often being well fed and watered by Mum. Their home was a welcoming one; no wonder it was one of Buster's favourite places to visit.

Buster tags along on an early morning hack

Dad, Roger and I sometimes took a late afternoon stroll with Buster across the fields, particularly following harvest, crunching through the short stubble. Walking away from the public footpaths, there was a visible change in Buster: he was happier, lighter on his feet and, off-lead with the freedom to do his own thing, he quickly became engrossed in snuffling. Deer were frequently seen

Mum and Shirley with Fee-Bee at animal farm

in the distance but they seldom ventured too close to the back gardens of the houses bordering the fields. Once, however, in the fading afternoon light, one silently stepped out from the cover of the hedgerow, head down, more interested in finding succulent green shoots than taking note of us. Buster was some distance ahead and too far away to reach before his hunting instincts cut in. He raced off towards the deer, ears flapping wildly as he voiced an earth-shattering 'barooo', which sent the deer leaping across the field in fright.

"Buster," Roger yelled, taking off after him.

"You're wasting your time; just leave him." But he was gone. Dad and I watched and laughed as Roger gave chase. I knew Buster would most likely circle back. By now, the deer had disappeared back into the hedgerow. Roger's voice sounded desperate as he raced across the uneven stubble. He fell, hit the ground hard and began to roll about, grasping his leg in both hands. Dad and I were bent double with laughter, tears streaming down our faces. But when Roger did not get up, we hurried over to him.

Buster was heading back; after losing his quarry, he had completed his loop and was looking dejected. We all reached Roger at the same time.

"I've broken my foot." Roger was rolling around on the ground, doing an excellent impression of a fouled footballer.

"Don't be stupid, of course you haven't," I snapped. "Get up, stop rolling about, you'll get filthy." Buster thought this looked like a great game and sniffed at Roger's ear.

"Get him off and help me up, will you?" By now, I thought I would die from laughter. My tummy hurt and seeing my dad with tears down his face in mirth was not helping matters. "You two can bloody laugh." So, we did!

Roger clambered to his feet and stumbled back across the field, partly leaning on me, partly hopping. Dad and I found it hard to hold in the laughter and Buster, bored by it all, ran ahead, hoping his dinner would be ready. All evening, Roger complained about his injury. Dad and I erupted into laughter each time but Mum and Shirley took pity on him.

"I need to go to hospital," Roger exclaimed.

"Go on then; you must be mad going there on a Saturday evening. You'll be waiting all night and, besides, there's nothing wrong with your foot," I insisted.

"I heard a bang; it sounded like a bloody gun going off."

"That'll be when your teeth fell out," sniggered my dad, erupting once again into a fit of laughter.

In the end, Shirley decided to take Roger to the local hospital and, as expected, they were gone for several hours. Finally returning home, poor Roger was sporting a plaster cast; he had indeed broken his foot chasing Buster. In years to come, this was an injury that would return to haunt us.

Chapter Six

A BOAT OF OUR OWN

"What's her name?" I whispered in Roger's ear. He was on the telephone to the owner of a Sagar Dutch barge who had advertised on a website selling boats of all shapes and sizes. Roger was chatting about things that meant little to me, whilst I was becoming more agitated, only hearing one side of the conversation.

Putting the phone down, he turned to me grinning, his eyes sparkling and said, "You're never going to believe this; the boat's name is *Lily*!"

Lily was my nan's name and we had already discussed the possibility of using it for our own boat. However, being superstitious, I was not keen on changing a boat's name as it was considered unlucky. We had found the type of barge we wanted with the right name – surely this was too good to be true?

Roger and I had taken numerous boating holidays in England and overseas but had never owned a boat. The closest we had come was joining Challenger Syndicateships, purchasing a share in *Silver Steel*, a Stevens 1120 cruiser based

in Burgundy, France. The boat handling course, information and cruising experience gained proved invaluable and, although the company did all the hard work, having the share provided our first insight into ownership.

Silver Steel on the River Saône in France

We came across many styles of boats holidaying on *Silver Steel* but it was the Dutch barges which caught my eye. It was fun daydreaming about owning one, talking about liveaboard life, where to travel and what we would do. One icy cold and snowy Christmas at Saint-Jean-de-Losne, we were invited onto a Dutch barge for sherry and homemade mince pies by a couple of expats. We were smitten by their beautiful barge but never sampled the mince pies as their lively Springer Spaniel, Einstein, devoured the lot.

After several fantastic years exploring the French waterways, we gave up our share in *Silver Steel*, using the funds as a deposit for a house and our forthcoming wedding. However, being without a boat soon began to take its toll and the search for our own home afloat began.

Finding a boat within our budget and providing plenty of room was important. There was also Buster to think about and our cat, Dusty, too.

However, due to Roger's work commitments in England, this immediately put a size limit on considerations. Most English canals were built to accommodate 7ft (2.1m) wide narrowboats. Other waterways were wider but this dimension varied across the country to fit the local style of boat. Whilst something spacious would be nice, we wanted to access as many waterways as possible. Hoping, at some stage, to cruise in Europe, ideally something more substantial than a narrowboat would be needed. It was these requirements which led us to Sagar Marine.

The family-run business of Sagar Marine was established in 1975 when they began building narrowboats from Victoria Works on the Calder & Hebble Waterway in West Yorkshire. In 1991, they constructed their first replica Dutch barge and went on to specialise in these. Roger and I were instantly drawn to their Mini-Luxe barge. Based on a 1920s Luxemotor, a Dutch trading vessel, it featured the same proportions of wheelhouse and back cabin but with a front superstructure replacing the cargo hold. With a long waiting list for new builds and a price tag above our budget, we looked at secondhand but finding one was not easy – those who owned Sagar barges held onto them. We waited patiently, the weeks slipped into months but, eventually, our patience paid off.

With Buster in my parent's capable hands, Roger and I made the four-hour drive to Shardlow Marina, Derbyshire, to view *Lily*. Seeing her for the first time was amazing; she sat in her berth, squeezed between other craft but still standing out from the crowd. Roger reached for my hand and squeezed it tightly. Our eyes met and it was hard to contain our excitement. From outside, *Lily* looked fantastic: extremely clean and tidy but also very large. Could we really handle a boat of that size?

Measuring 48ft (14.63m) long with a beam of 10ft 6in (3.20m), the size allowed access to almost all our country's wider waterways and provided ample living space. The high build quality of *Lily*'s steel body was immediately obvious, the almost invisible seams and gentle curving lines a joy to brush my hands over. She had all the fine lines and solid body looks of a larger Dutch barge but in miniature. Finished in ivory and deep green enamel with scarlet hull stripe and

Dutch barge Lily

roof edging she portrayed a traditional appearance. Her decks were wide; I could easily picture Buster trotting contentedly around them.

Lily's wheelhouse, constructed from iroko, an African hardwood, provided the entrance and could be dismantled, reducing *Lily*'s height from 9ft (2.74m) to 7ft (2.13m) for lower bridges. Stepping inside, the scent of sun-warmed varnish filled my nostrils and my heart skipped a beat. She was beautiful. At the helm stood a wooden and brass steering wheel, a single lever engine control and an instrument panel. To one side, a handy chart table; to the other, steps to below decks.

Her owner lifted a hatch in the wheelhouse floor. Roger gazed into the depths of the engine room; inside there was plenty of space to store tools and equipment. He grinned broadly and did not need asking twice to take a closer look. Before I could object, the two men disappeared below, talking about power output, cooling systems and service intervals. Together, they removed the sound-insulation panels surrounding the engine, revealing a shiny, bright red, five-cylinder Beta diesel. I was not mechanically minded but even I could see this was a beauty. There was also a diesel-powered generator: a handy

SCHEMATIC LAYOUT OF "LILY"

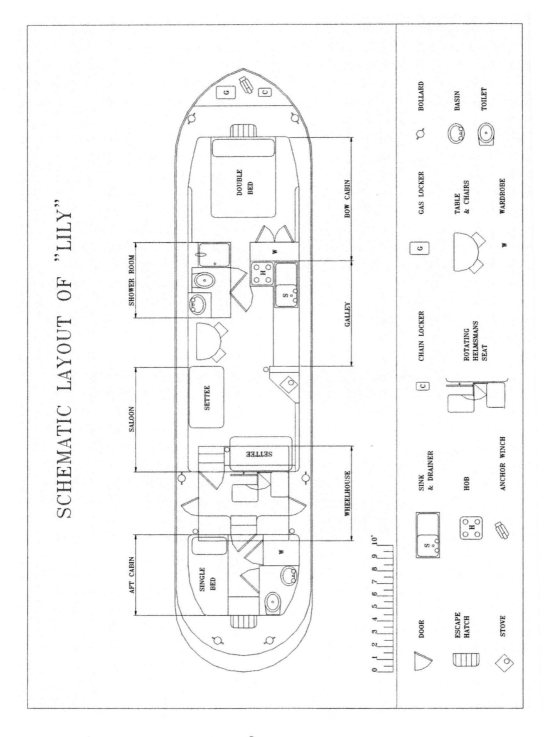

BOW CABIN

DOUBLE BED

W

SHOWER ROOM

H

S

GALLEY

SALOON

SETTEE

WHEELHOUSE

SETTEE

AFT CABIN

SINGLE BED

W

G

C

0 1 2 3 4 5 6 7 8 9 10'

BOLLARD

BASIN

TOILET

GAS LOCKER

TABLE & CHAIRS

WARDROBE

W

CHAIN LOCKER

ROTATING HELMSMANS SEAT

SINK & DRAINER

S

HOB

H

ANCHOR WINCH

DOOR

ESCAPE HATCH

STOVE

addition for time spent away from port.

Lily's country cottage-style main saloon

Below decks, *Lily* had a distinctly more feminine feel. The cream-and-pink back cabin provided guest accommodation with its own small bathroom. The main saloon was light and airy; the cream, panelled walls and ceiling reflected the light flooding in through the arch-topped windows and roof hatch. Watery patterns of dancing light glistened and glinted everywhere, bouncing off richly varnished iroko joinery and brass fixtures and fittings. A Morsø Squirrel stove with integral back boiler sat snugly in one corner. I adored this feature and thoughts of warm, cosy winter evenings on board flooded my mind. There were also radiators throughout, heated by an Alde gas boiler; the best of both worlds as far as heating was concerned. The loose furniture created a feeling of spaciousness, pretty floral prints and rosy pink soft furnishings reminiscent of an English country cottage. It was perfect.

The compact galley housed everything needed to live happily and comfortably on board. Adjacent to this was space for Buster's crate and bed, from where he could see the whole of the living area and be near the warmth of the stove but not so close he would overheat; his own safe place in the heart of the barge. Beyond the galley, a doorway led to the en-suite master cabin containing a good-size double bed, cupboards and a large built-in wardrobe with mirrored doors. Portholes engraved with a pretty starburst pattern allowed light in and the large Houdini hatch to the bow offered protection from breaking seas and provided an alternative escape route.

Lily had been built as a part-finished fit-out for the owner. Being a skilled carpenter, the standard of finish was high. He had considered the future of the boat's cruising life, installing good quality products, many of which would enable her to tackle estuary and coastal waters. *Lily* had character and a heart and had spoken to us. She was everything Roger and I had dreamt of, plus she was ready to go. All we needed to do was raise the cash and our adventures could begin …

Arriving at Shardlow Marina, the stresses and strains drifted away. Roger and I wore broad smiles from dawn to dusk, revelling in being boat owners for the first time. People were friendly: interested but not nosey, non-judgemental and full of helpful boating tips. *Lily* looked beautiful, felt safe and homely and was a pleasure to be aboard.

Buster took to his new surroundings immediately. He watched in fascination as a little black Staffie ran along the pontoon and threw herself into the marina's waters, doggy paddled to the banks thick with yellow irises, scrambled up them, doing the same all over again. Getting Buster to *Lily* along the floating pontoon had not been easy. Despite taking him to sample many moorings, we had missed this type. The movement was new and unsettling, caused him to freeze to the spot, place his legs wide apart and brace himself as the platform wobbled. After he had walked a few steps and froze, Roger lifted him into his arms.

"Well done, my boy, that'll do nicely for your first attempt," he praised, nuzzling his face deep into Buster's neck before carrying him to the firmer deck of *Lily*. Over the next few visits, we encouraged Buster to walk further along the pontoon until he eventually walked the whole way himself. Jumping onto *Lily*'s deck, he turned, gave us his best doggy grin and never again worried about moving pontoons.

Buying our first boat was scary. Raising the cash had meant re-mortgaging our house and it was different cruising in a vessel that we owned – a huge responsibility. Leaving the marina to head along the River Trent on our initial trip to Sawley, I had sweaty palms, a lump in my throat and butterflies in my stomach but nothing could wipe the big grin from my face. Roger took the helm as Buster sat on the chart table to watch the world slip silently by. Together we were beginning a new chapter in our lives and it felt good.

Chapter Seven

BETWEEN THE DEVIL AND THE DEEP BLUE SEA

One month after purchasing *Lily*, we reluctantly bid her farewell and headed to Lancashire and the Lake District for a two-centre holiday: the first week on the Lancaster Canal, the second at Church Brow Cottage, another one of the quirky properties I adored.

When booking the holiday, I had no idea that we would have a boat of our own by the time it came around. Taking Buster on another boating adventure was part of the plan to prepare him for life afloat. I also had special reason to visit the area, in particular Kirkby Lonsdale. As a child, my family had spent holidays there with my Great-Auntie Eileen and -Uncle Len, housekeeper and gamekeeper respectively. We stayed at their employment-tied cottage, which sat opposite the estate grounds of Newton Hall, a stone's throw from the River Lune. Over the years, they had been privileged to live and work in some amazing places and I believed it was this early exposure to grandiose estates that sparked my interest in follies and odd architecture. Rattling across open estate grounds in Great-Uncle Len's Land Rover, wedged between my sister and Cindy Loo, his black Labrador, dodging the rancid collection of dead pheasants and rabbits swinging to and fro, I would catch tantalising glimpses of a gazebo, an ornamental dovecote or a castellated stable block.

Arriving at Ashton Basin in the mill town of Preston, there was a short wait to board our hire boat, *Heron*. Buster pulled on his lead, eager to get on board.

"You'll have to be patient, Buzzy."

Being afloat was as exciting for him as it was for me. This was Buster's first trip on a narrowboat with a cruiser stern, an ample open space at the rear of the boat allowing passengers to sit out with the helmsman. Buster's bed fitted safely against the guard rails encompassing the open deck, where he could enjoy the delights of cruising in comfort. I ensured there was a safe place inside with familiar toys but Buster preferred being outside, snoozing in the sun and grumbling at passing ducks.

We awoke to swirling mists backlit by a hazy sunrise over the beautiful Lancashire landscape, the small villages and hamlets portraying peaceful scenes reminiscent of a bygone age. The early morning was a magical time to be on the move, the gentle ripple of water around *Heron*'s bow musical in the stillness of the new day. The Forest of Bowland and its distant fells, sprinkled with pale pink and

Roger guiding Heron along the delightful Lancaster Canal

lilac shades of flowering rhododendrons, added a splash of colour to the welcoming spring day. Easing into canal-time, the atmosphere gently enveloped us. Occasionally, I jumped off the slowed boat, Buster following, and we strolled the towpath. Alongside, Roger guided *Heron*, his arm lazily draped over the tiller, lost in reminiscences of childhood days on the cut. Buster delighted in these interludes, happily trotting along, nose on the ground, bottom in the air, tail on high waving joyously.

Spending a day off-water, we rewarded Buster with a walk along the Glasson Branch Canal. Descending the pretty Conder Valley for three miles, it linked the Lancaster Canal to the sea at Glasson Docks and was an oasis of calm. The yellow irises were in full bloom, attracting butterflies and insects, which, in turn, drew flocks of swallows. Buster ran through the grasses, skipped and frolicked, every now and then lowering his body into the still waters for a drink before racing off again.

Heron slipped silently into Deep Cutting. Hewn through glacial deposits, it was bordered by dense vegetation where wild garlic and ferns thrived in dappled sunlight and cool, damp conditions. Buster's nose twitched, drawing in the pungent, earthy smell of fungi, leaf mould and rotting wood. Kingfishers sped by at low level, creating explosive flashes of electric blue as they flew through the shafts of sunlight to punctuate the way ahead.

I liked the Lancaster Canal; it was lazy and laid-back and thrilled me with stunning views and architectural gems. *Heron* wound effortlessly around meandering curves, slid across aqueducts and carried us over the tumbling River Lune as, below, it rushed seaward, unlike us in a hurry to reach its final destination. At Hest Bank, we marvelled at the views across Morecombe Bay and the deep blue sea towards the mountains of the Lake District. The sea breeze enticed Buster out of his sleepy stupor to drink in the coastal scents and watch seagulls reel. Perhaps he was thinking how nice a paddle would be but the sands and mud flats revealed at low tide were treacherous. I had no intentions of venturing onto them.

"Can you help me?" I fluttered my eyelashes at Roger and tried not to laugh as we approached Carnforth. "I have something in my eye and need to bathe it."

"I'll bathe *you* in a minute, right in the canal," joked Roger as I played out the scene from David Lean's film *Brief Encounter*. Carnforth was high on our list of places to visit. It had shot to fame in 1945 when it was used as the location for this well-known film. With Buster in tow, we visited the railway station where the visitors' centre showed the film throughout the day. Buster yawned and stretched his neck in boredom, thinking, *I've seen this film before.*

Pulling into Tewitfield, we went to explore the Northern Reaches. Many years had passed since the last barge climbed the flight of locks, passed through Hincaster tunnel, over the impressive skew aqueduct at Sedgewick and beneath the only change-over bridge in Cumbria, to reach the terminus in Kendal. Now disused, its remains provided enticing glimpses into what the canal once looked like.

In the small Cumbrian market town of Kirkby Lonsdale, Church Brow Cottage sat perched on a promenade, high above the gloriously beautiful River Lune. An enchanting miniature cottage, originally built as a summer retreat, it sat in terraced grounds filled with birdsong, fragrant flowers, wildlife and peacefulness. One of the best rooms was the ground-floor bathroom. Relaxing in a deep hot bath of bubbles with the French doors flung open onto the garden and beyond the fells was idyllic, blackbird song the only

Church Brow Cottage and Ruskin's View

accompaniment needed to enhance the scene. After a week of narrowboating, the ultimate luxury.

The outlook was known as Ruskin's View after the leading Victorian art critic described it as one of the loveliest scenes in England. It was easy to see why. The River Lune twisted and turned through lush meadows bordered by woodland set against a backdrop of fells. The scene was forever changing. Clouds scudded across the sky, creating dark, racing shadows on the slopes as the wind pushed them ever onwards.

Below Church Brow Cottage, a riverside footpath led to Devil's Bridge, a name used for centuries for ancient crossings associated with a mischievous tale. The one crossing the Lune was no different. Reputedly, an elderly woman who lived on the banks of the river came across the Devil after her cow strayed to the opposite shore. He promised to build a bridge, allowing her to retrieve the beast but only in exchange for the first soul to use it. When the bridge was completed, the woman threw a scrap of bread across, which her dog chased after, outwitting the Devil, who vanished in a cloud of brimstone. Knowing the way Buster loved a scrap of food, I am sure if we had needed his assistance, he would have done the same but we never met the Devil, only a group of Hells Angels as the site was a popular weekend meet for motorcyclists.

Taking a trip on the Ullswater Steamer

During our stay, the weather threw everything at us yet was unable to provide the unseasonably hot days we had had on the canal. Days of warm sunshine were followed by pouring rain, a constant fine drizzle which my parents would have described as having the ability to go straight through you. When the sun made a brief appearance, a trip on the Ullswater Steamer was in order. Buster sat cuddled between us, his nose in full twitch as the scents hit his nostrils and sent his brain whirling into overdrive; the wind lifting his long velvety ears to make them flap gently in the breeze.

Talk in the evenings in front of a blazing coal fire, with Buster happily snoring at our feet, always returned to boating and canals: what the future held now we were first-time boat owners and, if we were brave enough to take the next step, what a full-time life afloat would entail. Keeping both a house and a boat would mean struggling financially; something would have to give. As with the Lancaster Canal, we too were stuck between the Devil and the deep blue sea.

Chapter Eight

RANGERS AND RAGAMUFFINS

With the Lake District diversion over, a routine was established with Buster and *Lily*. Weekdays were spent at home in West Sussex, attending to everyday tasks and commitments. Buster and I continued to walk and spend time at my parents'; he attended his dog training classes, passing exams, proving to many sceptics that a Beagle *could* be trained. Whenever I felt down, he was there to give me a warm nuzzle or a knowing glance and his escapades helped lift my spirits. As the week progressed, anticipation slowly grew in the household and, by Friday, it was complete chaos as everything needed for the coming weekend was crammed into the car, ready for the mad dash up the motorway to *Lily*. Buster dragged his bedding across the floor, leaving it in a heap by the front door, a reminder to pack his essentials too.

It was during this period that the vet discovered Dusty, our cat and Buster's companion (though there was no love lost between them), had a leaking heart valve and suggested she would be better off as a house cat, free from overexertion. This was a bitter blow. We were forced to readdress our dreams of sharing life afloat with her; a boat just did not seem suitable for Dusty but neither did being shut in a house all day. There was a perfect solution – Dusty

could go to live at animal farm. My parents would love and cherish her as much as Roger and I; we could still see her and she could have regular, monitored outdoor activity.

Buster and Dusty had been companions since a very young age

Buster greedily snacked on warm, buttered toast and Marmite which the staff of the Trent Lock Tearooms had lovingly prepared for him. Sitting outside and sipping steaming tea, Roger and I watched boats lock onto the Erewash Canal. As gongoozlers, we were critical yet knew we would do no better ourselves. Buster licked his lips, trying to gather escaped strands of yeasty spread attached to his chin. Across the wide River Trent, the River Soar beckoned.

The Soar was a delightful river navigation, it meandered through countryside so quintessentially English that one could be gliding through a descriptive

St James' known as the Boatmans Church, Normanton on Soar

narrative for a tourism campaign. Pretty villages spilled down to the waterfront. Normanton was particularly attractive with quaint little holiday homes – a ramshackle collection of properties more like glorified sheds with well-tended gardens and all manner of pretty planters overflowing with summer bedding.

I delighted in entering the Soar, its gentle, roving waters contrasting with the wide expanses of the Trent it flowed into. Beyond the thundering noise of the waters spilling over Thrumpton Weir, if rivers could speak, I believed the Soar would encourage helmsmen to throttle back and take it easy as the route gently hugged the shady, wooded slopes of Red Hill, where tall willows slowly swayed and danced in the breeze. It felt a kinder, more intimate river. However, appearances could be deceptive; the existence of Redhill Flood Lock was a clue to the river's more menacing side.

Ratcliffe Lock was the first lock Roger and I took *Lily* through ourselves. Unlike the locks on Sawley Cut, there were no automated procedures or a lock keeper to help with the tasks at hand. Buster had been happy to sit in his bed on the chart table and watch the ascent and descent in the Sawley Locks, one of us always close by to reassure him. The stable doors on *Lily's* wheelhouse allowed us to keep Buster safe inside but still have close communication with him. Now things were different as we had to operate the locks. There were heavy, creaking gates to push and stiff paddles to wind, as well as all the usual locking procedures which included ensuring *Lily* was safely roped in. We knew how locks worked, had operated many in the past, but getting to grips with our own boat took a little time. The three of us were on a steep learning curve.

Buster wanted to explore the surroundings. We walked him around Ratcliffe Lock, finding a safe place to tie him from where he could watch. Roger walked to the far side of the lock and together we slowly pushed on the balance beams and opened the heavy lock gates. Buster, wanting to join in, strained to see.

"Shall I take *Lily* into the lock?" I did not fancy the idea of winding paddles and opening hefty gates alone.

Roger set me off, holding *Lily*'s long bow rope, bow-hauling her towards the lockside where Buster was waiting. I lined *Lily*'s bow up with the entrance. From the helm, the vacant space looked tiny and soon disappeared behind *Lily*'s buxom body. She slipped into the lock chamber and, as Roger fastened off the rope around the furthest forward bollard, I put *Lily* into reverse, swiftly bringing her to a halt. Carefully, I made my way to the stern and threw the rear rope to Roger, who wound it around the bollard and lowered it back to me. I was going to control the stern rope and engine controls; from the lockside, Roger would operate the paddle gear and take charge of the bow rope. After closing the gates, Roger slowly wound the windlass to lift the paddles, releasing a gush of water into the chamber, and *Lily* began to rise. Soon I was eye-level with the top of the lock and could see Buster sitting patiently, watching with curiosity. Once he spotted me, his tail began to wag furiously and he let out a bark.

"We won't be long now, Buzzy," I called out, which made him bark even more.

When the lock was full, Roger opened the gates and I drove *Lily* out, with the help of him bow-hauling, and fastened up at the moorings.

"We did it!" I shouted as he approached. "I'll get Buzzy and help you shut the gates." It was a huge relief to get through the first lock. Leaning my back into the balance beam, straining against the weight, to my surprise, Buster stood on his rear legs and pushed too.

"That's it, Buzz, help Mummy shut the gates." He pushed and jumped forwards as the gate slowly began to swing, then did the same thing again. "Look at this, Rog."

"Well, what d'you know, perhaps he fancies himself as the Soar's lock keeper."

As part of a flood relief scheme, both Ratcliffe and Kegworth Deep Lock had been replaced. The old locks remained close by, their wooden gates still intact, hidden in the undergrowth. Exploring the remains of industrial archaeology was a favourite pastime of ours and Buster was no stranger to accompanying us on such expeditions. These sometimes involved pushing through dense undergrowth, climbing fences and wading through ditches at a time when the right to roam was wishful thinking, all to seek out a lost canal route. Buster usually found the remains of locks, wharves and bridges first and liked nothing better than being rewarded with a tasty treat after showing off his superior skills in sniffing out a find. He also bore the brunt of many encounters with officious landowners, a scapegoat in the form of a Beagle. When faced with the words "What the bloody hell are you doing on my land; this is private property?" we only had to point at the dog and shake our heads to be let off the hook.

"He saw a rabbit and chased it, sorry." We would beat a hasty retreat as Buster flashed us a glance of contempt.

The Devil's Elbow at Sutton Bonington was a popular weekend destination for boaters. The sound of leather on willow and calls of "How's that?" rang out across the countryside on Sunday afternoons as cricket was played. Taking Buster around the perimeter, he one day decided to take a shortcut by running diagonally across the middle of the cricket pitch whilst a game was in full swing. Luckily, the bowler spotted him before releasing the hard ball, pausing the game to allow our snuffling Beagle right of way.

When time allowed, we ventured further. Once through the lock at Zouch, a cut bypassed the natural river for a short distance. This was traversed by a low footbridge which required *Lily's* wheelhouse to be dismantled. *Lily's* previous owner had demonstrated how the wheelhouse folded down; it was an easy enough procedure but, in this open spot, it could quickly develop into a battle with the elements as the winds tried to whip the aluminium roof panels out of our hands.

The Soar was once one of the most prosperous river navigations in the country, carrying coal as its main cargo, but, with the arrival of the railways, freight inevitably declined. The Victorian Central Station, Loughborough, marked the start of the restored Great Central Railway to Leicester. Buster loved the train ride through countryside to the terminus at Birstall on Britain's only mainline steam railway, the cause of the Soar's demise as a trade route.

"Think there's something round the prop; the engine's stalled." Buster and I were sitting up front as *Lily* gently chugged through the southern outskirts of Loughborough. I had felt the shudder but, as *Lily*'s engine was quiet, had not realised it had stalled. Roger guided *Lily* into the bank and fastened off.

Access to the prop was gained through the inspection hatch in the back cabin. In the short time we had had *Lily,* this had become full of items thought essential but in fact they rarely were. The back cabin had been christened 'the shed' and, as Roger fought to empty the small space, stacking items on the towpath, it became obvious the situation had to be addressed. Tins of paint and varnish, buckets, camping chairs, wellingtons, fishing gear, odd pieces of rope, old coats, a yard broom, jet washer, dog blankets, sacks of firewood, a tool box, then finally a bag of compost and a collection of seed trays and flower pots emerged. The towpath resembled a jumble sale; passersby stopped to eye the items sprawled bankside. Roger was exhausted before even opening the inspection hatch but Buster was pleased to discover a long-lost toy in the growing heap. He sat on the towpath and gnawed at it as if it were a bone.

"How much d'you want for the dog?" a cyclist shouted. Buster dropped his toy and grumbled.

"Bloody cheek," I muttered under my breath.

"I'm going to need a saw," Roger boomed from the back cabin as I stared unbelievably at the pile on the towpath. Had all these things really come out of such a small space?

"Oh no, I think it's buried in amongst the pile on the towpath. D'you know what the problem is?" I climbed back on board, peering into the gloom.

"Fabric of some kind, wrapped so tightly around everything I can't move it." As Roger spoke, he raised his wet arm out of the inspection hatch and let the dirty canal water drip all over the pale pink carpet.

"Watch the carpet, will you; put a towel down for goodness' sake or you'll ruin it!" After retrieving the saw, Roger spent the remainder of the afternoon removing a fleece from the rudder and prop. It was amazing an item of clothing had totally incapacitated *Lily* but thankfully it happened on a still canal section rather than the open river.

The river beyond Mountsorrel Lock was bordered by lush, nature-rich water meadows and led to picturesque Sileby Mill, where there was a small marina. Roger phoned ahead and booked *Lily* a berth but, despite giving her dimensions, on arrival the owners were unable to accommodate her – *Lily* was too large. Instead, we were offered a canalside spot adjacent to the marina, with no facilities. Knowing I would be alone with Buster for a week as Roger was returning south to work, we topped up with water from the marina before taking up the mooring. Once the tank was full, we prepared to move off. Roger knocked the throttle into gear but *Lily* would not budge. He tried to reverse and a thick, muddy wash bubbled up beneath the stern. *Lily* was firmly stuck on the bottom, the weight of a full tank of water grounding her. The only way to escape the muddy hold was to turn on the taps, emptying the water just added.

Buster and I explored the local countryside and villages, rising bright and early in the mornings to walk along the river to Junction Lock. As the name suggested, this was once an important junction, the entrance to the former Wreake Navigation close by. Other times, we struggled up the steep incline of Castle Hill. Topping the scant remains of the former castle was a war memorial constructed out of local quarried pink granite. At one time, the granite accounted for much of the goods passing through Mountsorrel Lock, transported by barge to London. The forecourt of Buckingham Palace was constructed from this stone.

When the sun shone, we sat outside together. Buster snoozed contentedly and I occupied myself with writing articles, reading or, now that the compost had been found, planting chilli pepper, aubergine and tomato seeds. On occasion, dark clouds rushed in on gusty winds to bombard us with short, sharp showers that sought forgiveness by offering sweeping rainbow arcs spanning the lock cut, enthralling us with their beauty. The red brickwork of Sileby Mill gave the illusion of a penetrating warmth against the cold, grey, stormy skies. Large globes of angelica bordering the mill race somehow withstood the force of the downpour. May blossom, not so successful in this endeavour, coated the water with tiny petals.

Despite Roger's absence, I felt secure on board thanks to Buster. Although not generally considered good guard dogs, Beagles were bright and alert. Buster would warn me if someone was close by, a muffled grumble under his breath quickly gave way to a bark if need be. For a relatively small-sized dog, his bark was deep and loud, enough to warn off any would-be intruder or inquisitive onlooker. Roger joked, "We had to roll up his bark to get it inside him."

During our time on these waters, we stopped frequently, indulging in friendly chats with the riverside rangers who formed part of the Leicester riverside programme, created to redevelop and encourage more people to use the waterside amenities. On one visit, we were approached by a ranger who was surprised to hear a boat of *Lily*'s size had successfully made it to

Dark skies and double rainbows at Sileby Mill

Leicester. *Lily* had touched bottom in a few places and he was keen to record where for a future dredging programme.

"Next time you're heading to Leicester, can you give us a call? It would be really helpful if one or two of us could come along and record the depth and problem areas." Roger and the ranger swapped contact numbers. He then went on to ask us if we had had any unwanted attention from unruly youngsters. Thankfully, our travels on the Soar had been trouble free.

Limekiln Lock was occasionally used by youths as a swimming pool and, although a dangerous practice, one could not help being impressed by their imaginative use of local facilities. Returning from a trip to Leicester, we found ourselves confronted by a group of bare-chested youngsters, jumping and leaping about, throwing themselves into the full lock chamber. Roger and I liked to think we were streetwise but, after the recent conversation with the ranger, our senses had been heightened to the evidence of antisocial behaviour. Buster, in his elevated position on the chart table, was usually enough to put troublemakers off but having a camera or pretending to talk on a mobile phone were nifty tricks to keep bored youngsters from using us as target practice.

"Great," I muttered, "looks like trouble up ahead." Roger was already eyeing up the situation, windlass in hand.

"Drop me off and stay in the middle of the canal."

"No, what if there's trouble? I won't be able to reach you." As we got closer, I could see the group were only young so my fear subsided a little. "Just be nice and ask them if we can go through." We moored up loosely in case I needed to move off quickly.

Roger put on his boldest swaying walk, swinging the windlass as if a weapon of war. I was too far away to hear the conversation but the group had divided. Some were talking to Roger, a couple continued jumping into the lock chamber and the remainder came rushing over to me.

"Cor, look at this boat. It's fantastic. Is it yours, missus?" The over-excited voice came from a dark curly-haired boy. He wore baggy shorts, a damp towel draped around his shoulders and nothing on his feet. "C'mon," he shouted to his mates. "'Ave a look at this." In no time at all, there were six boys at his side, eyeing me and *Lily* up and down. Buster shuffled in his bed, sat bolt upright, tilted his head and observed them closely. He was a great judge of character and, from his behaviour, I knew there was nothing to fear. However, that did not stop my heart racing and a sense of dread building. Beyond the boys, I could see Roger and a couple of older lads were talking, leaning together on the balance beam.

"Look at those little mats." One boy pointed at our 'Welcome Aboard' coconut doormats. "Cor, they're really nice, aren't they?"

"Thank you." I wished Roger would hurry up and open the gates.

"Can I stand inside with you, missus?" the curly-haired lad asked, his eyes atwinkle.

"Well, I'm just going so it's not a good idea." I stroked Buster more out of trying to block the doorway than nervousness.

"Oh please, I won't touch anything." He seemed upset. "Go on, please, just for a minute." I was not one to be taken in by youngsters but this lad was as angelic as a street urchin from a Charles Dickens novel as he grinned at me and pleaded, "Go on, missus."

"Just quickly then and don't touch the dog."

"Why's that, missus, does he bite?"

"Well, he hasn't had his dinner yet." I tried not to laugh, this was one of my dad's favourite lines.

"Oh right, I see," the lad stuttered and stepped back, obviously growing worried. His mates realised it was a joke and erupted into laughter, one of them giving him a quick nudge in the ribs with his elbow before he cottoned on and fell about, joining them in the joke.

"Come on then." The lad stepped into the open wheelhouse.

"Look at me in the boat. I can be captain." The smile on his face was broadening with each second that passed. "Oohh, look down there, it's like a house." He almost screeched in excitement as he gazed down the steps into the main saloon.

"Where, let's see?" Another lad stepped on the boat and peered downstairs. Then another stepped on and sat down behind me.

"This is lovely, what a nice boat you got, lady."

Before I knew it, all the lads were in the wheelhouse. They were no bother, just wide-eyed and astonished. They looked at the gauges, the steering wheel, my pot of herbs and, of course, Buster but not one of them touched him.

"Hey, get off the bloody boat now." Roger's voice boomed into their enthusiasm, stopping it dead. There was no hesitation; they hurriedly left the boat, leaving me to calm the situation.

"It's alright, Roger. I said they could stand in the wheelhouse."

"Oh, alright then." He looked at me as if I were mad. "We're off now anyway. Sorry about that, lads." He ate humble pie at breakneck speed, fearing his over-reaction could flare up trouble.

"That's OK, mister, got a really great boat there and you will fill the lock back up, won't you?" one of the boys asked.

"You know it's dangerous, don't you? I shouldn't really. I could get into trouble."

"Yeah, I know," he sighed. There was a chorus of moans and sighs by his mates, followed by pleas. As Roger stepped back on the boat, the lads thanked us for letting them on board and then helped us lock through, chatting all the while. Buster never took his eyes off them but neither did he growl or give reason to think there was a danger. Exiting the lock, we waved goodbye to the fresh-faced, full-of-life youngsters.

"Pull over," Roger said.

"Why?"

"I'm going back to fill the lock for them."

In the early days of boating with Buster and *Lily*, we visited the Soar many times. Most weekend trips involved a pleasant cruise to the Devil's Elbow, evening walks and barbecues along the riverbank, kicking back and relaxing. It was on a trip back to base from here when Buster, in pursuit of a Border Collie on the bank, forgot to stop on reaching *Lily*'s stern and found himself in deep water. We were beginning to learn plenty about boisterous Beagles and bothersome boats.

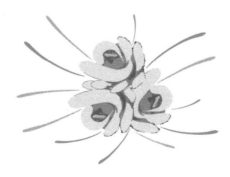

Chapter Nine

THE TRESPASSER

The River Trent, one of Britain's greatest rivers, was the third longest in the country. So far, Roger and I had only seen a small fraction of the upper reaches but, with *Lily*'s mooring expiring, we decided to find her a new home; somewhere allowing exploration of the waters further north. Whilst we enjoyed Shardlow and its surroundings, the bottlenecks caused by the locks at both Sawley and Cranfleet cuts meant a lot of time was wasted, eating into our already-limited weekends as a famished, shipwrecked sailor would a good square meal.

The navigable river was split into three parts: the upper reaches from Shardlow to Beeston, the middle reaches from Nottingham to Cromwell and the tidal reaches to the Humber Estuary. The Beeston and Nottingham Canals linked the upper and middle reaches. Locking onto the canal at Beeston, the wheelhouse needed dismantling to pass beneath Nottingham's low bridges. Dubbed the knife capital of England, following several crime-related incidents, it was somewhere we had previously avoided. Without the wheelhouse, we were vulnerable — sitting targets for trouble makers — and I was nervous about the journey. But it was not unruly youths brandishing weapons which caused fear and mayhem. With a sudden fluster, several pigeons flew out

from the low-level bridge beyond Castle Lock, skimming Roger's head as *Lily* slid beneath. With no wheelhouse offering protection, Roger was immediately sent into a blind panic due to his fear of birds.

With *Lily* safely secured in Meadow Lane Lock, we walked to the edge and peered down on the river below. Roger and I eyed each other with nervous grins, each knowing what the other was thinking. This was similar to some of the wide, fast-flowing rivers we had navigated in France. Buster teetered on the edge of the coping stones, looking at the scene before him. Slowly, he raised his head to look at us. *Are you guys **serious**? Do you really think we are taking the boat out there?*

Holme Lock was overshadowed by the massive Colwick Sluices, constructed to prevent the city of Nottingham flooding. As if by magic, the lock gates slowly and silently opened as *Lily* approached. With a green light displayed, I motored into the vast expanse and, being the only boat in the chamber, allowed her paddle-wheel effect, which favoured the portside, to dictate her position.

"Hello, everything alright and are you secure?" came a loud but friendly voice from the control centre. Buster started, glared over his shoulder.

"Hi, it's our first time here but, yes, I think we're all set." I finished gathering in *Lily*'s stern rope.

"I'll be right out." The lock keeper smiled broadly and, a few seconds later, was at the lockside, clutching a handful of literature about the river and its surroundings. Roger tied *Lily* off at the bow and joined us for a chat about the Trent and how things worked. The lock keeper told us he would radio ahead, informing the next lock keeper to expect us. Buster listened, taking it all in, loving the attention given to him. "Now settle in and enjoy the ride. It's a slow, smooth descent, relax and welcome to the middle Trent." The descent was indeed slow and extremely smooth. As daylight retreated, Buster settled down and fell asleep. A few minutes later, a thin crack of light appeared between the vast lock gates. It was time to push on.

"That was a friendly welcome." Roger had joined me at the helm.

"Yes, wasn't that nice? I think we're going to be happy here." Buster opened one eye and, with a gentle murmur, nestled his muzzle into the comfy blue jumper lining his bed.

"Think Buzz approves too," Roger chuckled.

The Trent appeared a different river below Nottingham, growing wider and deeper, with more rural surroundings. Approaching Stoke Lock, steep cliffs began to rise from the bank and the wooded landscape closed in around the river. The woods surrounding the lock, originally planted to supply fuel for shipping, formed a nature reserve; a haven for wildlife. Bat boxes had been mounted and, in the evenings, pipistrelle bats could be seen skimming over the water. Flowing on, the Trent made several sweeping curves, passing the pretty village of Burton Joyce before reaching Gunthorpe, where the long weir arced across the river to the lock.

Yellow fields of rapeseed, as tall as me, tumbled down the steep slopes of the Trent Hills above Gunthorpe. The public footpath, dry and dusty, ran through the middle of the field then plunged out of view in its descent towards the cooling waters of the Trent. Half hidden and far below, it hugged the tree-lined bank in an almost desperate search for shade. The strong, musky, bitter-sweet scent from the crop was overpowering but, as it bore such a delightful flower, I was happy to forgive this shortcoming. As Buster walked in front of me, his white paws slowly began to turn a rosy shade of pink from the dusty soil he kicked up. Above, skylarks sang as if their lives depended on it, shattering the otherwise silent scene. On the river, waterfowl had paired and raised their brood of hungry chicks. They fussed about them and tried their best to keep them safe from the slinky mink or steel-like jaws of the pike. Late spring at Gunthorpe, there was nothing better.

Leaving Gunthorpe Lock, white-painted clapper gates punctuated the riverside path. Gliders from Syerston airfield circled silently on thermals, as if giant birds of prey patrolling the skies over Hazelford Lock. Sitting midstream on

a small island, known locally as The Nabbs or Rabbit Island, Hazelford Lock became our second home and Buster adored it. The resident

Walking through rapeseed fields on the Trent hills above Gunthorpe

colony of rabbits kept Buster entertained, amongst them a golden one which was only ever seen on a couple of occasions, its bright, ginger-coloured fur standing out against the undergrowth. How it got there was a mystery; was it an escaped pet from the lock keeper's cottage or maybe an oddity of nature?

Buster rushed off in a flurry of excitement, sending rabbits scurrying in all directions. They desperately sought shelter in the dense blackberry bushes as our marauding hound bellowed in pursuit. One, sitting in the middle of a grassy pathway, was slow on the uptake and, instead of diving for the blackberry bushes, turned and raced along the path. Roger and I stood and laughed as we watched the pair of them disappear. Then it went quiet.

"D'you think he's alright?"

"Yes, of course he is." But we both quickened our pace, weaving between the blackberry bushes, although still no sign of Buster. There were several ways which he could have gone but, knowing he could not get off the island, neither of us were overly concerned. We heard the gentle tinkling of Buster's name tag on his collar before he raced around the corner of the narrow pathway, brushing the blackberry bushes as he came, a huge, burnt sausage in his mouth.

"Oh no, where did you get that from?" Buster skidded to a halt at my feet. Looking at me, his eyes twinkled with happiness.

"I always knew that dog was special," said Roger. "Not only can he catch a rabbit, he's a skilled butcher and chef to boot."

Heading to the barbecue area, we discovered a family enjoying their meal. I felt awful, Buster at my feet, licking his lips, no doubt hoping for a re-run as I nervously stumbled through an apology on behalf of my food-stealing hound. The father in the family stood up. My heart sank. I sensed a lecture coming on and tried to prepare myself.

"There's no need to apologise. Your dog didn't steal the sausage. I gave it to him; it was too burnt for us. Hope that was alright?"

I let out a huge sigh and looked down at Buster. He met my gaze and frowned. *Why do you always think the worst of me?*

People usually developed a liking for Buster; either that or they felt sorry for him. He had an uncanny knack of looking bored, hard done by and constantly hungry, frequently resulting in offerings of food, much to Buster's delight. Boat crews approached with leftover chargrilled items from barbecues or wandered back from the local pub clutching a doggy bag.

"We thought your dog would like this," plunging a soggy napkin of their pub meal remains into my hand.

"Lovely, thanks very much." I would grin as the greasy juices oozed between my fingers. You name it, Buster got it, from a gristly cut of steak to a hot roasted potato, and he loved it.

This, unbeknown to me at the time, was all therapy. Whilst *Lily* and the waterways produced a calming effect, Buster encouraged me to go out and have conversations that, otherwise, I would avoid. Combined, they soothed and healed, gave me back some of the confidence I had lost. I found solace in them. As flotsam on a flowing river, I was happy to go along for the ride, to discover what watery adventures life had in store for me.

We spent hot summers and cold winters at Hazelford as well as everything in between. We had hung on until flood waters levelled the highest point of the quay before slipping moorings, speeding back to safety in the gravy-brown, swirling waters. Many Christmases we had the place completely to ourselves

and could not understand why people packed up their boats in October and went to hide in their brick-and-mortar boxes. We were spoilt rotten. The years on the Trent were magical, she became our river, our home and we loved her.

Newark Castle

The Trent rounded the pretty village of Farndon, cut through Newark, overshadowed by its castle ruins, and wound on to Cromwell Lock, marking the start of the tidal reaches. It had been used as a means of navigation since the Bronze Age, forming a trade route between the metal-working industries of Ireland and Europe. The Romans called it Trisantona – the trespasser – which referred to the frequent times the river flooded, spilling its waters onto the surrounding landscape and, just as a trespasser would, the Trent silently crept in and stole my heart.

Chapter Ten

A NEW HOME FOR LILY

*L*ily's new home was Farndon Marina, in my opinion the best on the Trent. The grounds were beautifully maintained, grassy banks and blossoming cherry trees bordered the water's edge. Birds and wildlife thrived in the haven of still water. Kingfishers visited daily and, from the galley window, we looked out onto a small island where a pair of grey heron nested and raised their young. *Lily* was in good company, sharing the marina with three other Sagar barges: *Our Millie D*, *Peridot* and *Doris*. We forged friendships with their owners, shared stories, cruising itineraries, help and advice on maintenance. One of the finest places we ever had the privilege to call home, we stayed for over four years.

Two of the first people we met there were Viv and Bryony. Also new to the marina, their powerful sports cruiser, *Buoy-o-Buoy*, was a few berths from *Lily*. Their boat was a swish, glass-fibre beast with tinted glass, thick pile carpets and a round double bed; all very glamorous in that Hollywood-movie way.

When an opportunity arose for Buster and me to accompany them on a short trip for lunchtime drinks one Friday, how could I refuse?

Lily moored at Farndon Marina

"Don't you get used to that," shouted our neighbour, Ken, from the decks of his barge, *Helianthus*. I had made no secret of the fact that I would have liked *Lily* to have a little more power. Buster and I sat on *Buoy-o-Buoy*'s rear deck and lapped up the slow potter through the marina. Passing the newly arrived weekenders with bags of supplies and bottles of booze, all eyes were on the handsome boat or, as Buster would say, 'the handsome hound'.

A forty-five-minute trip in *Lily* took just ten in *Buoy-o-Buoy*. We sat outside the Bromley Arms with large glasses of silky-smooth red wine and looked down on the river and fields of yellow rapeseed stretching into the distance. Buster drank long and slowly from a fresh bowl of water delivered to him personally by the bartender. A couple of hours passed along with the consumption of a few more glasses of wine, which slid down like velvet, soft and fruity, leaving us wrapped in hazy warmth similar to the day itself.

Before the journey home, Buster and I stretched our legs whilst Viv and Bryony returned to prepare the boat for departure. Buster was happy with the unexpected change of scenery on a weekday. I thought of Roger toiling away at work, missing out on a perfect afternoon, the long four-hour commute still ahead of him. Returning to the boat, the engine was already throbbing loudly, attracting the pub's clientele to look over the quayside railings at the 'mean machine'. Buster and I enjoyed the walk through the crowd, down to the pontoon and onto the rear deck, knowing we were being enviously watched. Perhaps Viv was thinking the same from the helm because, turning the boat in the river, he fully opened the throttle.

The boat's bow rose steeply out of the water. From my sitting position, I could no longer see anything through the front cabin windows, only the sky. Bryony and I held onto our seats and giggled. Buster, his feet slipping and sliding on the shiny, smooth deck, appreciated the wind beneath his ears. He backed up, wedging himself tightly and securely between my legs, screwed up his eyes, lifted his nose in the air and sniffed deeply as we shot down the Trent at goodness knows what speed. Looking back towards Fiskerton, people were dots in the distance, jostling to watch our progress and the wash created. It was topping the quay wall, sending splashes into the air. People stepped away to avoid a drenching.

Viv did not not let up; boy oh boy, could *Buoy-o-Buoy* move! We sped along, rounding bends without slowing. The thought of encountering a large barge flashed into my mind but did not linger. Luck was on our side; we encountered no other craft, only dropping the revs on the final bend into Farndon, having reached the village in record time. It was a moment of madness, of foolish irresponsible behaviour but, for me, after pottering about at five knots, a naughty treat.

Lily's neighbouring boat was a glass-fibre Nimbus cruiser, the owners rarely seen, their names a mystery but we gave the man in the partnership our own nickname after a certain incident …

I was with Buster on the sofa, an old black-and-white movie playing on the television, when the mains electricity died.

"Sorry, Buzz, must be a power cut." I pulled myself away; Buster loved draping his entire body over me. Glancing out of the window, I saw my neighbour madly flicking switches in the electric box. Heading into the wheelhouse, I opened the window.

"Hello, have you got a problem with the electric?"

"Yes, I haven't got any. Have you?" he replied without taking his eyes off the switches.

"Mine's fine but I think you may have switched it off." He spun around, staring at me as if I had sworn at him.

"You say you have power?"

"Yes, it's been fine all day." He flicked several switches on and off before returning to his boat.

Snuggling down to continue my afternoon with Buster, the same thing happened. My neighbour was back, flicking the switches.

"D'you realise you've turned my electric off again?"

"You have electric, do you?"

"Yes, I did but now you've turned it off."

"I think there's something wrong with it. Best go and tell them at the office." He scratched his head.

"There's nothing wrong with it; my electric's fine when you don't turn it off."

"But you said you didn't have electric?"

"Yes, that's right. You've switched it off."

"So, you did have electric earlier?" Opening the door, I stormed over to the electric box and flicked the switches on.

"There you are. Now *you* have electric, *I* have electric and so does everyone else on the pontoon." I turned to see Buster in the doorway. He leaned into a long stretch, no doubt thinking, *Not that idiot again.* I beat a hasty retreat before my hound could make matters worse. A few minutes later, the same thing happened again. I watched from the window, knowing sparks would fly if I went out.

Whenever our neighbour arrived, the same thing happened. He spent more time flicking the switches of the circuit breakers than boating. Flick, flick, flick, he drove most of us on the pontoon mad and was soon referred to as 'Sparky'. The cause of Sparky's constant power failure turned out to be a rapid-boil kettle tripping the system.

Further along *Lily's* pontoon was Colvic cruiser, *Ambergris*, which belonged to David and Wendy. The couple were well known in the marina and befriended almost everyone. Looking back, it was hard to imagine the place without them; they were almost part of the fixtures and fittings. Like us, they were dog people so, when invited to each other's boats, it was fine for our respective dogs to go too. Evening drinks at the marina and along the Trent's moorings became treasured events, barbecues lasting long into summer nights, spicy mulled wine warmed on the stove as snow softly fell. We shared so many wonderful occasions with them.

"Here comes Bertie Basset," the sing-song voice of *Lily's* new boating neighbour rang out. *Not again,* I thought to myself. Buster threw me a glance. *Why does he insist on calling me a Basset, can't he see I'm a Beagle?* I had corrected the man several times and was as fed up as my hound but laughed it off. Our new neighbour had relocated from a marina upriver following an unfortunate encounter with rodents. Leaving his boat with a window open over winter to allow ventilation, he had returned in the spring to discover a family of rats had moved in. They had revelled in the unoccupied boat, gnawed at fixtures and fittings, chewed on soft furnishings and plucked out the stuffing of seating, creating a luxurious nest fit for any king rat and his extended family. With the rodents successfully evicted, refitting the boat had begun in earnest. Returning from morning walks, we would find the pontoon littered with all manner of boat contents. Despite trying my best to give it a wide berth, Buster's nose homed in on the ratty rubbish, almost pulling my arm out of its socket to take a closer sniff. After listening to the story, I ensured *Lily's* windows were firmly shut when leaving her for any length of time and, feeling sorry for the man, let the Bertie Bassett mistake slide – much to Buster's disgust.

Chapter Eleven

TIME AND TIDE

Roger and I stood on the lockside, staring into the empty chamber. It was a long way down.

"It's huge," I gasped. Buster sat down next to me and scratched his neck. I leant down and stroked him. "It's alright, Buzz, nothing to worry about. You're safe with us." He stopped scratching and looked at me, loving and trusting.

"It's like being back on the River Saône." Roger's comment helped. We had navigated the French river in all seasons and conditions, laughed at our thoughts of not tying into lock chambers. They were so huge we could have motored the length of them and still not have reached the far gates before the locking process was complete. But it was not Cromwell Lock which was bothering me. It was the Trent's tidal waters.

My initial nervousness of venturing onto tidal waters was not due to lack of knowledge – inshore cruising off West Sussex had given me some experience – it was the thought of taking *Lily*, my safe haven, onto them which was causing concern. Whilst I was happy planning trips, Roger was the calculator and mathematician; it was his responsibility to time everything correctly. A lot was at risk; inaccuracy could result in *Lily* being left high and dry whereas accuracy could reveal a whole new world of cruising opportunities. Tackling the tidal Trent as far as Torksey would allow access to the Fossdyke and Witham Navigations and one of the country's greatest masterpieces of Gothic architecture – Lincoln Cathedral.

Cromwell was always busy with craft; it was the place to take stock of the tidal route ahead. There was usually a dog or two for Buster to play with, someone with an unwanted snack suitable for him to take off their hands and plenty of sticks. The trees bordering the lock site dropped twigs and Buster loved to romp off with a great mouthful of them, enticing one of us into a game of chase.

"Roger, he shouldn't have all those twigs. He'll hurt himself running about with them in his mouth." We knew the dangers – how a stick could easily cause injury – but it was difficult to stop Buster playing the game. I had collected a heap of twigs – once dried, they made good kindling for the stove – and had gone to fetch a basket from the boat. I returned to see Roger chasing Buster. He was laughing so much he could hardly run. Buster was frolicking, leaping, teasing Roger into thinking he had almost caught him before taking off in a double-the-speed blast. Buster stopped, turned to face Roger and promptly spat out a mouthful of soggy, chewed-up twigs, jumped on the spot a few times and raced through my kindling pile, grabbing a mouthful.

"Oh no, what a waste of time," I yelled, dropping the basket. Twigs flew everywhere, scattering all over the grass from where I had spent the last hour collecting them. Roger was in fits of laughter and still giving chase. Buster dodged him, dropped the mouthful of twigs and returned, doing the same again. Hands on hips, I sighed, shook my head and watched my boys play. They were having such fun I went to join them. Winter was a long way off. The kindling could wait.

For Buster, Cromwell became the place to let off steam and take a toilet break before the two-hour trip to Torksey. Toilet training during his early days was now paying off. At the command "Quick wee-wee," he would promptly cock his leg and do his duty, rushing back to take pride of place in the wheelhouse. Buster never relieved himself on board *Lily*, against boater's ropes and mooring pins or on any type of jetty, always waiting until reaching dry land. We were proud of him.

Once through Cromwell Lock, Roger and I were immediately into route-finding mode. The navigable course constantly changed position. The tidal guides

HUMBER RENOWN

showed shoals, shallows, sunken islands and training walls, many lying unseen at certain states of the tide.

A commercial barge grounded on the tidal Trent

"Be careful," I would gasp or, "Get over," as a feeling of panic descended when tackling a tricky section. Buster looked at me as if I were crazy for raising my voice. He could not see what all the fuss was about. Gradually, I grew to love the tidal Trent almost as much as the middle reaches; I became confident navigating it but never complacent. I adored seeing the wading birds, became intrigued by the local names for specific stretches of the river and its reaches – milking boat and the fleet; racks, stakes and dubs. Every time *Lily* was lowered onto its waters, I felt she was undertaking a great voyage.

There were also commercial barges carrying aggregates to contend with. These leviathans appeared quite intimidating, especially if encountered on a blind bend. Fully laden, they pushed a great wall of water before them, the bow wave often as high as the vessel itself. Our years in France, boating alongside péniches, had stood us in good stead; we were not nervous encountering such huge vessels, simply in awe. The Trent skippers were kind and considerate, always throwing a wave, and it was a great joy sharing the waterways with them. Buster stirred when he heard the thudding of their engines. Watching them pass, he would gaze down into the waters as *Lily* crossed the wash. But even the professionals got it wrong sometimes. During a particularly low tide one year, we passed two commercial barges beached across the width of the Trent. It was a shock rounding a bend to find them sitting midstream. Roger called one of the skippers on the VHF and he instructed us to pass in the deeper water lying off their bows. They had to wait for the next high tide before the Trent released them.

The tidal journey was not so much a boring trip for Buster as a chance to relax, time to have two hours uninterrupted snoozing in the knowledge that something nice awaited him at either end. Torksey Cut was known locally as 'The Arm' and led to the entrance lock on the Fossdyke. There was usually an optimistic atmosphere on the moorings with plenty of storytelling as people awaited the right state of tide to continue their journey. Once ashore, Buster displayed his thanks by shimmying along the pontoon, head on one side and bottom in the air, travelling for a few yards in this position before collapsing and rolling around on his back, legs waving in the air. What this behaviour signified was hard to define – happiness, relief or just celebrating life – but it became one of his trademarks, attracting the attention of other boaters and always raising a smile. He was enjoying life and so, finally, were we.

The Fossdyke was constructed by the Romans to join the River Trent with the River Witham in the heart of Lincoln and was the oldest man-made waterway open to navigation in the country. Collectively known as the Fossdyke and Witham Navigation, it provided a through route from the heart of Britain to the North Sea. For centuries, it played an important part in our country's history: used by the Danes when invading Britain and by the Normans for shipping stone used in the construction of Lincoln Cathedral. From the tidal Trent, it was accessed through Torksey Lock but there was only sufficient water over the cill for a few hours either side of high tide, which meant liaising with the lock keeper and getting the timing right was essential.

I slowly eased *Lily* along a series of straight sections; she appeared extremely large on the narrow waterway. Hemmed in by the high flood banks, Roger thought the Fossdyke was boring but, after the intense concentration needed on the tideway, its simplicity was welcomed.

"You can tell the Romans built this. It's just like their roads: dead straight." With that, he took Buster for a stroll around the deck, which was a mistake because all he wanted to do was jump ship; he was bored too. There was no towpath or anywhere for him to get off until, rounding a corner and passing under a railway bridge, we entered Saxilby.

Not far beyond Burton Waters Marina stood the Pyewipe Inn. Pyewipe was a local name for the lapwing, an attractive wading bird and a familiar sight on the surrounding farmland. It was more commonly referred to as the peewit, due to its distinctive call. After a belly-blowing Sunday roast in the Pyewipe, a doggy bag of leftovers was delivered to our faithful companion left tethered in the open wheelhouse.

"What a good boy you've been, Buzzy." I reached down to praise him but he was only interested in the smell of still-warm leftovers. Buster quivered in excitement and tried his best to nuzzle the bag.

"You'll have to be patient and wait until it's in your bowl. Now sit." Buster immediately obeyed the command; it was amazing the hold food had over him. Instead of having his usual Bonio biscuit for lunch, he tucked into a succulent bowl of roast beef and vegetables, sleeping soundly all afternoon.

The River Witham flowed into Brayford Pool in the heart of Lincoln, where it mixed with the waters of the Fossdyke to form a navigable waterway. Until the late 1840s, this was the main means of transporting passengers and goods between the towns of Boston and Lincoln. Leaving Brayford Pool, the navigable Witham followed a narrow, one-way channel through the heart of Lincoln. This short section was controlled by traffic lights, advising boaters to proceed with caution or informing the navigation was temporarily closed, depending on the force of the current. It was crossed by High Bridge, the oldest bridge topped with medieval timber-framed buildings in the country. The dark passage underneath was known to boaters as the 'Glory Hole' and, to pass through, *Lily*'s wheelhouse needed to be dismantled. Once through, she emerged into the bustling city. The sounds of 'oohs and aahs' when people spotted Buster carried across the water and rebounded off the walls. Parents gathered toddlers into their arms and pointed at him, mobiles and cameras were sought and, knowing he was about to be caught on film, Buster would turn away with a 'No paparazzi if you please' expression on his face.

One chilly Easter, we took Roger's father, Les, for a trip to Lincoln, the first and only time he was able to visit us aboard *Lily*. He laughed at Buster's dismissive behaviour over would-be photographers.

"He really hates it, doesn't he?"

"Yeah, he doesn't really like me taking his photo either. I never know what I'm going to get. Sometimes he looks right in the lens and smiles, sometimes he turns away in a huff." Over the years, Buster's grin became known as his sometimes-smile. When it made a show, the world was a better place for it.

I hated the self-operated Stamp End Lock and sluice. Its guillotine gate always dripped cold water on my head as I steered *Lily* beneath. Roger was halfway through filling the lock one day when a small, wide, tatty-looking cruiser pulled up. An elderly man jumped out, his bow legs wide enough for his own boat to pass between. Swaying towards Roger, he adjusted his flat cap and sang out, "Morning, very slow this lock; it's governed you see," then promptly stuck a screwdriver into the workings of the control panel.

"Hey, what're you doing?" shouted Roger.

"Overriding it. Works much faster if you do this but of course you need to know what you're about."

"Hang on, isn't that dangerous?" The man continued to push and twist the screwdriver.

"No, I've been doing it for years. Look, I'll show you, then you'll know how to do it next time you penn through. It'll save a lot of time."

"Think I would rather take it slowly and live longer, thanks all the same."

"It's simple, no danger at all, look ..." He pointed and explained the workings of the lock.

I stroked Buster's head and whispered to him, "It's OK, I think he must be a part-time lock keeper." Buster was busy watching the swirling waters around

Lily and looked uncertain at the newcomer's interference. I glanced over to Roger, who was in deep conversation with the man. Roger caught my eye and shrugged his shoulders, shaking his head at the same time.

At Washingborough, we stopped for a short break at the moorings to walk Buster. Information boards told how the village was bombed one night in WWI by a Zeppelin when the train it was following stopped short to save the city. The Lincoln to Boston railway had been converted into a cycle route known as the Water Rail Way, named after the shy bird that inhabited the river, and featured several interesting sculptures. Near Five Mile Bridge there were two fine Lincoln Red cows crafted from scrap metal and steel fittings. Following a previous incident with curious cattle in Stansted Park in West Sussex, Buster was extremely wary of bovine encounters, so it was

Buster gave the red cow sculptures on the Water Rail Way a wide berth

no surprise that he refused to walk past the sculptures without the behaviour of a pantomime farce.

Stopping at Kirkstead Bridge, we headed off for several hours at a time to explore the Water Rail Way. Alongside most of the path was a deep dyke separating it from crop fields. Having Buster off-lead felt safe; he was unlikely to dip his feet into dirty ditch water. However, one morning he proved me wrong. Ahead, a bold hare hopped out of the hedgerow. Buster went into stalk mode and walked slowly, silently, deliberately, willing himself invisible to his prey. I knew it was a lost cause as I launched myself at him. Sensing my nabbing plan, Buster leapt into full throttle, thundering along the path in pursuit of the hare. The ground vibrated from Buster's thudding paws; his frustrated cries rang out, breaking the silence, sending birds into flight from treetops.

Sighing, I made no great haste to follow. The hare had disappeared through a gap in the hedgerow leading down to the fields. Buster would stop at the deep dyke having lost the scent, be scurrying back and forth in frustration, enabling me to retrieve him. I reached the gap and looked. Buster was nowhere in sight. I stood and waited, listened, but there was not a sound. I scanned the scene, the mile upon mile of flat, never-ending fields, and a movement caught my eye, a white flash in the distance. Buster was working a field, nose firmly on the ground, flag waving frantically. I stood and watched, amazed he had covered so much ground. I could not see an easy way of crossing the dyke and prayed I would not have to retrieve him. Suddenly, he paused and looked up.

"Bussssssterrrrrr," I called. "Buzzzzzyyyyy," I dragged the name out in a high-pitched tone. Buster looked at me and I raised my hand, waving the red handle of the retractable lead in wide arcs above my head. With eye contact made, I felt better. Buster would be back soon.

Two hours later, Buster returned to the dyke, puffing and panting. He paced alongside it, reluctant to get his feet wet for a second time.

"Come on, Buzz, you'll have to get across yourself. There's no way I can get to you." I tried to sound encouraging but I had had enough of my hound's

antics. Buster sat down and looked at me, dirty and wet, tired and no doubt hungry, his lunchtime snack well overdue. I walked to the edge of the dyke, lost my footing

Fun and games with the boat bike at Kirkstead Bridge

and plummeted to the ground, my feet and legs sliding into the ditchwater. Winded, I lay there and burst into tears. "Come on, Buzzy, do it for a biscuit, there's a good boy." Buster barked as I struggled to get up. I had hurt my back and my feet squelched in my saturated trainers. Reaching into my pocket, I rustled a bag of doggy treats. Buster threw himself into the black, stinking water and waded through. Scrambling out, he galloped at me, smashed into my legs and jumped up, snatching a biscuit from my grasp. Munching, he shook himself and I looked down to see I was covered in as much dirt and grime as he.

Arriving at *Lily*, we discovered she had company. A narrowboat had moored in front and a couple were enjoying an al fresco lunch and bottle of wine, the table neatly laid with a white cloth and vase of fresh flowers. Buster peered up at me with an 'I'll just pop over and introduce myself, see what's for lunch and all that' kind of look in his eyes.

"Don't you even think about it," I said aloud, staring hard at him. The couple looked up and eyed us oddly. Giving **them** a wave, I gathered my dirty dog in my arms and hurried inside, heading **straight** for the shower.

I liked the moorings at Tattershall and the pretty, red-brick bridge. Buster preferred Dogdyke with its dog-friendly pub. Roger did not have a preference as, from either, he could pull up a camping chair, sit back and watch his very own personal air display from nearby RAF Coningsby. *Lily* was buzzed by Eurofighters – fast-moving, noisy jets. Buster was not concerned about the noise but his eyes would flick about all over the place as he struggled to focus on them.

Long straight sections of canalised river faded into the distance. Reaching the end and turning the corner, an identical one stretched ahead.

"I'm sure we've just cruised this section," I joked; the Witham was a déjà-vu of a waterway. Anton's Gowt marked the entrance to the Witham Navigable Drains, which stretched for miles, leading to small

Boston Grand Sluice and the Stump

hamlets and villages but only the smallest of craft could access them. Ahead was Boston. The huge tower of St Botolph's Church, known as the Boston Stump, was the largest parish church in England. Visible across the flat countryside, it was used as a navigation marker for craft on The Wash.

Boston Grand Sluice marked the end of the non-tidal Witham. Beyond, the course of the tidal river wound through Boston, finally flowing into The Wash at Tabbs Head, but it would be a few more years before *Lily* undertook that voyage.

Chapter Twelve

LIVING WITH LILY

Unable to sell the house to finance the purchase of *Lily*, we had had to remortgage. This had proved expensive and purely a short-term fix. We were delighted when finally we sold it, despite the controversy this caused. Some family and friends were shocked, thinking we were running away. We could not continue to tread water; we had to move on with our lives. Sometimes you have to run away in order to start to live.

We left the relative warmth of the South Coast to move aboard *Lily* at the beginning of a bleak December, the car loaded with essential items. The temperatures plummeted to -13°C. Roger and I became compulsive wood collectors and, with the Morsø Squirrel stove pumping out heat, the cosy atmosphere inside *Lily* was heart-warming, homely. At times, it was too warm. We would often find ourselves rushing to fling open windows and doors to release the heat. If we had a pound for every time someone asked, "Isn't it cold on board during the winter?" we would have been revelling in riches beyond our wildest dreams.

Tap, tap, tap. Tap, tap, tap. I was woken by muffled noises coming from outside. Ducks and swans would come alongside and peck at the weed which had taken hold on the waterline of *Lily*'s hull but this was deeper, further beneath the surface and more pronounced. Tap, tap, tap, it went again.

"Did you hear that?" I whispered into Roger's ear. At the same time, Buster let out a raucous chorus of snores.

"All I can hear is the dog."

Climbing out of bed, the tapping continued as I headed into the galley. Through the window, in the grey winter dawn, I saw a small flock of tufted duck. They were shy and wary; spotting me, they headed off. Over the following weeks, the tapping continued. Eventually, through cautious approach to the galley window, I spotted them diving below the surface close to *Lily* and the tapping would begin.

"They must be picking off weed," said Roger. The noise was not a nuisance; the ducks were entertaining and had adopted *Lily*.

With Christmas approaching, *Lily* was decorated in fairy lights and, with carols echoing from the stereo and mulled wine gently warming on the stove, we cruised the Trent in complete contentment, seeing no other craft on the river for over a week. We headed to Hazelford Lock seeking solitude and were not disappointed. On Christmas Eve, we revelled in winter sunshine and a sausage sizzle at the barbecue area but the real icing on the cake was waking up on Christmas Day to a pristine, snow-covered landscape. Roger chopped wood and Buster explored; snow-encrusted molehills needed much investigation and the odd rabbit bold enough to brave the chill was soon chased back into its burrow. Buster amused us for hours playing in the frozen landscape, basking in the freedom of the lock island. I managed adequately in the compact galley, cooking a fabulous Christmas dinner of roast duck with all the trimmings.

At the stroke of midnight on New Year's Eve, we stood on the frosty lockside and watched the distant towns send showers of multi-coloured fireworks into the sky. Only the Trent spilling over the weir and the popping of a champagne cork broke the silence. Buster snuggled into the side of my leg and watched the chrysanthemum-like images of the fireworks.

River Trent watch dog, Buster keeping an eye on Lily at Hazelford Lock

"It feels good to be here." Roger put his arm around me. Looking down at Buster, he said, "I can't imagine life without Buster or *Lily*, can you?"

"No, I don't know what I'd do without them or you." I sighed, long and deep. "This feels so right. I guess we've been lucky in our unluckiness." I gazed up at Roger who leant down and kissed me.

"Uhrrrrrrr, what is *that?*" Roger winced and drew away, an abrupt halt to his romantic gesture.

"What's up?" Surely my breath did not smell that awful? Then it hit me, a most putrid rotting smell rising from around my legs. Buster had broken wind.

"I knew he shouldn't have had those Brussels sprouts with his dinner." Roger was waving his arms around, trying to clear the air.

"Buster, was that you?" He looked lovingly up at us with a 'Happy New Year' greeting.

The following spring, during one of the coldest months on record, *Lily* was lifted for hull painting. I had spent weeks unpacking boxes only to pack them up again but I thought it necessary to protect valuables during the lift. I was not prepared for the hollow feeling in the pit of my stomach as I watched *Lily* lifted from the comfort of the water into the grey overcast sky. To see 20 tons of steel being raised was bad enough but knowing most of my belongings were inside made it worse.

It became evident where the tapping sounds had come from. *Lily's* hull was completely covered in zebra mussels apart from a large oval section on her offside. The tufted duck had been diving beneath the water, plucking off the mussels to feed on, clearing *Lily's* hull in the process.

A team of professionals painted *Lily*'s hull with two coats of black comastic and fitted new anodes at the bow and stern. The friendly team at Newark Marina made the experience of lifting *Lily* a good one, informing us of procedures and keeping our minds at ease. With *Lily* out of the water, we replaced the bow and stern rope fenders with new black nylon ones and added ten new bottle fenders. New matching black ropes were ordered and learning how to splice kept us entertained for many evenings, with Roger becoming a dab hand at it. Buster thought having ropes indoors was a great idea and constantly gave them sharp tugs, pulling the working ends out of Roger's grasp at the most inopportune moments.

The iroko woodwork of Lily's wheelhouse needed regular maintaining

During this time, we did not want to live on *Lily*, balanced high on wooden blocks, so we stayed at Mill Hill Cottage, a vernacular 'mud and stud' thatched building at Little Steeping in the heart of rural Lincolnshire. This decision soon proved to be correct when we realised how difficult it was to get Buster up and down the ladder to access the boat.

With our home safely back in the water, better weather followed and Roger attended to the iroko woodwork. The window frames needed to be rubbed down and stained as did the folding wheelhouse and mast. Three coats produced a rich glossy finish in a dark teak shade and enough protection to last many years. On days when the weather was good, we tried to work

Buster in his mug shot pose whilst cruising or find a nice mooring spot to work from. Buster had developed a love for reclining in our canvas camping chairs, dozing off with his chin resting on the arm, which earned him the title of chin-strap-woey. Fed up being constantly pipped to the post to our outdoor seating, we had purchased Buster his own camping chair, although he never stuck to it, preferring to make his way in and out of all of them during the day. Another of his favourite positions was on the wheelhouse seats. They were too short for Buster to lie down on but that did not stop him from trying. With his legs dangling, he would snooze noisily, teetering on the edge. *Lily*'s British Waterways Board (BWB) registration number plate was affixed beneath the side window of the wheelhouse and, when Buster sat upright, he looked like a criminal having his mug shot taken.

Being close to nature was one of the best discoveries of living with *Lily*; daily visits by kingfishers, seeing foxes play in fading evening light and coming face to face with inquisitive mink made me realise how beautiful our countryside was. The calming atmosphere of being afloat added a new dimension to working from home; being able to take my office with me and work from wherever *Lily*

was moored was liberating. I felt happy with life and with the choices made. Being afloat was the way it was supposed to be but it was not all plain sailing. We were still newcomers to boat ownership and there was a lot to learn.

With the early days came several teething problems but, with each one, we learnt how *Lily* ticked and became more confident. The loss of the bow thruster on a trip was a wake-up call, making us realise we should never count on electronic gadgets to get us out of sticky situations. When awoken in the early hours to a pulsating fridge, a quickly defrosting ice box and flashing fridge lights making the inside of *Lily* resemble a disco, our inexperience turned this into one of the most stressful situations. The fault was eventually traced to a sticking float switch on the bilge pump causing excessive drain on the batteries.

Buster settled into life on board easily. He made his way around the decks surefootedly and loved to lie on the side decks which were wide enough for his chunky body. Turning around was not possible amidships. He would either continue to the bow or stern to turn but found this tiresome and developed a backward walk which later developed into a trot. He learnt to lift his rear leg to avoid bashing it on the bollard situated close to the wheelhouse. It was a sight to see, especially when done quickly.

"What are you doing, Buzz?" He was lying down on the side deck and looked almost stuck in the tight-fitting space. Once he knew he had my attention, he began grumbling under his breath and then propelled himself along the deck, his back on the superstructure, his stubby claws fighting to grip the inside lip of the gunnel. "Will you look at this crazy dog of yours." Roger stuck his head out of the wheelhouse in time to see Buster's sideways shimmy come to an end.

"That dog's crazy." Buster must have heard Roger because he lay down and did the same thing on the way back, grumbling all the time.

"It's the Buster Back Buffer, a super soft buffer, gives a shine like no other."

Roger laughed as we both watched Buzz put a shine on *Lily*'s cream bodywork. Unfortunately, the same could not be said for the inside of the gunnels, which bore the marks from his stubby claws.

Chapter Thirteen

HALCYON DAYS

Buster led a privileged life whilst based at Farndon Marina. Set at the beginning of a large, sweeping loop in the Trent, bordered by farmland and public footpaths, he could roam freely and safely with the doggy companions he made. We forged many friendships during our years here but one special one was to bloom.

I first met Hilary and her bouncy Boxer, Bunty, opposite the Staythorpe Power Station. Buster and his doggy mate, Boots – the first dog he befriended in Farndon – were enjoying their daily walk around the river loop. Boots was a great swimmer, heading out unafraid into midstream. Buster would run up and down the bank, furious at him for going into the water, but would never venture in himself. Toes were fine but no further than the tummy-line, not since his complete submersion in the Soar. Bunty sat quietly and patiently, watching the two crazy dogs playing. Her glossy, red coat, the colour of a ripe horse chestnut, shone in the sunlight, the stub of her docked tail constantly twitching in excitement. Her eyes – deep, dark pools – glistened as she gently tilted her head inquisitively. As the dogs did not know Bunty, Hilary asked if she could let her join in and soon the three of them were friends, running and playing without a care in the world as if they had known each other all their lives.

For years afterwards, Hilary and I would meet at 9:30 each morning, come rain or shine, on what became known as Alison's Corner. Living on *Lily* meant there was no garden for Buster. No matter what the weather, I had to tog up and give him some exercise. On average, Hilary and I would walk for a couple of hours; there was always much laughter and time-wasting as we stood and watched Buster and Bunty play. As time went on, we were joined by others and sometimes a great group of us, dogs tearing wildly around our feet, could be seen tracking the river loop. I wondered what we looked like to other people. Did they say, "Watch out, here comes that group of women with their uncontrollable dogs?" Although the dogs may well have seemed uncontrollable, they were, on the whole, well-behaved but I am sure we must have frightened some people as they saw us approaching.

There were many dog tales, or dog tails as I liked to call them, from our time spent on the Trent. Over the years, time blurred many of these together; it was not possible to recollect exact dates and times when we cried with laugher or sometimes frustration at the doggy escapades of our mutts. Interspersed with weekends away to Hazelford or longer trips with *Lily*, the reunions became treasured events, not only for Buster and Bunty

Bunty Boxer

but also for Hilary and me. Her friendship came at a time when I needed it most and she unknowingly helped to put my life back on track. Hilary did not mind if I wore the same dirty, dog-walking clothes all week, did not brush my hair or, on 'down days', looked like death warmed up. If she did, it was never mentioned. If I did not feel like talking, we would walk in silence; it was never uncomfortable and, at times, Hilary was more in tune with my feelings than I was. I adored the firm, closing click of her silver cigarette case, the warm, sweet smell of tobacco from the hand-rolled cigarettes, her short shrift with fools and passionate love of dogs. We shared good and bad times, traipsing along footpaths and fields, battling through hedgerows and wading along damp riverside tracks. No matter how either of us felt, the dogs soon made us laugh.

This was the beginning of a time which came to be known as the Halcyon Days. The term derived from ancient Greece, when the Halcyon, now commonly known as the European Kingfisher, made a floating nest in the Aegean Sea, which created a period of calm seas and balmy weather whilst she nested. The Halcyon Days referred to the endless sunny days of youth; for Buster and Bunty that was exactly what they were.

The Log Field, so called due to the huge tree trunk which lay across its entrance, was a set-aside meadow full of tall grasses, young shrubs and brambles. For Buster and Bunty, it did not fall far short of heaven on earth. They loved to chase each other through the swaying grasses. Bunty would leap and jump, taking on the actions of a gazelle on the grassy plains of the Serengeti, whilst Buster charged after her, flattening everything in his path with all the grace of a rhino. Bunty was a clever dog; she would suddenly drop and lie still, hidden from sight. Buster would try to jump up over the grass to spot her, his long ears flopping up and down but he rarely found her.

As well as open fields to walk around, there was also the Willow Holt, a few grassy meadows with retting pools, a willow plantation and a wooded riverside section. It was a pleasant combination and made a nice change from the river loop. When time was of no concern, Hilary and I would add the

The best of friends. Buster and Bunty at Farndon Marina

Holt to the river loop but we always had to be careful as the black muddy retting pools could tempt one of our dogs into its murky depths.

In early spring, the green spaces of Farndon were awash with drifts of snowdrops; it was one of the most beautiful times to wander aimlessly through the interconnecting alleyways and **along** the neatly laid-out streets. We were totally spoilt, both on and off the **waters of the** Trent.

As Buster and Bunty ran wildly across the pathway, they nipped at each other and grumbled in delight at the game they had created. Becoming more excited, they left the grassy path and river's edge, heading onto a ploughed field. Bunty managed to trip Buster and firmly trap his podgy body into one of the furrows.

She stood astride him as he wriggled and writhed to escape, and threw us a look of utter satisfaction. She had her playmate securely trapped and was relishing the moment. Buster squirmed and jerked, grumbled and growled but, no matter how hard he tried, he could not get up from the muddy confines (not that Bunty had any thoughts of allowing him to do so). Hilary and I were in fits of laughter. If there was one thing Buster hated, it was being laughed at. To him, it was adding insult to injury; he hated being the brunt of a joke and I knew he would sulk for hours afterwards. He grumbled his displeasure.

"Oh, you are funny, Buzzy," cried Hilary. Bunty then had a brainwave and began nibbling on Buster's privates. "Get off him, Bunty!" Poor Buster, tired, frustrated and covered in mud, made another attempt to right himself and this time managed to turn onto his side, enough to hide his privates from Bunty's reach. Looking very pleased with herself, she finally relented and let Buster struggle to his feet. The look he gave was enough to send us all six feet under.

There was a certain bend on the river loop where an apple tree grew which always produced an abundance of fruit. Bunty would race ahead and sit patiently beneath, waiting for Hilary to scrump a juicy apple from the branches for her to play with. On this particular day, Bunty ran ahead with Buster following when, suddenly, he stopped, raised his hackles and growled fiercely. Bunty, sitting beneath the tree, tilted her head and eyed Buster curiously. It was plain to see she had no idea what he was making such a fuss about and neither did we.

More grumbling under the breath was followed by a slow, sideways walk away from Bunty and her apple tree. Barking followed and I noticed the cause of all the excitement. In the river, partly submerged, having come down with the recent flood water, lay a tree trunk. A large branch rose from it, resembling some kind of strange river monster. The sight of this new 'creature' sent Buster into a wild panic. He tried his best to frighten it off, gave it his deepest barks and most lip-curling growls but they were not enough to send the wooden monster to the depths. As time went by, Buster got fed up with constantly showing the log who was boss and, each day, the carefully played-out scenario became less and less until, finally, he passed by without noticing it.

The fishermen we met were a temperamental bunch. One day, they would be happy; the next, as miserable as a wet winter's day but the Trent was a draw for them; they could not be avoided on our daily walks. One or other of the dogs would frequently find a dead, rotting fish to roll on, heading back to us with a look of pride on their faces and the putrid smell on their coats which took several baths to remove.

On one occasion, we passed a fisherman sitting in front of a huge bucket; inside a mix of red groundbait, which looked and smelt revolting. The dogs walked by, taking no notice but, after a few hundred yards, Buster had one of his 'nose-taking-over' moments and raced back to sink his head into the bucket. He had munched his way through as much of the contents as he could before I descended on him and wrestled to remove his red-stained head and neck out of the bucket. At this point, the fisherman heard the commotion, turned and moodily shouted, "Bloody hell, that was sirloin steak in there." Well, no wonder Buster ate it – no fish was ever going to be good enough to waste a prime piece of beef on!

But it was the encounter with a fisherman at the old ferry crossing in Farndon village which always stuck in my mind. The fisherman was in an area where the dogs went down for a drink and paddle. Not seeing him, I took no notice of Buster's rear end disappearing down the bank until the sound of shouting filled the air. Buster had stumbled upon the maggots being used as bait, which had been rather stupidly laid

Dirty dog, Roger giving Buster a hose down on the pontoon

out on a steel tray and placed on the ground. There was no waiting for an invite; Beagles have no table manners and Buster dived straight in, swallowing up as many as possible. The fisherman grabbed at the tray, lifted it into the air and maggots fell like rain to the ground. He turned away from Buster towards the bank so my dog could no longer reach the tray but Beagles were quick thinkers and Buster jumped up on the bank, sinking his head back into the tray of bait, much to the fisherman's frustration.

The fisherman's temper was quickly fraying. He thought Buster was going to attack him, which was nonsense; all he was after was a free meal. Instead of pushing Buster away with his hand whilst keeping the tray to one side, he used the whole tray. This was the most ridiculous thing to do because, as he tried to push him away with it, he only succeeded in putting the bait under Buster's nose. Each time he did so, Buster took a huge mouthful. Back and forth, back and forth, the routine went on for an eternity. Buster was taking such massive gulps of the maggots that the wriggling things spilled out of his mouth onto the grass and all over the concrete quay; the place was alive with them and Buster was hoovering them up as fast as he could. I had always said that the name of Hoover or Dyson would be most appropriate for a Beagle. Everyone with me was in fits of laughter apart from the angry fisherman and me. Finally catching the little rascal, I could not help but break down in tears of frustration.

Many dog owners knew the time Hilary and I met each morning so would come along or time their walk to meet us somewhere on the circuit. The dogs in our group were as diverse as their owners. There was Missey, a plucky little Border Terrier who barked constantly at Buster and Bunty's play fighting. Barney, a young miniature Schnauzer, who practised escapology until one day he got his head stuck through the cast iron railings of a gate and had to be rescued by the local fire brigade. Gillie, a black Tibetan Terrier, who, despite having most of his face hidden behind a long fringe, we could always tell was happy by his white toothy grin. Carrie, a cross-breed rescue dog owned by Hilary's older sister, was the matriarch of the group; kind and gentle, she kept law and order amongst the dogs and was respected by them all. Bella, a chocolate Labrador, who shook, shimmied and rubbed against us in sheer uncontainable excitement whenever she met us and, on occasion, the gentle Izzy, a polka-dot-spotted Dalmatian. There were others we met regularly and, although they did not walk with us, the dogs played with each other. Amongst them was Buster's namesake, a beautifully broad British Bull Terrier like Bill Sykes's 'Bull's-Eye' in Dickens' novel, *Oliver Twist*. This Buster came to an unfortunate demise after reputedly attempting to eat his owner's shed whilst left unattended in the garden. Milo, a crazy Spaniel who would rather swim than walk, constantly pounding in and out of the Trent sending sprays of water all over us or driving his owner to a frantic despair by swimming into the middle of the river and ignoring calls for his return. Toby, a chocolate Doberman with which Buster had a love-hate relationship and Tess, an elegant, curly-haired Airedale.

In the afternoons, Buster and I walked more locally to Farndon Marina and met up with different owners and their dogs: Theo, a black Pug with a curly, little pig tail and a love for racing around in ever decreasing circles, his actions sending Buster into a spin, and, on rare occasions, the rather splendid, wiry-coated Italian Spinone named Harrington.

Hilary's other sister, Val, lived in London but would often visit, bringing with her Flora, a Brindle Boxer with attitude. Buster was not keen on Flora and would quickly begin to sulk in her presence. One day, we met Val near the bridge over the entrance to Farndon Marina. As she waved merrily to us, Buster stopped dead in his tracks and, realising this was the lady with the Boxer he disliked, ran away and hid in a hole in the riverbank. When Flora sadly passed away, Val got herself a new red Boxer puppy, a bundle of fun named Ruby but, despite the change in dog, Buster still viewed Val with caution, running back to the safety of the boat on the first occasion he met her with Ruby.

Chapter Fourteen

THE NORTHERN LIMITS

The Trent downstream through Newark and the tidal reaches to Torksey were by now well known to us but beyond, like the ancient mariner's map, lay uncharted territory and there be dragons! When Roger first suggested visiting Ripon, I thought the idea splendid. When he mentioned tackling the notorious Trent Falls, where the Trent and Ouse merged to form the treacherous and unforgiving Humber Estuary to get there, I thought him bonkers.

We had left Torksey early in the morning with the tide high and slack, pushing north with the beginning of the ebb tide to Gainsborough for an overnight stop. After settling down for the evening, we heard footsteps and voices. Buster was quick to react with a growl.

"I hope we're not going to have trouble," I whispered as muffled voices continued outside. We had heard rowdy youths sometimes caused problems for boaters staying overnight. I was hoping there would be other boats for company – there was usually safety in numbers – but we were alone. A loud splash made us jump and Buster erupt into a deafening bark. Outside, there was screaming, running, a thunderous thumping on *Lily*'s door. Buster leapt off the sofa and gave it his all, rushing up into the wheelhouse behind Roger.

"Be careful, Roger," I warned, following them. At the door stood a distraught girl in her mid-teens. High above on the quayside, illuminated by street lights, two young lads looked menacingly down. Buster's barking caused the girl to back off but desperate, almost hysterical, she approached again.

"Please, you've got to help, my friend's in the water; we can't get her out." Roger rushed out the door, shouting to keep tabs on the boys and stay with *Lily*. At this point, I was unsure if it was a serious request for help or a way of drawing us outside. Watching, my eyes grew accustomed to the darkness and I saw a figure kneeling at the end of the pontoon, arms outstretched, holding onto someone in the water. Roger and the girl ran up behind and I saw them all pulling. This was serious.

"Stay here, Buzz, guard *Lily*." Buster looked at me meaningfully as if to say, 'No worries, you go help, I've got this covered.' He directed his gaze on the lads above and curled his top lip. I grabbed *Lily*'s life buoy but, by the time I reached Roger, a plump teenage girl had been pulled from the water and was sobbing uncontrollably. Everyone was cold and soaking wet but our offers of towels, tea, warmth and phone calls were quickly refused, leaving us concerned when they wandered off.

"Well done, Buzz, you've done a good job," I praised. Buster had protected us; I was proud of my boy. Looking up, it appeared the lads had fled but Roger went to check. We were not sure what had happened; had the girl jumped or been pushed? But, thank goodness, she had been able to hang on as the tide had turned and was rushing in. Back on board, concerned, we telephoned the police and explained the incident. They did not seem bothered and, despite saying they would send someone out, **we** never saw anyone or had any other disturbances again that night.

It was a 6 a.m. start the next day; if Roger had calculated correctly, it was going to be a twelve-hour cruise to Naburn. Being on the tideway meant limited access to shore; to cater for Buster's needs, we had cut a section of turf from animal farm, placing it on *Lily*'s front deck for use as a doggy toilet.

"Here you go, Buzzy, this is for you." I walked him to the bow and showed him the ingenious invention but he did not look too impressed. He placed a paw on the turf, bent his head and sniffed before promptly trotting back to the wheelhouse. "You'll be glad of it later," I shouted after him. We excitedly left Gainsborough and by the time the water was falling away rapidly towards lowest ebb, Keadby Lift Bridge loomed out of the morning murk. The hefty, iron lift bridge no longer opened; the lifting section was sealed shut in 1958 following a decline in shipping. Ironically, trade later picked up and the bridge set the height for vessels venturing upstream.

Beyond, we were plunged into the throngs of commercial craft, docks and warehouses, damp and dismal yet totally spellbinding. The dull weather added to the atmosphere of the ramshackle jetties, their skeletal cranes silhouetted against the blank sky. We cruised on in awe, passing huge coasters lining the wharves, perched high and dry, waiting for the incoming tide. Their crew stopped to wave, the sight of Buster bringing smiles to faces. Hidden between the wharves was the entrance to the Stainforth and Keadby Canal. For less sea-worthy craft, it offered an alternative route; for us, it marked the last safe refuge before reaching the Humber.

"There's no going back now," chimed Roger as *Lily* passed the lock gates.

"Well, let's pray you've got your sums right then."

Approaching Burton Stather, we should have hit the flood but had made better time. Not wanting to anchor in deeper water to await it – a common practice for craft taking this route – we slowed. Roger had purposely chosen a neap tide to give *Lily* best water level at lowest ebb but we still needed to meet the flood about half an hour before reaching Trent Falls. Passing prominent power lines, Roger switched banks, feeling for deeper water towards 'the cliff', a well-known landmark signifying the run-in to the estuary. Slowly, the land fell away, sinking and transforming into marshy mud flats and, with the flood making good, we were surprised not to see any other craft at this desolate spot.

The end of the Trent was marked by the Apex Light, which signalled the start of the mighty Humber Estuary. Together with its tributaries, it drained over 10,000 square miles (25,900km²) into the North Sea and had a tidal range of over 20 feet (6.1m), coming second only to the River Severn. With Apex Light in view and the greyness of the day lifting, we headed into the vast expanse of the Humber. We had been warned about turning too soon; the fast tides could throw craft back onto the training wall separating the two river mouths. Once sure there was plenty of space, Roger turned *Lily* into the flow and, in no time at all, we were flying, caught up in the rushing flow of the tidal Ouse,

its muddy brown waters carrying *Lily* along as if she were weightless. We had rounded Trent Falls in a matter of minutes and were left wondering what all the fuss was about.

Buster sitting at Lily's bow as we head up the tidal Yorkshire Ouse towards Goole

The early flood swept us towards Blacktoft Jetty, where there was an opportunity to tie up and take Buster ashore. Sensing a stop looming, he made his way to the bow and sat looking hopefully at the approaching jetty. I joined him but, as Roger slowed the engine, *Lily* was still travelling at a rate of knots. With no easy way of stopping, the idea was abandoned and the flow carried us onwards, following the river's wide arc towards the busy inland port of Goole and beyond.

"Never mind, Buzzy, you can use your doggy toilet instead." He screwed up his muzzle and skulked off.

Passing beneath the first of the famous Ouse swing bridges at Skelton, we realised how small *Lily* was compared to the huge vessels regularly using the river. Onwards, at the tidal barrage marking the confluence with the River Derwent, Roger became aware of the rising water level. With the river's diminishing width, he called ahead to Selby Bypass Bridge to check headroom and was assured there was plenty of clearance for *Lily*'s wheelhouse. It had been a long day and

97

we had only grabbed sandwiches for lunch. With stomachs rumbling, I left Roger to navigate and placed a pre-prepared chicken casserole in the oven.

At Cawood Swing Bridge, we caught up with two narrowboats that had entered the Ouse at Selby after taking the alternative route through the canal system. With the flood slowing, we took up a place behind them, forming a small convoy. At Naburn, we locked off the tidal river together, entering an enchanting scene of workshops and bygone equipment whilst the smell of home-cooking wafted up from the galley. The short canal cut above the lock was the ideal place to moor and gather our thoughts. Throughout the day, *Lily* had handled well and we had been safe and comfortable on board. As for Buster and the turf, well, that was a waste of time. Remarkably, he held on for twelve hours until *Lily* was securely moored, allowing him access to dry land, where he finally relieved himself.

The next morning, it was a short cruise to York. Whilst other cities were built on steel, coal or wool, York owed its rise to something sweeter – chocolate. At one time, deliveries of cocoa beans regularly arrived by barge to supply the city's confectionery manufacturers. The Terry's, Rowntree and Cravens brands were synonymous with York, home of Britain's best-loved chocolate bars, although, sadly, the river no longer provided the transport.

Walking York's walls, Buster stayed as close to the edge as he could. It was a strange habit he had adopted, one which saw him always heading for the kerb or quayside. It made my mum laugh and say, "That dog likes to live life on the edge." I was thinking of her when a voice boomed, "Dogs aren't allowed on the walls." I looked around to see a stern-looking man standing in the doorway of a souvenir shop.

"Oh, I'm sorry, we didn't know. Are you sure?"

"There are enough signs up saying so. Where did you get on the walls?" He was grumpy.

"By the river, along there." I pointed towards the spot. "I never saw any signs." Roger and Buster had carried on walking; I was alone.

"There are signs up at each entry point," he snapped. "You need to get the dog off the walls immediately," he said, raising his voice.

"He isn't doing any harm; he's well-behaved. Besides, I haven't seen any signs." I was not going to let him intimidate me.

"His behaviour isn't the point. He shouldn't be on here in the first place. Now get him off."

I was cross now and replied, "I'm afraid I haven't packed his parachute today, so you'll have to wait until we walk around to the nearest steps then I suggest you spend the rest of the day walking the walls yourself and checking there really *are* signs because there certainly isn't one over there." Angrily, I stomped off. Roger and Buster were waiting a few hundred yards away.

"Why did you stop and speak to him? You should've kept on walking."

"Why? We haven't done anything wrong; he just didn't like dogs."

"Didn't you see the sign on the steps where we came up?"

On the Ripon Canal, a narrowboat was in Bell Furrows Lock, preparing to penn through. Mooring and gently lifting down Buster, we went to greet it. At the tiller was a young lad whilst an older lady prepared the gates. I passed the time of day with her and Roger nipped over to the opposite gate to help. Her son had purchased the narrowboat to live on whilst studying at college. His mum was concerned; he wanted to give up his mooring in Ripon Racecourse Marina, take a year out and travel the waterways but she was afraid he would not find something suitable on his return. Reading between the lines, I could see there were other concerns on her mind: that he was about to choose an unconventional life, that he may miss the chance to get onto the property ladder or that he may sail off into the sunset and never be seen again. Not being a mother, I could only guess at the heartache this kind-faced lady was going through, listen and tell her of our experiences, try to put her mind at rest. Buster instantly took a liking to this worried mother figure and gently nuzzled up to her legs. She leant down and stroked his head. He lifted his soulful eyes and met hers; they held each other's gaze for a short while. When she looked back at me, she smiled and said, "It's hard for me; he's my only son. I don't want to stand in his way but I want him to be safe." There were tears in her eyes.

"He will be," I said reassuringly. With a nod, she leant on the gate and it slowly gave way under the pressure.

As the narrowboat chugged away, the lad raised his hand and shouted his goodbyes. His mother walked away from the lock, windlass in hand. Together, they drifted into the distance as if fallen leaves on the flow of a river. I was left wondering what life had in store for these two people. I will never know but, from time to time, I thought of them both, of that moment when our lives touched and for a while we became one on the rotating wheel of time.

Nearing the terminus, *Lily* received some surprised glances; people pointed, stopped and stared. Wide-beam craft rarely reached this point. I should have been proud *Lily* created such reactions but I found it embarrassing. After winding in the basin, we took up a place at the moorings, jubilant at reaching Ripon, the furthest point north we would travel with *Lily* on English waters. We set off to purchase our Head of Navigation plaque, which subsequently took pride of place in *Lily*'s wheelhouse.

Fountains Abbey and Studley Royal Water Gardens were easily reached from Ripon and provided Buster with a full, off-water, doggy day out. On the bus there, Roger and I sat side by side, Buster nestled between our legs. After exploring the impressive grounds and enjoying a picnic lunch, we began walking the four miles back to Ripon. The sky looked heavy and, before we were halfway back, it poured with rain. Arriving at *Lily*, we resembled drowned rats; huddled in the wheelhouse, we stripped off wet clothing and towelled ourselves dry. Buster's fur was waterlogged; he resembled a threadbare teddy who had been loved hard, its fur over-crushed with cuddles. When it finally dried, his coat became soft, springy, sweet smelling – my rain-soft doggy.

Chapter Fifteen

SWINGTIME

An alternative route back to base had been planned. I did not think it would be as exciting as rounding Trent Falls but we were in for a few surprises. Before departing Ripon, *Lily*'s water tanks needed topping up at the sanitary station. To reach, *Lily* needed to be positioned across the canal, blocking the waterway; fortunately, no traffic disturbed us. Travelling down the Ure and the Ouse, autumn was in full swing. Another day was spent in York, revisiting places we liked best and baking on board. Roger was a dab hand at breadmaking and rustled up some ciabatta rolls whilst I turned my hand to fruit scones. We both had great fun cooking and Buster was only too willing to sample new recipes.

To access the tidal Ouse passage required booking twenty-four hours in advance with the Naburn lock keeper, who worked a flexible day around the tide times. He then informed the Selby lock keeper of our ETA and, between the two of them and the Cawood bridge keeper, our progress on the fast-flowing tidal reach was monitored.

The name 'Ouse' derived from the Anglo-Saxon 'clear water', however most of the tidal section was murky brown and littered with rubbish. Apparently, it could take months for floating debris to reach the sea as it was constantly

Lily at the Ripon Canal's sanitary station   swept back and forth on the tides. On the way upriver, we had not seen any debris but, on the journey down, we spent the trip looking out for, and dodging, large tree trunks and branches, as well as the more unusual fridge and gas cylinder – empty, we hoped!

Reaching Selby, the river narrowed, forcing the flow through at speed, assuming a more aggressive character. Lining up for the road bridge immediately after a sharp bend was tricky but, once through, Roger had *Lily* on course for the next bridge. The Naburn lock keeper had explained the procedure of locking up at Selby and Roger and I were anxious about it. Once clear of the railway swing bridge, *Lily* had to be turned 180 degrees so she was facing into the flow.

"What the hell do you think you're doing?" I yelled at Roger as I fought to stand upright whilst the force of the river swept *Lily* along on her side.

"It's alright, I know what I'm doing. This is what the lock keeper at Naburn told me to do." Roger was amazingly calm, considering our predicament. Buster sat upright in his bed, as bold as brass, looking like he was supervising the procedure.

"Are you sure? I don't recall him saying anything about this."

It was scary drifting sideways down a fast-flowing river and, with an audience of gawpers, was not my idea of fun. *Lily* hung in a stagnant position until the power of the engine cut in, driving her bow forcefully into the flow. Time to breathe but only briefly; we needed to keep our wits about us. Roger let the flow carry *Lily* backwards until her bow was almost level with the lock.

"Now, hang on tight." Roger powered *Lily* forwards towards the lock entrance. I held on tightly to the chart table with one hand; the other had a firm grasp on Buster. At the edge of the quay, the lock keeper peered down at us bobbing about in the murky depths and gave us the thumbs up as *Lily* safely charged through the lock entrance. It was not over yet though. As *Lily* was hurtling into the lock chamber on full power, we were completely reliant on reverse cutting in to prevent her bow from headbutting the far gates. Roger slammed the engine into reverse. It roared like a starving lion and *Lily* came to an abrupt halt with inches to spare. We had made it safely into Selby Lock; no bangs, marks or scratches on *Lily* and our lives intact. Buster groaned and shook off my vicelike hold. Roger put his arm around my shoulder and gave me a grin to cherish. I patted *Lily*; she had done us proud.

"See you have done this before," the lock keeper boomed from the top of the chamber.

"Errrr, no, can't say that I have," Roger shouted back, shaking his head. "It was definitely more luck than judgement."

"Well, either way, you did well. Hang on and I'll have you safely up here in no time." With that, he disappeared from sight. Soon we were high above the turbulent waters; looking down on them, it seemed incomprehensible that we had been there only moments earlier. I mopped my brow and turned to Roger with my adaptation of some words from *The African Queen*: "It's no wonder you enjoy boating, Mr Allnut."

"It's the Yorkshire Ouse, not the Ulanga," was his ironic reply.

With a temporary canal licence purchased, we joined the short but sweet Selby Canal. *Lily* slipped easily beneath the bridges without need to dismantle her wheelhouse. Buster hopped on and off as and when he fancied a stroll along the towpath. We moored for the night at West Haddlesey Junction, where the Selby Canal joined the River Aire.

"Hurry up and get a move on; we've gotta go BWB," shouted Roger the next morning.

"Gotta go what?" I was puzzled. What on earth was my husband talking about?

"BWB."

"British Waterways Board?" Now I was growing concerned, thinking that *Lily*'s river licence had expired without me realising.

"No!" He laughed, "Boating with Buster!"

Traversed by commercial barges, the Aire and Calder Navigation was not for the faint hearted. It was a joy to see a canal being used for the purpose it was originally intended; however, after passing several barges, I could not help thinking the canal could do with being slightly wider.

Before 1819, Goole was a small hamlet but, with the construction of the Aire and Calder Navigation built to link Knottingley and ultimately Leeds with the Ouse, the area began to flourish. Coal was the main cargo, transported by compartment boats known as Tom Puddings, and the only remaining hydraulically powered hoist used for loading was undergoing restoration. It was a fair walk into town but the views across the docks to the impressive hoist were worth it.

Lily spent the night amongst a motley collection of commercial barges, tankers, Humber keels and fellow Dutch barges. In the small hours, an engine roared into life, followed by another and yet another; the unmistakable deep thudding which could only be generated by a commercial vessel. Buster let out a warning bark and followed it with a grumble. Rain was falling; its soft pitter-patter on the roof had woken me before the engines had. Pulling back the curtains, the windows were covered with transparent droplets through which navigation lights and spotlights of vessels preparing to depart distorted and reformed, then distorted again. I watched, transfixed by the scene: men in waterproof leggings and thick, black donkey jackets pulled and heaved on ropes; capped men leant out of wheelhouse windows giving instructions. The occasional horn sounded and the revs rose as, one by one, the group of craft surrounding *Lily* released lines and slowly headed towards the lock. *Lily* jostled, their wash sweeping into her hull, surrounding her in waves of bubbling water.

"The tide must be right for locking through; they're off out to the Humber," said Roger. "Come on."

Grabbing some warm clothes, I headed to the wheelhouse, followed by Roger and Buster. Taking a place on the seat, Buster pressed his head against the cold window and watching in astonishment, muttered under his breath. To some it would seem a strange event to be passionate about but, to me, it was fascinating, as if stepping back in time or watching a scene from an old Pathé newsreel. Vessel after vessel prepared to head out, heavy loads making many low in the water. Leaning out of the wheelhouse to look along the canal, I saw pinpricks of light as a procession of trading craft approached Goole to access the river and the sea beyond.

The impressive Went Aqueduct, New Junction Canal

Both ends of the New Junction Canal were marked by aqueducts; at the northern end, the impressive Went Aqueduct and, at the southern end, with huge guillotine gates used as flood barriers, the Don Aqueduct. At a swing bridge, we met two of Waddington's barges. Being working vessels, we gave them priority, happy to stand back and watch the professionals at work. A cold tingle of goosebumps crawled along my arms as motor barge towing dumb barge passed, dwarfing *Lily*. Despite being only five miles long and dead straight, the canal had been far from boring.

After a day in Doncaster, we joined the Stainforth and Keadby Canal and wished we had not bothered; with its numerous swing bridges, it was an obstacle course. Some bridges were easy to operate, automated designs; others, incredibly heavy, hand-operated contraptions which Roger had the unenviable task of struggling with.

"I never want to see another swing bridge in my life," I moaned as we neared Keadby. Buster groaned; even he was fed up with constantly jumping on and off to help. The unusual sliding railway bridge, one of only three in Europe, raised our enthusiasm a little, albeit briefly. Mooring at Keadby, the place looked as if it could do with a good scrub and, devoid of any shipping at the wharves to keep us entertained, was very dull.

The following morning, the final swing bridge was swung and we were penned down to re-enter the Trent. It felt like meeting an old friend for the first time in many years. We were penned onto the tideway much earlier than expected but, thinking the lock keeper knew better than us amateurs, did not question it. As Roger motored *Lily* out of the lock, there was a shudder.

"We've touched bottom. I knew we'd left too early." Roger knocked *Lily* into neutral and, luckily, she brushed over. We both turned to remonstrate with the lock keeper but he was hurriedly dashing away to his car.

"He's in a hurry; must have an urgent appointment. Perhaps that's why he put us through early?"

About a mile upriver, we passed a narrowboat heading downstream. The crew looked cold standing on the exposed counter but gave a friendly wave. Over the VHF came the voice of the lady skipper, trying to raise the Keadby lock keeper. Before disappearing from our sight, I could make out the narrowboat circling in the vast expanse of the river, the woman's voice becoming more frantic, willing him to answer her call. We monitored the radio until it fell silent but never discovered if he answered or if the narrowboat had to make a temporary mooring. Either way, that fearful voice stayed with me.

Making our way up the Trent, clouds closed in and it was not long before rain fell. Miserably, Buster eyed the raindrops collecting on the windows of the wheelhouse, putting paid to doggy deck time. We arrived at Cromwell Lock as daylight faded and spent the night above the tidal river before heading back through Newark and on to Farndon the following day. Our first major trip with *Lily* had proved quite an adventure.

I had arranged to meet Hilary and Bunty on Alison's Corner the morning after returning. Buster was excited; he ran ahead with a cocky hop, skip and jump, knowing he was going to see his favourite playmate. When they appeared and started walking towards us, Buster stopped. Hilary let Bunty off the lead and the two dogs ran towards each other but, before meeting, paused. Buster went down, flat on the ground. Bunty looked away and there was a brief stand-off before they ran at each other. Standing on their back legs, they hugged and sparred as if boxers in a ring.

"Hello, Buzzy!" Hilary called. Buster ran at her and leapt into her open arms, wriggling away, pleased to see her yet knowing how uncool his actions looked. Bunty nuzzled up to me before jumping high in the air, giving me her best bouncing Boxer routine. All four of us strode out across the fields. It was the happiest of reunions.

Chapter Sixteen

KEEPING UP APPEARANCES

Contrary to popular belief, being a boat owner was not just about cruising. To enjoy time away exploring the waterways, a safe, well-maintained boat was required and the weather had a huge impact on our ability to carry out work on *Lily*. Roger and I liked to cruise all year and in all weathers but our second winter on board turned out to be completely different from the previous year. Instead of cold, frosty mornings and sprinklings of snow, we were bombarded by rain, which set the scene for most of the coming year.

Lily's roof desperately needed a repaint; some sections were beginning to flake and show signs of rust. Having never painted *Lily* ourselves, we firstly concentrated on the smaller back cabin. After rubbing down, a coat of red oxide primer to blank out the patches and give a good base was applied. White undercoat was added and finally topped off with white gloss and edges cut in with a brush. All went well and soon the rear cabin roof was sparkling in fresh white paint. Finishing off, we painted the roof edge in glossy bright red. We only had time to apply the red oxide primer to the front roof; finishing off had to wait for better weather.

Roger stood back to admire the finished result of the back-cabin roof. "Looks good, Al, doesn't it?"

"Um, yes, but I'm not keen on those red blotches along the bodywork."

Recrimination followed with both of us blaming each other until Buster appeared, wagging his red-tipped tail.

"There's the culprit. Buster's been painting with his tail." Swift application of white spirit resolved the issue for dog and boat although, even after rinsing off, Buster was not impressed with his 'high-octane' tail. "Think you'd best stick to the role of foreman, Buzzy; being a worker doesn't suit you." Buster jumped into his camping chair and nuzzled his chin into the armrest as if to say, 'I was only trying to help.'

In preparation for our next adventure and to improve security, Roger added brass reinforcing rods to the opening rooflights. It took a little time to find what we were looking for; in the end, a Leicester-based clockmaker, who used brass rods for counterweights when restoring antique clocks, supplied them, cut to the correct length.

Roger carried out the annual servicing in the autumn but, as we cruised with *Lily* all year and she was not winterised, it could be undertaken any time. Servicing involved changing the engine oil and filters on both the main diesel engine and the diesel

Roger racing rain clouds to get the roof painted on Lily's back cabin

generator. Although the service intervals for the gearbox were longer, Roger always changed the gearbox oil at the same time.

The window frames were resealed to the superstructure as some had developed leaks and painted with a wood preservative. The wheelhouse bore the brunt of inclement weather and harsh sunshine all year round. It needed to be partially dismantled and, with all the doors, panels and sections, took a full week of fine weather to complete. There always seemed to be a plague of small insects, wind-born dust or a sudden release of fluffy tree pollen to stick to the wet paintwork, usually just as Roger stood back to admire it.

It was not easy 'keeping up appearances'. *Lily* bore a few knocks and scrapes since Roger and I had acquired her but they were all part of her character and each one had a story to tell. I liked to call them her battle scars. Roger said, "They're to be expected. After all, boating is a contact sport."

Chapter Seventeen

IT WILL ALL COME OUT IN THE WASH

Despite early summer proving a washout, we had a schedule to keep. Months of planning had gone into the trip and nothing was going to stop us. We were heading for the beautiful flatlands of the Fens, where the Inland Waterways Association (IWA) were holding their annual National Festival and Boat Show at St Ives, Cambridgeshire. Reaching the destination would involve crossing The Wash, a bay of the North Sea.

It was *Lily's* first festival and sea voyage, a milestone event for all of us as I had been commissioned to review new boats at the show with the promise of our trip covered in a series of articles for a mainstream magazine. Best of all, Roger received payback for his many evenings at night school to gain his Royal Yachting Association Day Skipper qualification, which had enabled him to successfully plot our sea crossing.

An overnight stop at Cromwell Lock allowed an early-morning departure on the tidal Trent. With river levels already exceedingly high and more rain due, the lock keeper was convinced passage would be closed later that day. Travelling down the tideway, we could see over the flood banks; the Trent was full to the brim. At Torksey, we encountered the first of many problems – jammed lock gates. Roger was quick to offer a hand to the lock keepers on duty. I am not sure if he was help or hindrance but, in no time, the problem was fixed and we were on the Fossdyke.

At Saxilby, moorings were lost beneath flood water, the few spaces usually available on a section of high wall already taken, with many craft doubled up. There was no choice but to push on. It did not sit well with Buster; he was rather partial to cooked white fish and knew we had been contemplating a fish and chip supper courtesy of the local take-away. There was some space between the BWB yard on the outskirts of Lincoln and the University Moorings, enough to squeeze *Lily* in. It was just as well as we later discovered that water pouring through the Glory Hole, resembling a white-water canoe slalom, had closed the navigation. As the rain began, so did a waiting game.

There was no telling how high the water would rise or how long the holdup would last so we settled in for the long run. Roger commuted to his day job, leaving Buster and me to fend for ourselves. We became experts at walking the plank, a necessity for getting on and off the boat in the extreme conditions. Three days later, Roger spotted a green light at the entrance to the Glory Hole and, by 6 a.m., with *Lily's* wheelhouse dismantled in record time, we were through the city centre and onto the remote River Witham. Buster sat in his usual spot, taking in the scenery and scents, happy to be on the move. With the sun finally making an appearance, we cruised all the way to the moorings at Kirkstead Bridge with the wheelhouse down, soaking up the warmth and early-morning birdsong. The stop allowed a walk into Woodhall Spa to catch the bus back to Lincoln and collect the car. When we got there, the Glory Hole was again displaying a red light, white water gushing through.

Buster and I spent a week on *Lily* at Boston whilst Roger commuted from her to work. I celebrated my fortieth birthday with bottles of bubbly and helium balloons, seafood supper with friends and long-distance phone calls with loved ones. There was an old seafarer's saying that, if you stood on the steps of the Witham Tavern, looked at the trees on the opposite bank and saw their tops moving, you should not venture out on The Wash. The day of our crossing, I went to look and wished I had not. The trees were indeed moving and not just the tops; almost every branch was bending and swaying in the breeze. A force 5 dropping to 4 had been forecast; not ideal but the following day looked even worse. I prayed the winds would drop before departure.

Because of *Lily*'s length, we needed to pass through Boston Grand Sluice Lock at free-flow, about two hours after high water, when both sea and river were level, allowing both sets of lock gates to be opened, eliminating any restriction on boat length. Time was limited so, once joined by David, our friend from Farndon who was the extra crew member required for insurance purposes, we moved up to the lock, ready to leave when instructed. The *Boston Belle* trip boat headed back into port. As she passed, I managed to have a few words with her crew about the conditions at sea. This, along with a friendly chat to an elderly lady on the towpath, who used to sail on The Wash, gave us the final confidence to forge ahead. "Go on, it will be lovely out there. I'd come with you if I were younger." With a friendly wave and the bells of Boston Stump ringing away in a frenzy, we finally headed out onto tidal waters.

The Witham wound through Boston town and passed the docks. Dealing with goods from overseas, including timber from Scandinavia and the Baltic countries, the enclosed docks were accessed by huge lock gates. During the thirteenth century, Boston was the second largest port in Britain and owed much of its prosperity to the wool trade with Flanders. Keeping constant checks of the GPS and the course Roger had plotted on the chart, by the time we reached more open water the wind had subsided slightly. We were now on The Wash, heading along the marked channel known as Lower Road, running parallel with the South Lincolnshire coast.

"We're on the sea," I squealed in joy. "Buster, you're on the sea. What have you got to say about that?" He was not impressed. Roger and David were too engrossed in following the buoyed channel to share in my glee as I hummed 'A Life on the Ocean Wave'. Rounding the Boston Roads fairway marker, with no further buoys visible, we were truly on our own, following a course towards a prominent water tower south of Hunstanton on the North Norfolk coast.

The prevailing south-westerly force 4 caught *Lily* on her starboard beam. She handled the conditions well and, with no need to hurry, we settled at a comfortable speed. Buster started looking a little worse for wear. Watching him lying in his bed wearing a deep frown, I grew concerned for him.

"I don't think Buster likes this," I said to Roger as he returned from a walk around the deck with David.

"Perhaps he needs to go for a wee?" As with our last extended cruise, Roger had placed a freshly cut roll of turf on the front deck for Buster's toilet needs but that was not what was bothering him. Roger looked at Buster, then at the charts.

"I don't want him to be ill, Roger. If this isn't fun for Buster, there's no point doing it."

"We can tack for a bit; that will give him some respite from the swaying. The wind is dropping all the time. I think it will calm soon." After a ten-minute tack to the north, Buster retired below and fell asleep. At the end of the return tack, the wind had dropped to a comfortable breeze and we rejoined our original course.

Passing Sunk West cardinal buoy on our port beam, we entered the channel towards King's Lynn. Ahead, seals basked on huge sandbanks. Buster must have smelt them as he excitedly returned to the wheelhouse, wagging his tail.

Lily swinging at anchor off Buoy 7, Blackguard Sands

"Are you feeling better, Buzzy boy?" He looked brighter now the wind had dropped. He rubbed himself against my legs before sitting in the open doorway of the wheelhouse, gazing longingly at the sandy land. With depth running out, Roger searched for a safe place to drop anchor. We needed to await a turn of tide to carry us safely into King's Lynn for our overnight stop.

Nose on the ground and bottom in the air, Buster snuffling on the sandbanks

"This area looks good." Roger slowed *Lily*. "The sandbanks are dry; they'll be firmer for going ashore." I was impressed by his observation. After passing the tide gauge in the Bulldog Channel, Roger picked his spot and dropped the anchor just south-east of No. 7 buoy. It was the first time the anchor had been used other than in practice sessions and an anxious few minutes followed as *Lily* came to rest. After ensuring she was holding fast, we climbed into the dinghy and went ashore onto Blackguard Sands.

Buster ran and splashed through the shallows, all thoughts of sea sickness extinguished from his mind. He claimed the sandbank as his own, chased off the seals and guarded his patch by barking as they continuously bobbed their heads in and out of the water, trying to catch a glimpse of the intruder. The two-hour break gave Buster the chance to let off steam; he ran until he became a tiny speck, the sun picking out the sprays of water his paws threw up, encircling him in a shower of silvery, sparkling dots.

"Crazy dog." Roger was setting up the barbecue but Buster's barking had distracted him. We watched as he sent a small flock of seagulls into the air, jumping after them as they screeched and reeled.

With a sausage sizzle underway, Buster was quick to return, exhausted, damp and covered in sand but as happy as I had ever seen him. He was soon asleep, recumbent at my feet, imitating the beached seals he had chased off earlier. Slumped in camping chairs, we ate chargrilled sausages, the sea salt on my lips adding seasoning to each bite, and watched *Lily* gently swing in the slowly turning tide. When she had fully turned, we headed back on board to prepare for the last run of the day. By the time everything was shipshape and the anchor raised, the huge expanse of sandbank was no bigger than a double bed. The sea had raced in and made it easy to see how people found themselves stranded by rapidly rising tides.

Motoring into the mouth of the Great Ouse on a strongly flooding tide, the light was fading fast. As the haunting cry of the curlew carried over the diminishing sandbanks, the sun was no more than a dull red orb, low in the sky. At the docks, a large ship was berthed, its lights flickering on as we passed. As there were no public moorings at King's Lynn at that time, we had spoken to the harbour master a few days previously for advice. Navigating the tidal river to Denver Sluice at night was not recommended; he suggested mooring against the fishing boats, alongside the pilot boats if space allowed, or on the Great Ouse Boating Association's (GOBA) floating mooring buoys. Having already joined GOBA, we concluded their moorings the best option.

"There they are," David shouted from the bow whilst pointing at the buoys bobbing and dancing in the tide.

"Will we be able to do this? The tide's raging in." I did not wait for Roger's answer. I stepped out of the wheelhouse and looked into the speeding water. It looked menacing. "I'll have to help David. This is going to be tricky. Will you be alright here with Buzz?" I asked.

"Yes, of course, but listen, I'm not going to see a thing over *Lily*'s bow. You'll have to direct me, be my eyes."

At the bow, a chill had descended. It was growing dark and I prayed Crew *Lily* would get it right first time. Roger motored *Lily* past the buoys. I watched him eyeing them up, seeing how they sat in the water, the best way to approach. Buster was sitting at his side, attentive, knowing some action was about to happen. Just beyond the buoys, Roger turned *Lily* into the flow and slowly began approaching them.

"Here goes," said David, grabbing the boat hook and a rope. Roger had a good line of approach so I waved him forwards.

"Keep coming." I was not sure he could hear me so kept waving him on. David leant over *Lily*'s high bow and tried to reach the mooring buoy with the boat hook.

"I can't reach it," puffed David, leaning as far over as he dared, his arm fully outstretched, desperately trying to catch the buoy with the boat hook.

"Let's try and get *Lily* alongside." Her side was slightly lower and would give David more room for manoeuvre. "Roger, can you keep her coming?" *Lily* moved forwards slowly, fighting the driving tide. As her bow slowly began to pass the buoy, David tried again.

"Can you hold onto me so I can lean further over?" It was time to get intimate. I grabbed hold of the belt and waistband of David's trousers. Waving Roger forwards and shouting at him to keep the power on, I grasped hold of *Lily*'s steelwork with my free hand. There was no way I was letting David fall into the water; his life was in my hands but I was struggling to keep hold. He had leant so far over, I was sure he would topple. I could not see the mooring buoy; David's body was blocking my view but I knew by the flow that Roger would have to keep powering *Lily* on so shouted at the top of my voice, "Roger, motor forwards." I screwed up my eyes and gripped hard. *Lily* shot forwards and the tension I had on David was released. He had attached the rope and was busy pulling it back on board. He had done it.

"Phewwww, well done, David." I glanced back to the wheelhouse and gave Roger the thumbs up.

"You can let go of my trousers now," said David, smiling.

Chapter Eighteen

AS I WAS GOING TO ST IVES

The following morning, Roger checked *Lily*'s oil level, bilge and weed hatch before setting off. Leaving on the incoming tide, *Lily* still found many shallow spots. Denver Sluice and Lock were a welcoming sight; beyond lay the gentle, non-tidal waters of the Ely Ouse. We had successfully crossed The Wash and could breathe a sigh of relief. With a newly purchased, three-month Environment Agency (EA) licence, the waterways of the Fens could be explored at leisure.

Mooring opposite the lock, Buster was excited at the prospect of terra firma, squeaking and making shallow under-his-breath barks until Roger lifted him down from the chart table and placed him outside. David joined them and they went for a stroll, David clicking away taking photographs whilst Roger fought with Buster on the extending lead. Wendy was due to meet us later to collect David and was bringing along her father, Dick. I went below to prepare some light refreshments.

Dick was a man we were in awe of. In his eighties, he was still nimble on his feet and knew his way around a boat, taking ropes and hopping on and off with no more thought than stepping off a kerb. During WWII, Dick joined the RAF and became a 'tail-end Charlie', sitting precariously and rather vulnerably in the aft turret of the Lancaster bomber with little protection save four Browning machine guns. Dick was one of the few lucky survivors and listening to him recount stories always had us totally absorbed.

When our guests departed, and with chores complete, we returned to Denver and the Ely Ouse, where we decided to take a well-earned break on the River Wissey.

From the helm, we appeared to be in a scene from the classic movie *The African Queen*. I had no view of the water, only a wall of pale green rushes and a threatening sky. At any moment, I expected Roger to leap over the side and, braving leeches, bow-haul *Lily* through the forest of reeds. The entrance to the River Wissey gave the impression it was not the place for broad-beam craft but we bit the bullet and forged ahead. Roger walked to the bow and kept an eye out for oncoming traffic. With the reed beds brushing and swooshing against *Lily*'s hull, I slowly edged her on; despite the narrowness, depth was good and charts promised wider waters ahead. Small metallic flashes of turquoise whizzed around *Lily* as she ventured forwards; the chattering laughter of the kingfishers mocked, almost dared us to enter their domain. Emerging onto wider waters, it was difficult to know where to focus: on the pretty surroundings, abundant with wild flowers, or into the depths. The Wissey was a beautiful chalk stream, its waters crystal clear revealing fish and swaying aquatic plants in all their glory. Only 10 miles (16km) of the lock-free river was navigable. Less than a mile in, I knew it would not be enough; the Wissey was already a truly magical waterway.

The moorings at Hilgay were full but I managed to edge *Lily* in at a recreation ground using the gangplank to access land. It was there that George Manby invented the Manby Mortar, a rocket-like apparatus used to fire a line to ships in distress to which a Breeches Buoy could then be attached. Being Church Warden of the village, he took advantage of the role by practice-firing his invention from the tower of All Saints' Church. Thousands of lives had been saved by the device, a powerful gift bestowed upon the world from a Fenland village resident.

"Why have we stopped here?" Roger asked.

"I want to go and see the grave of George Manby."

"Is it an unusual grave?"

I was about to answer when I realised Roger was making fun of me, picking up on a story from the novel *Three Men in a Boat*. I turned to walk away and tripped over Buster, who let out a groan.

"Bloody hell, Buzz!" He looked up at me innocently. "Oh, I see, you're in on it too. Don't tell me, getting in the way and being sworn at is your ambition in life?" I walked off in a bit of a huff then, as an afterthought, shouted, "Perhaps we should have called you Montmorency after all."

The next morning, we continued to the head of navigation, passing the rusting framework of the Wissington sugarbeet factory and crossing by aqueduct the Cut-Off Channel, constructed to carry excess water to the Flood Relief Channel. There was just room to wind *Lily* at the confluence with Stringside Drain. After doing so, we moored at Grange Farm Caravan and Campsite close to the village of Whittington and spent a glorious afternoon painting the remainder of *Lily*'s roof. The vast expanse of it looked daunting so Roger and I tackled it together, using rollers and sharing a tray of thinned paint.

"We're getting this covered fast, aren't we, Al?"

"Yeah, but there seems to be one problem." I stopped painting and looked at what we had done.

"What's that then?" Roger put down his roller to see what I was looking at.

"Look how much better my side is than yours."

"Oh, very funny, ha ha."

I tipped Buster a wink. He was staying well out of the way after his last encounter with open paint tins, lying on the grass and chewing daisies, waiting impatiently for the barbecue to be lit.

We were no sooner relaxed and replenished from our sea crossing when another, more unexpected, tidal journey was undertaken. The derailment of a freight train approaching a bridge crossing the river near Ely had caused considerable structural damage and was preventing craft from onward navigation. The only way for *Lily* to reach St Ives was to take the tidal One Hundred Foot Drain. It was late afternoon when we locked through Denver Sluice onto an incoming tide and settled down for a three-hour cruise. There was plenty to see and

Navigating the One Hundred Foot Drain   not all was hindered by high banks as expected; some parts were very narrow, others formed a nature reserve. On this section, a hare pottered alongside for several hundred yards, completely unaware of our presence, although Buster knew he was there, nose twitching in excitement as the sun faded on another tidal adventure.

Finally arriving at St Ives, we moored at our allocated show spot, elated to have achieved so much. The elements had been against us from the start; at times, it had been hard work but, having arrived at our destination, nothing was going to dampen our spirits … until the IWA informed us we were two feet off our allotted mooring space and had to move up. If only they had known what we had been through to get there.

Buster was in his element at the festival site on Hemingford Meadow. It was a dog's playground and, as the week progressed, we savoured the wide-open space to walk and play in. We made friends and were asked to keep

Buster and Alison with Lily at Hemingford Meadow

watch over the little Wilderness trail boats which had breasted up along from *Lily*'s mooring whilst their owners returned home to attend work prior to the show weekend. The festival site slowly took shape; large white marquees were pulled and pushed into shape, show stands erected and transporters with boats arrived, turning the showground into a quagmire. With my heart in my mouth, I watched the boats lifted into place. Ken and Josie, our neighbours from Farndon, often stopped by for a chat. They were IWA members and involved in the preparation of the showground site. Buster made friends with Bosun, another Beagle, who was at the show with his charming owners on board their narrowboat.

By the time the show began, Buster considered Hemingford Meadow his home. As he sat in the wheelhouse, surveying his surroundings, most passersby admired him rather than *Lily*, who had been decked in bunting and given a polish especially for the occasion. From his elevated position, Buster gave the appearance of authority, looking down on people as if scrutinising them or about to give orders.

"He looks like he's in charge," a man called from the bankside.

"Well, he likes to think he is," I replied with a chuckle. Buster gave me a stare as if saying, 'What do you mean, *thinks* he is; you know I am.'

The man stepped closer and Buster turned, ignoring him.

"He's a little aloof, I see. He's very much the captain, isn't he?" he added. "No, no, he's not a captain; that isn't the right …" There was a short silence. "Admiral, that's the word I am looking for; he's more like an admiral!" He smiled proudly at me then said to Buster, "That's what I shall call you from now on – the Admiral." And so, it came to be. Every time the man passed, he would greet the Admiral, who always returned the same offish look only Buster could perfect. It quickly spread through the showground and soon more people knew our dog as the Admiral than by his real name.

With calls of "bring out your dead" from the floating rubbish disposal operatives, chats to inquisitive members of the public and posing for photographers, we slowly eased into show life. From being a lone barge on a sweeping river bend, we became one of many. *Lily* was hemmed in front and back by breasted-up narrowboats sporting beautiful bright paintwork, murals of roses and castles, planters of

The look which earnt Buster the title of the Admiral

Colourful narrowboats at the IWA National Festival

summer flowers and polished brasses, creating a floating fantasy dream world. It was not until later we discovered *Lily* was the only Dutch barge to attend.

The night of the illumination parade, we had the best views, sitting on *Lily*'s roof as the Wilderness boats performed their ballet-on-water routine to astonished crowds. A couple came and joined us. I cannot recall their names, only that of their narrowboat, *Norfolk Lass*, moored at Buckden Marina. But it did not matter; that was the spirit of the show – people with similar interests drawn together for a short period, passing ships in the night. Living on the waterways, people constantly drifted in and out of my life and I liked the fact there were no expectations. From a brief encounter to a long-term friendship, there was room for all.

Chapter Nineteen

THE FENLANDS

With Hemingford Meadow returned to its former state, old friendships rekindled and new ones forged, it was with a hint of sadness that we prepared to move on. We were going to explore the upper reaches of the Great Ouse; Priory Marina in Bedford our eventual destination, where Roger had provisionally booked *Lily* a berth. However, taking it up depended entirely on whether she could pass through Cardington Lock, which, according to waterways guides, was exactly the same width as her.

The charming Hemingford villages were straight off the lid of a chocolate box: timber-framed cottages with thatched roofs; country gardens bursting with rambling roses, towering hollyhocks and fragrant sweet peas. From Hemingford Grey, the river described a sweeping arc as it headed towards Houghton Lock. It was pretty beyond belief and backwaters and mill races joined the main river, attracting wildlife. Buster sat on the chart table, looking very much the Admiral, delighting in the wind beneath his ears. He revelled as one would in a topless car speeding along on a hot summer's day, drinking in the scent of wild flowers, freshly mown grass, warm straw and tumbling water in weir pools.

I was eager to show Roger Houghton Mill and Tea Rooms, perhaps purchase some flour for breadmaking. Buster and I had walked there from St

Ives previously and, on our way back, passed through a gate into an enclosed meadow where I had let Buster off-lead. Halfway across the field, he turned back and went bounding off at a steady pace, ears flapping, tail held high. I stood, hands on hips, watching him shrink into the distance. The meadow was securely fenced; he was safe and would return, eventually. Buster reached the gate and began barking. *What's he up to?* I thought to myself. People on the riverside path turned to look at him and I could not help but giggle over his antics.

Buster's barking became louder. Some people approached and he began jumping up, demanding their attention. I watched in disbelief as one of them stepped forwards, opened the gate, stood back and let him out.

"Nooooooo!" I screamed. Plunging into panic mode, I ran as fast as I could to catch up with Buster, who was already out of sight, lost along a curving footpath entering woodland. My heart thumped hard, banging as if it would jump out of my chest; the pretty pastoral scenery, previously pleasing, now a green blur. Reaching the far side of the meadow, the guilty gate-opener had vanished. I continued over the lock bridge and into the woods, passing the last place I had seen Buster. People in front heard me and moved to one side.

"Have you seen a dog, a Beagle, pass this way?" My question was met with blank expressions. Perhaps my flustered appearance had startled them into silence. "Yes, no?" Still no answer. "Thanks!" I realised Buster must have come this way; there was no other path unless he had gone off-track. I was exhausted, my legs were shaking and I had to slow to a fast walk to try and catch my breath. I rounded a corner. There was the mill and tea rooms and, by the picnic tables, next to an overflowing litter bin in sight of the doorway, sat Buster, his nose twitching at the inviting smell of afternoon tea and cake.

Thankfully, my visit with Roger passed without incident.

Great Barford Lock, with its tumbling weir, pretty village and seventeen-arch bridge, was my favourite spot on the upper reaches. Negotiating the bridge required care; headroom was tight and the sharp turn on exit was not easy for long craft. Over the years, the bridge had undergone numerous alterations, resulting in the downstream side being faced in stone whilst the other was plain

Passing beneath Great Barford Bridge

red brick. A short distance upstream, Roger moored *Lily* behind the former lock island. I wanted to see Barford Old Mill Lock with its scalloped chamber walls.

A little black-and-white Border Collie appeared on the towpath ahead of *Lily*. Running back and forth, she enticed Buster to play. I feared a repeat of Buster's drenching in the Soar but he had obviously mellowed during the intervening years as the two of them played nicely together. A short while later, her master arrived. "Oh, it's the Admiral. I wondered where my dog had got to." Roger and I had never seen the man before but he certainly seemed to know Buster.

We idled away the afternoon in the sunshine before an evening stroll along the riverside path. Watching hares play in stubble fields, Buster caught a whiff of them and, unable to contain himself, ran through in full cry, sending the hares racing into the distance. When he sauntered back, we walked on to The Anchor at Great Barford. A few drinks sharpened our appetites and discussions of what to conjure up in the galley followed. Most options lacked one vital ingredient – onion. Unbelievably, we had passed a small field of them earlier, fat and bulbous, protruding out of the dry soil. On the way back, Buster, full of mischief after forty winks in the pub garden, proceeded to attack one of the dry stems, yanking the golden globe from the soil.

"Roger, get it off him. Onions are bad for dogs." Roger retrieved the chewed and battered bulb from Buster's jaw. He held it high as Buster jumped and fussed, trying to reach it.

"D'you think the farmer will miss one?"

"No, I shouldn't think so; anyway, it's damaged goods now!"

"We'll eat well tonight; after all, what's a bit of dog slobber between friends?"

A difference of opinion existed regarding whether or not Lily could squeeze through Cardington Lock. Some local boaters believed the lock was slightly wider at the upstream end; if we placed Lily towards the head of the lock she would get through, with her return requiring backing into the chamber.

Others thought lifting the man-overboard chains out of the lock would allow enough room. Not wanting an audience, we waited until early the following morning to try. It was still and quiet as Roger directed me in. *Lily* gently touched the chains a few times but, carefully motoring her forwards, there was slightly more space; she fitted like a glove. Roger penned us through, slowly and gently; there was hardly any room to spare. It was an anxious few minutes; butterflies flittered in my stomach but we were soon exiting.

"We did it." I clapped my hands and grasped Buster's face, plastering

It was a tight fit for Lily
in Cardington Lock

him in kisses. He grunted and shook me off. It was far too early in the day for that sort of thing.

Before taking up the berth in Priory Marina, I could not resist heading on towards Bedford to see how far *Lily* could get but was aware headroom on the bridges would be a problem. The first, a disused railway viaduct, required us to duck as *Lily* glided beneath. The Engineers Bridge marked the end for *Lily*; the height of the mast tabernacle hindered further navigation and, although a little disappointed at not making the final run into Bedford, we consoled ourselves that *Lily* had at least made it to Priory Marina.

Reaching the end of the navigable route played on our minds and, not ones to give up easily, we packed a picnic and set off in an attempt to reach it in the dinghy. Buster sat at the bow, ducking beneath the low-hanging branches on the river above Bedford, observant and inquisitive. When Roger nosed the dinghy into the bank for our picnic lunch break, Buster leapt off and rolled about in a meadow, full of excitement and mischief. Just short of Kempston Mill, the dinghy ran aground on gravel shoals, having reached the limit of navigation, reputedly some 88 miles (142km) from King's Lynn and the sea.

On the upstream journey, eager to reach the showground, the section between Earith and St Ives had been swiftly passed. Returning, there was time to linger, stopping at the pretty village of Holywell, which took its name from a spring in the local churchyard. It was a novelty having the wheelhouse erected after weeks of daily dismantling for low bridges. Buster basked in the warm sunshine glinting through the glass, legs hanging out of his bed, snoring loudly. The scenery began to change; the wooded banks faded away, revealing far-reaching views topped with big skies, room to breathe – real East Anglian flatlands. By the time Brownshill Staunch was reached, the wind whipped selfishly across the open landscape and I was glad to have the shelter of *Lily*'s wheelhouse.

Reaching the tidal waters at Earith, instead of taking the One Hundred Foot Drain, we entered Hermitage Lock and joined the non-tidal waters of the Old West River, linking the upper reaches of the Great Ouse to the Ely Ouse. It was a narrow, meandering river, alongside which cattle lazily grazed and paddled in the shallows amongst flowering water lilies. There was plenty of depth for *Lily*

The charming village of Holywell but width was tight when meeting other craft. All of the oncoming boaters knew of our pending arrival, which they said had come via the local jungle drums – VHF radio. Despite *Lily* being on the large side and taking up a lot of room, we were met with kindness and consideration from fellow boaters. As a couple passed in their cruiser, the lady threw some photographs, weighed down in a bag by a scented candle. They had taken pictures of *Lily* earlier in the season and made copies, keeping them on board in the hope they would see us again. They were one of my most treasured items from *Lily*'s epic 102-day adventure on the waterways of the Fens.

Entering the wider, deeper waters of the River Cam, *Lily* sprang into life as we headed to the village of Upware and a pub with a fabulous mouthful of a name: the Five Miles from Anywhere No Hurry Inn. Upware was the entrance to a network of small waterways known as the Cambridgeshire Lodes, which we did not venture onto with *Lily* as there was not much depth and they were so remote we would have had a problem had she become grounded. High winds and grey days made even the prospect of a jaunt in the dinghy unappealing. With Roger and I togged up in wet weather gear, exploring on foot suited Buster better. Much of the area formed the National Trust's Wicken Fen Nature Reserve, one of the oldest in the country. The undrained Sedge Fen offered an amazing insight to how the surrounding countryside would look if left to Mother Nature.

Shirley drove up from West Sussex, bringing my mum to visit. It was good to catch up on gossip and feast my eyes on the familiar faces of loved ones. Buster was ecstatic to have their company; he adored the unexpected extra affection and treats they brought with them. When they were ready to leave, Buster and I walked with them to the car park. As they drove away, waving farewells, Buster tugged and pulled on the lead in a frenzied attempt to follow and howled in utter despair when they disappeared from sight.

When it was finally time to leave Upware, we were unable to; the wind had pushed *Lily* onto a bankside ledge, grounding her. Roger tried his best to free her. With the engine running in reverse, he pushed hard with the ash pole but it snapped clean in half, almost piercing his chest in the process.

"I saw my whole life flash before my eyes," he exclaimed dramatically when propping up the bar in the pub that night. *Lily* was rescued by a group of young lads who delighted in hauling her back into deeper water with their powerful cruiser.

Moorings for the cathedral city of Cambridge began at Midsummer Common but we pushed on, turning *Lily* in front of Jesus Lock, with its beautifully crafted balance beams fashioned in sweeping curves resembling cow horns, before taking up a berth. Navigation was restricted above the lock. It was home to the punt, which some considered the best way to view Cambridge. I had never punted along The Backs, the name given to the rear of the colleges, and was looking forward to the experience, but a steady drizzle set in and the thought of sporting a soggy bottom for the remainder of the day was enough to put me off. Buster looked thoroughly fed up; wet through and paddling through city streets was not a Beagle's idea of fun. We scurried back to *Lily*.

Joining the Ely Ouse at Pope's Corner, winds pushed in grey clouds heavy with rain, forcing us to seek shelter at Little Thetford. The flood banks towering above *Lily* offered protection, albeit limiting the view. After stopping early due to the weather, we made an early start the next morning, falling in behind two hire boats. It was late September and the derailment stoppage which caused problems for craft trying to reach the showground during the early summer remained the talk of the Fenlands. Being in a small convoy would hopefully avoid an extended holdup. Restructuring of the bridge was forging ahead and there was only a brief wait as engineers moved the floating platform they were working from, allowing us passage.

Ely was once surrounded by marshland and known as the Isle of Eels. In the past, this snake-like fish used to form part of the staple diet and was a source of income for many local families. Ely was small and compact with an inviting appearance that continued into its very heart, the narrow streets, old-world buildings and pleasant green spaces culminating in the stunning cathedral. Famed for its unique Octagon Tower and known as the Ship of the Fens, it was considered one of the country's finest Norman cathedrals. Although Buster was not a town dog, the small winding streets, parks and heritage trails pleased him, as did meeting and playing with a distant relative – another Cliffmere Beagle.

Before heading back to Denver Sluice, there was time for a couple of diversions. The first was on the River Lark where the Prickwillow Drainage Engine Museum was celebrating its silver jubilee with a year of special events. After visiting the museum and enjoying the hospitality of custodian Joan Stacey, we lingered for the following day's event – Village Crafts and Trades. Brick and tile making, eel trapping with traditional handmade willow traps, thatching and wool spinning were a few of the local trades exhibited. Joan was welcoming and took quite a shine to Buster, providing him with drinking water throughout the day and allowing us to leave the car on her driveway whilst continuing to explore the Lark.

Strolling around Isleham Marina, Buster began hanging back on his lead. This was not like him; usually he was way ahead or pulling to one side, checking out a delicious smell.

"What's up, Buzz?" He did not look very happy but walked on after I had given the lead a gentle tug. When I next turned to look at him, I noticed blood on one of his front paws. "Buster's hurt himself." His expression was telling me he needed help.

"Come here, my boy, let me have a look." Buster slowly lifted his paw towards Roger but, despite us both looking closely, we could not see an injury. "Let's get him back to *Lily* and bathe it. We'll be able to see more clearly. I'll carry him the rest of the way."

Back on *Lily*, we discovered Buster had pulled off a claw and was in pain. Roger fired up the internet – the first time it had been used for help – and was soon in touch with a local vet. Luckily, Joan's house and the car were not far away and Buster was soon at the surgery. He was given a check-up and the injury assessed. A painkiller and antibiotics were administered and dressing applied. Buster was grateful for the pain relief but was not impressed with the bandage. It was blue for a boy but printed with images of fish – obviously meant for a cat.

On reflection, Roger and I recalled signs on a new bridge at the marina, warning that care should be taken with dogs as the non-slip surface was made of sharp metal spikes. Meeting a gentleman on the bridge, Buster needed to be pulled in tight to allow him to pass. Had we unintentionally inflicted the injury on our beloved boy? Guilt ate away at us and the incident terminated the cruise on the Lark.

The River Little Ouse was also known as Brandon Creek, a title I preferred as it seemed more romantic and conjured up images of Daphne du Maurier's pirate ship, *La Mouette*, in *Frenchman's Creek*, and the folly of a long-lost summer. However, the macabre tales linked to the river entrance and inn built by Dutch engineers in 1640 meant it was far from that. Prior to the construction of the first Denver Sluice, the river was tidal; errant prisoners of war, used during the construction of local drainage systems, were buried up to their chins in the river's mud and left to drown in the rising waters. Rumours of hauntings and sightings of ghostly figures on mist-shrouded nights were rife.

Buster recuperating on board

Buster's injury was healing but he struggled to walk far so finding moorings to keep him amused became a priority. At Hockwold Fen, the low-lying, soft, grassy banks were ideal and he sat and watched kestrels hovering high above him all afternoon until a buzzard appeared, panicking birdlife into fleeing for shelter. In the distance, Lakenheath runway was visible; during the week, aircraft from here and nearby Mildenhall shattered the silence, treating us to an aerial display of another kind. The remoteness of Brandon Creek was intoxicating and we enjoyed watching the sheer power of man-made flying machines competing with nature for our attention.

With exploration of the Fenland tributaries completed, in the early-morning darkness Roger reluctantly headed off to work in the car. I returned to bed and snuggled up to Buster, only to be awoken by the jazzy tone of my mobile. I instantly knew something was wrong. Roger had collided with a deer. He was shaken but thankfully unharmed, which was sadly more than could be said for either the vehicle or the deer. The insurance company provided a replacement car, allowing Roger to continue working during the day and help move *Lily* towards Denver in the evenings. A few days later, having exhausted the three-month EA licence, we bid farewell to the Fens.

Chapter Twenty

HOMEWARD BOUND

Wedged into the wheelhouse corner, David's legs were astride, his feet firmly pushed onto the floorboards, toes gripping a non-existent ledge. He battled to keep his balance with outstretched arms and hands, his splayed fingers constantly slipping on the shiny, polished wood panels. As *Lily* took another hit of cold, grey seawater, she pitched sideways, poised suspended, before rolling off the wave into a sickening plummet. Roger fought with the steering wheel, knuckles white from his tight grip. Gazing ahead into the unrelenting force of the sea, a worried look washed over his face. Bracing, he turned the wheel into another fast-approaching wave but the angle was not enough to save *Lily* from another pounding.

The wind roared and lashed, tried its best to dislodge the wheelhouse, which slopped and slewed against each knock, imitating a drunken sailor wending his way home. Water flew at the windows, hitting them with such force I was sure they would shatter. Another hit on the side and down we plummeted again, scrabbling for hand- and footholds wherever we could find them. Bangs and crashes from below battled to be heard above the wind's bellow.

Buster sat bolt upright on the chart table and gazed in fascination as the waves slammed against the hull, sending spray against the windscreen, smearing it with salty droplets. With sparkling eyes, he turned towards Roger and gave him his sometimes-smile. He was taking his newly administered name and role of Admiral far too seriously for my liking. What had happened to the seasick hound from a few months ago? Despite our dog's enjoyment at being buffeted about at sea, this was not a good situation; a Dutch barge on The Wash in a strengthening wind was worrying. Would we escape the raging waters with our lives or was it going to end in disaster?

Four hours previously, out of courtesy, Roger had telephoned the King's Lynn harbour master informing him of our intentions, only to discover that the friendly, polite gentleman we spoke to on our way over had been replaced by a harsh, unhelpful individual. As before, we had planned to head to the GOBA buoys and swing on them overnight but, when Roger mentioned this, there was an audible intake of breath. "No, I'm afraid not, you can't hang off them. Far too heavy, you'll rip them up," he declared.

"We're only a small barge, twenty tons, and have permission from GOBA," came Roger's pleading reply.

"I laid those mooring buoys; I know they won't take your weight. You must make other arrangements."

"What! We used them on the way over and there wasn't a problem."

"No, it's out of the question. You'll have to moor elsewhere."

I sensed this harbour master was enjoying his new-found role of dictator.

"Where do you suggest? Can we moor next to your craft?" Roger took a mouthful of tea and slammed down the mug in frustration.

"No, you can't. I'll see if you can moor next to the fishermen. It will cost around £50 for the night." He grunted.

Roger almost spat his tea all over Buster, who was sitting close by, intently listening to the conversation.

"Fifty quid! You've got to be joking?"

"I'll call them and see if it's possible, then get back to you." The line went dead as he rang off.

Gazing at each other in disbelief, a hollow, empty feeling developed in the pit of my stomach. It had been my suggestion to contact the harbour master.

"There's no way on earth I'm paying fifty quid to moor next to a smelly old fishing boat which will most likely want us to move at the crack of dawn," Roger said.

"I agree; that's a lot of money and may go straight into their pockets for all we know."

"I think we should just go on down there and tie onto the mooring buoy."

"No, you can't do that; he'll watch for us. If he asks us to move, then we'll have no choice. Let's stay here for a few more days."

Roger looked at the time and the headroom remaining in the lock. Passage had to be closely timed; with the Fens being below sea-level, we would be locking onto rising tidal waters through a lock constructed into a sluice system. It resembled a short tunnel more than an open-topped lock.

"Let's go," he said. "Lock through and I'll call David; we'll go now."

The phone rang; it was the harbour master.

"It's possible to moor against the large fishing boat on the quay. It will be fifty, cash, for the night but you'll have to let them out early in the morning." He sounded as if he was revelling in the good news.

"Are you certain we can't use the GOBA buoys?" asked Roger. "We're paid-up members."

"No, you're too heavy. There's only the fishing boat suitable for such a vessel."

"OK, I'll have a think about it."

We had left it late; there was hardly any headroom as I locked through. The lock keeper, who did not seem surprised by the awkwardness of the harbour master, did all he could to cheer our spirits; he even checked the weather forecast and told Roger the winds were due to rise later.

"Go now, go all the way and don't stop until you get to Hobbs Hole," he advised. "Look, I'll show you on the chart." David arrived with lifejacket in hand and wearing a warm grin. I was pleased to see him. David had no more experience than us but he was calm and could act as the voice of reason; plus, he provided an extra pair of hands, which was always welcome. As Roger explained the situation, he agreed we should go; the thought of parting with £50 did not sit well with him either.

The lock keeper waved us off, saying he would inform Boston Sluice. We headed out towards the sea, passing the GOBA buoys bobbing free of boats.

David took the wheel as Roger double-checked the course, ensuring he knew where to anchor. The fishing fleet were toppling this way and that as they made their approach to the harbour.

"It's going to be rough," said Roger "We spent too much time trying to reason with that idiot; we may hit the winds before we make the anchorage."

"We could go back." I was concerned.

"What, and give him fifty quid for the privilege?"

"It's our lives and our boat. *Lily*'s our home now."

"Right, I say we go on. David, what do you think?"

"We've come this far already so we may as well continue." David was enjoying being at the helm.

"Whatever you think," I said to Roger. "You're the one who's done the navigation course; only you know."

"I say we go on. I'll take the wheel now, David." Roger had decided.

Heading onto The Wash, the winds gathered pace and the seas began to build, becoming rough and uncomfortable. *Lily* was taking a hammering. The waves were large, the thumping violent as she smashed down them, making things move below. I beat a hasty retreat to discover the herb jars banging out of their rack every time we descended a wave. Roger, at the helm, had the best spot, using the wheel not only to steer but help keep his balance. He tacked *Lily* to gain some respite; it helped but was short-lived, back and forth, back and forth with little obvious progress.

"I'm going to have to take a longer tack," he shouted over the roar of the wind.

"OK," I yelled from below. "Is Buster alright or shall I come and get him?"

"No, he's fine. He loves it."

I looked at David and asked, "Are you alright?"

"Yes, but I feel a bit queasy."

"Me too." I nodded and then turned, desperate to catch a glimpse of the horizon from the nearest window to steady my nausea.

Roger made a huge tack, taking us off course and, for a while, bearings were lost. Spotting a buoy, Roger headed towards it to confirm our location. It was a shock; he had tacked as far in as the Nene Roads buoy. Now we needed to turn back into the full force of the wind to pick up the plotted course. The waves kept coming, pounding, unforgiving against *Lily*'s hull. Bang, bang, bang, one after another, a continual round of blows never letting up. Was this ever going to end? Could *Lily* really handle this?

After what seemed like a lifetime, the waters gradually began to calm, which enabled us to move about more freely, rest our tensed limbs. In fading light, we slowly crept into Hobbs Hole, selected a spot and dropped anchor. Roger took a bearing and made a note of a landmark on the shore whilst *Lily* bucked and wriggled as if a young steer lassoed for the first time. There were creaks, groans and dull bangs, strange noises new to us and lots of movement but she held firm.

Exhausted, we sat together in the wheelhouse and watched commercial shipping in the distance; their lights twinkled brightly as they were met by the pilot boat. Finally, we gave in and let sleep take us. Roger napped but kept watch most of the night, going out on several occasions to check the anchor chain. At some stage, in the deep inky blackness of the night, he carefully guided Buster to his piece of water-drenched turf so he could relieve himself on his soggy doggy toilet. It was a long, rough night. I lay sideways across the bed, fully clothed, finding it more comfortable to bear the knocks that way. Buster lay by my side, his warm body pushed against mine. Drifting into a disturbed sleep, my dreams were dominated by constantly moving blue-and-white swirling waters, flying fish and isolated atolls.

"Motor Vessel *Lily*, Motor Vessel *Lily*, Motor Vessel *Lily*. This is Boston Sluice. Do you read? Over."

All three of us stopped munching on our bacon butties and looked at each other, wide-eyed and surprised, as the VHF crackled into life. Buster let out a moan of despair, knowing this would delay his chance of receiving any scraps. Roger dropped his breakfast onto the plate and rushed up to the wheelhouse. Buster threw me one of his 'has he finished with that?' looks.

With a mouthful of bacon, Roger keyed the mike and replied as best he could. "Errr, yes," he managed to get out through a slapping of his chops. "This is Motor Vessel *Lily*, Boston Sluice," he said, followed by a lumpy swallow. "I am reading you loud and clear. Over."

A short conversation ensued; the Denver Sluice lock keeper, true to his word, had been in contact with Boston Sluice.

"I understand your predicament; I have been informed all about it so know you've endured a rough night out there. I'd like to get you in as soon as possible. Can you please make your way upriver?" The voice was friendly and understanding.

Roger put his head down the stairwell. "Come on then, let's go. He wants us in as soon as possible." Now Buster looked very hopeful. David and I quickly finished our bacon butties whilst Roger fired up the engine. As Buster edged forwards, lining up to receive his master's disregarded breakfast, Roger called out, "Can you pass me up the rest of my butty?"

The look of disappointment on our Beagle's face could have sunk the barge.

Having said our farewells to David, we headed on to Anton's Gowt, relieved to once again be back on still water. Making our way along the Witham, I often took *Lily* single-handed whilst Roger moved the car to our next destination or rode the fold-up bike back to collect it. On other occasions, we travelled together and made the return to collect the car

Buster enjoyed having the wheelhouse dismantled on the rural Witham

a nice walk for Buster, who loved the Water Rail Way running alongside the navigation. Late one evening, as we walked to the car, there were no lights along the track and, with little moonlight, Roger used his windup torch to light the way. All manner of night creatures must have used the pathway because Buster was in full scent mode throughout the walk, his constant snuffling and grunting sounds only interrupted by the regular winding of the torch or distant hoot of an owl. Buster strained to run on the lead, his grunts becoming louder as he began weaving across the path. I was about to ask Roger to take him from me when Buster whimpered and stopped.

"What's up, Buzzy?" I tried to feel for him but it was too dark to see. "Shine the torch on him, will you, Rog?" Giving the torch a wind, Roger shone it downwards. Buster was rubbing his muzzle with his front paws.

"He must have walked into something; a bramble I expect."

"No, it can't have been; he was in the middle of the path when he cried out." Roger arched the beam around and it illuminated a hedgehog scurrying away. Buster, totally engrossed with his nose on the ground, must have walked straight into its prickly spines.

Plenty of stops were made along the Witham, allowing Buster to perfect his pantomime farce routine with the various sculptures. We stayed longer at Bardney, where new floating pontoons and electric hookup had recently been installed. Back at Saxilby on the Fossdyke, the flood levels encountered in early summer had dispersed and the moorings were free to use. Buster and I enjoyed a few days exploring the area. It was late in the season; nights were drawing in and the sale of fireworks in preparation for Guy Fawkes Night was underway. One afternoon, the sound of bangers disturbed us. Buster had grown accustomed to such noises and was not fearful but the noise was close enough to cause a grumble under his breath. Alone on the boat, I was nervous and, after enduring the noise for an hour, knowing Roger would not be back until after dark, made the decision to move *Lily*. Buster watched me prepare the boat; he was calm and thoughtful, perhaps sensing the anticipation of our imminent departure. The hardest part was putting the mast down; Roger had tightened it as if in preparation for a tropical whirlwind. A pair of pliers and a tea towel wrapped around the nut finally did the trick. Lifting Buster up into his bed on the chart table, I had a quick word with him.

"Now then, Buster, it's time to show me you really are an Admiral." With Buster comfortably settled, I set off.

Slipping away, a small group of boys ran parallel along the waterside street, throwing bangers at each other. Buster turned to look at them and grumbled. I thought we were sure to come under attack and I silently prayed Buster would not draw their attention by releasing one of his deep barks. I opened the revs; Buster quickly settled down and I do not think I breathed again until rounding the bend leading away from the otherwise delightful Saxilby.

It was a pleasant, uneventful trip to Torskey, where I took up a berth at the beginning of a long stretch of public moorings. Mooring was probably the most dangerous part of being alone on a boat and I was not prepared to take any chances in fading light on a cold afternoon. It was an ideal choice; Buster and I were undisturbed and enjoyed a few peaceful days, warm enough to tempt us out into the camping chairs to soak up the diminishing rays of autumnal sunshine.

Heading back towards Farndon, Buster began recognising places and there was a noticeable shift in his behaviour. At Torksey, gateway to the Trent, he was beside himself. On daily walks, he raced around the fields and dipped his toes into the waters of our river, its swirling eddies welcoming us home.

One of the few places to moor on the tidal Trent was the floating pontoon at Dunham Rack. Roger and I had earmarked it as a possible break for Buster but not had the opportunity to take advantage. It was a lovely day; walking to Dunham Dubs, a double bend in the river, the watery sunshine bathed the scene in a hazy warmth.

Leaving the moorings, we headed out into the main channel, picking up speed when, without warning, *Lily*'s engine stopped.

"What's wrong?" Roger yelled from the front of the boat, where he was tidying the ropes.

"I don't know; she just stopped." Buster looked at me; he had snuggled down in his bed, knowing it was a long trip. I was concerned; we were midstream

Steaming Trent Valley power stations viewed from Torksey

on tidal waters without an engine. There could be commercial barges about.

In the engine room, things looked bleak; the vee belt was broken and there was no spare. Closer inspection revealed the water pump had seized, causing a toppling effect on everything else. Roger restarted *Lily* but the batteries were not charging and there was no cooling flow to the engine. *Lily* had to be nursed slowly up the tidal reaches to Cromwell, dropping anchor midstream to let the engine cool each time the gauges showed she was about to overheat. Roger radioed ahead to Cromwell Lock; there was no way we would reach there before it closed for the evening.

It was a frustrating cruise, taking double the usual time. Luckily, we met no commercial traffic and the sunny day helped keep spirits high. The lock keeper at Cromwell kept in constant contact, checking in before closing for the night, ensuring we could reach the safety of the pontoons under our own (slow) steam.

Safely moored on the tidal pontoon below Cromwell, we endured a disturbed night, constantly buffeted from the outfall of the weir. It was still possible to fire up the generator, prepare hot drinks and cook a good meal. After all the miles *Lily* had covered, we could not complain. Imagine if the failure had happened out on The Wash! Roger managed to strip down the water pump and effect a temporary repair, which, along with the fitting of a new vee belt obtained locally, allowed a safe return to Farndon.

"We saw Buster in the newspaper," shouted one of the Farndon Marina staff as I slowly backed *Lily* into her mooring. Not the welcome I had been expecting. I was more prepared for an intense question-and-answer session concerning our crossing of The Wash, rather than comments on the fame of my dog.

"See the Admiral has returned." It was Ken on *Helianthus*.

"Hello, nice to have you back. Saw Buster in *Towpath Talk*," a fellow boater chimed as he passed. The comments made me feel proud and generated a wide smile. Buster had already appeared in several articles I had written but attending the IWA show had introduced him to a wider audience. He was becoming well known on the boating circuit.

"Seems like Buster's stolen the limelight." Roger ruffled Buster's head. Buster was watching my mooring manoeuvres but glanced up at Roger and grinned. I gave the throttle a quick blast forwards, bringing *Lily* to a halt, then tapped the bow thruster, sweeping her gently into the side of the pontoon. Roger stepped out of the wheelhouse and roped *Lily* in.

"Well done, old girl." I patted *Lily*'s warm, varnished woodwork and switched off her engine. We were home.

Chapter Twenty-One

NEW DOG ON THE BLOCK

There was a new dog on the block: a red Boxer puppy with gangly legs and a whippy, uncontrollable tail. Roxy was instantly likeable and I soon grew to love her but the arrival of this extra dog in Hilary's household changed the dynamic between Buster and Bunty. He was no longer Bunty's adoring, all-consuming playmate; instead, she would run and chase her younger companion, mothering as if she were her own puppy, relegating Buster unintentionally to the sidelines. He, of course, bore no malice and was happy to go off and do his own thing whilst the two of them played rough and tumble but I felt sorry for him. I still enjoyed our walks and the company but the introduction of a third dog saw the sun begin to set on the Halcyon Days we had all come to love and cherish.

As time passed, Buster changed; gradually he began to calm and eased into adulthood. Despite this and the shift in the relationship between Buster and Bunty, an air of mischievous play still existed amongst our group of dogs. With the addition of Roxy, we had a new element of 'puppiness' and, with that, naughtiness, which sent us into belly-hugging fits of laughter or, on occasion, floods of tears, depending on our moods or the situation we found ourselves in.

Boxer puppy Roxy, by Maki Harris

Hilary and I were almost at the end of our morning walk, the dogs happily trotting along, taking it easy after having run themselves ragged. Roxy stopped and turned her head into the stiff breeze then made a bolt for it, running as fast as she could across the open fields.

"Where on earth is she going?" I asked Hilary as we watched Roxy's lean, slinky body quickly cover the ground. Gathering up Bunty, Hilary sighed.

"Oh no, here, Al, take Bunty, please." Handing me the lead, she hot-footed it across the fields in pursuit of her runaway ward. Slowly, it began to dawn on me what was happening. A couple of fields away, a tractor was muck-spreading; Roxy was racing towards it, the smell too tempting to ignore.

Bunty, Buster and I followed behind and arrived at the corner of the field in time to see Hilary racing across the uneven ground, almost breaking her neck, her arms waving frantically in a vain attempt to halt the tractor driver. Roxy was chasing the muck spreader, leaping into the air as if catapulted out of a gun, and catching in her mouth flying wodges of manure, having a great time playing poo frisbee. Occasionally, she grabbed hold of a lump so large that she could not eat it; instead, she shook it violently in her mouth, sending clods of manure showering all around. I could not help but laugh; it was a hilarious sight. Bunty and Buster sat calmly and quietly one either side of me. Watching events unfold, they both glanced up at me as if to say, 'Puppies, who'd have 'em?' then promptly turned their heads back to watch some more. What this story lacks in retelling was the smell; the overpowering, intoxicating aroma of manure was foul. When Roxy was finally retrieved, she was a mess; her beautiful, velvety face smeared in manure, lumps of rotting straw hanging from her jowly jaws, **but** she was one of the happiest dogs I had ever seen.

Buster came from a successful line of show dogs. In his early years, we had had some success at shows, mostly fun-level competitions, but he was never keen on them. When a dog show was organised in Farndon in aid of Boxer Rescue, we went along with Hilary and her girls as well as several others from our dog-walking group. Buster trotted off, happy as usual to be on a walk but, realising he was going to be in a show, immediately switched character. Gone was his confident, in-charge attitude; instead came the rarely seen I-want-no-part-of-it look. He sat down and would not move; he hid behind our legs or tried to squeeze beneath any nearby chair. When it was his turn to go into the ring, he projected such a look of misery that the judge awarded him a rosette just to cheer him up. It was no good; for the rest of the day, Buster hung his head and sulked. Even Bunty's and Roxy's gentle nuzzling could not reinstate the usual, playful Buster.

Finally admitting defeat, we said our goodbyes, whereupon a completely different dog suddenly appeared. The old, bouncy, happy-go-lucky Buster was back, trotting to the gate with his tail held high, waving from side to side, a show dog if ever there was one. Reaching the exit, we passed the judge, who did a double take before saying, "That's not the same dog, is it?"

"Yes," I replied. "He's happy to be going home."

"I can see that," said the judge, chuckling. Buster was such a fraud; on more than one occasion he pulled similar stunts. Far from being dumb, as some claimed, Beagles were extremely **clever.**

Throughout all these mishaps and misadventures, *Lily* was the calming effect in our lives. She plodded on, doing everything we asked of her, keeping us safe and secure. At the end of a hard day's boating or dog walking, there was nothing better than relaxing below deck in *Lily's* cosy, warm cabin. Her country cottage interior oozed peace as we settled down in front of the stove on chilly

evenings to listen to audio books or play a game of Scrabble. Buster would curl up by my side and, when fully warmed through, slide off to flop

Roger and Buster having a game alongside the River Trent

out on the floor at my feet. He would give a series of little snorting sounds, a sign he was content and happy before gently wafting his tail to disperse the wind he had just passed, the most putrid scent imaginable.

A simple pleasure was spending afternoons cuddled up with Buster on the sofa, watching a classic movie. Our all-time favourite was the beautifully filmed version of *Great Expectations* by David Lean. Roger and I liked to incorporate names and lines from films in our everyday life to make us laugh. The aged parent referred to as 'Aged P' in this Charles Dickens classic became our name for Buster in his later years. He became our aged puppy, our very own Aged P. We had slipped easily into boating life; the weeks faded effortlessly into months, the months into seasons, the seasons into years. Miss Havisham's words had been so apt – "I know nothing of days of the week; I know nothing of the weeks of the year" – and so, for a while, that was how it was for us.

The ability to travel, taking our home with us, was liberating; sneaking into city centres often unseen was a privilege, living close to nature and wildlife a treat. At Farndon, we felt comfortable; new and long-lasting friendships were forged. Buster was having a wonderful life, walking and playing freely with a large group of dogs. He was a lucky hound. We were happy. However, our world was about to be rocked. Fate had spotted us and was about to throw a spanner in the works.

Chapter Twenty-Two

A SPANNER IN THE WORKS

Roger was made redundant after only eighteen months in a job we thought would last and allow him more leisure time. Despite searching, a new position in his specific line of work close to *Lily*'s mooring could not be found.

With no work forthcoming, we tried to look at the positives rather than the negatives and began to think about the possibility of relocating somewhere that would fulfil our boating dreams as well as offer employment. With no ties and only ourselves and our well-being to consider, we felt this was the right thing to do. There was only one problem — where to go?

"You do realise we could go anywhere, don't you?" I said.

"I know but I was hoping to spend a bit more time here; it fits us so well and it's been good for you." Roger was right; life on the Trent had helped heal. I felt better than I had in years, more at one with the world. My confidence had improved, Buster had helped me make new friends, travelling the waterways with *Lily* had provided new and interesting topics to write about and I was holding my own, work-wise. I felt ready to take on a new challenge; with Roger and Buster by my side, as a family I knew we could make a success of it. "I'll get the European waterways map out."

Suddenly full of enthusiasm, Roger jumped up from the sofa and headed for 'the shed'.

"Good luck with finding that," I replied. Buster groaned.

Our long-term plan was to take *Lily* to Europe, in particular France, where we had spent many happy years boating earlier in our relationship. From a work point of view, France was out of the question; neither of us had good language skills. Scotland became our first choice and a likely position came up in Inverness. Roger applied, attended an interview and seemed happy with the outcome but, a week later, he heard the position had fallen through. It was a bitter blow but turned us towards Ireland. Within a matter of weeks, Roger had attended interviews, accepted an offer and found a pretty cottage to rent near Athlone in the heart of rural Ireland.

Section Two

IRELAND

Buster's travels in Ireland

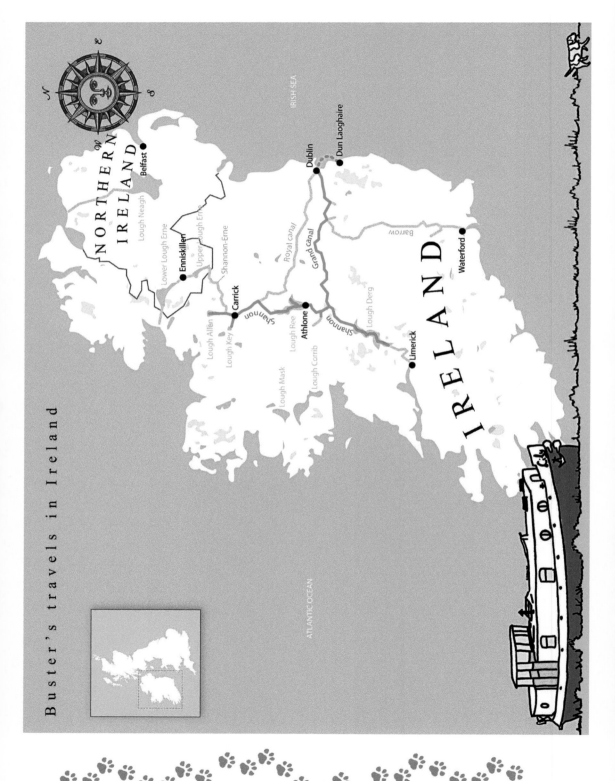

Chapter One

BOATLESS IN THE CALLOWS

Torc Cottage, in the sleepy village of Clonown, nestled on the edge of the callows, bordering the River Shannon. A traditional Irish longhouse, all rooms were on ground level. The large kitchen housed an oil-fired Stanley range, something I had never used before but which quickly became a favourite with Buster, who adored the constant warmth which permeated from it. There were outbuildings storing turf for the open fire and a pretty garden overlooking lower meadows where cattle grazed and hares boxed. Buster discovered a love of sitting on the very edge of the drop, watching the wildlife. The hares taunted him, racing close by. Breaking into full cry, Buster would tear along the fenceline, the frustration at being unable to reach them apparent in his voice. One hare was particularly fearless. He was almost the size of Buster with a daily routine which involved a trek across the meadow, onto the lane and up the hill towards the village. Encountering him face to face was a bewildering experience; I am sure, if he had raised himself up on his hind legs and thrown me a punch, I would have been out for the count.

It was rumoured that the people of Clonown slept with lake boats beneath their beds as the callows, the Irish name for water meadows, were prone to frequent flooding, sometimes resulting in devastating consequences. Wildfowl

155

Our new home Torc Cottage, a traditional Irish long house

flocked there; it was believed almost one seventh of Ireland's population of redshank nested on the callows. Not shy in coming forwards, these wading birds mobbed Buster in the spring, dive-bombing with shrill cries or hovering inches above his head, their scarlet legs dangling all aquiver. Buster meant them no harm but they did not know that; instinct told them belligerence was best. Buster took little notice as he walked along the gravelly track across the open landscape but neither did he wander into their nesting grounds so the message must have got through. Curlew, snipe, lapwing and the illusive corncrake all made their home on the callows, as a result of which farmers could claim an annual grant for delaying haymaking until after the birds had nested.

The callows were full of scent and sound; the latter made by the woodcock and corncrake, two of the strangest, closely followed by the trumpeting of the whooper swan. The almost constantly mushy ground and wild environment were a dog's delight and, once the breeding season was over for the ground-nesting birds, I would let Buster off-lead. The flat landscape made it possible to see him for miles, the tip of his tail waving frantically as he charged back and forth following some heady scent through marshy ground, water spraying around him.

"Ye knows there are bog holes out there, don't ye?" an elderly farmer took great joy in telling me as I watched Buster disappearing into the distance. "Swallow up a dog 'ole, so they will." I quickly learnt to take what the Irish said with a pinch of salt.

"Thanks, I best get him back then." I nodded and walked away as the farmer fired up the small tractor and rattled away in a cloud of black smoke.

Almost everyone in Clonown had a tractor and they were not used solely for farm work, often assuming the role of the family car, driven for the weekly shop or a trip to the pub. As tractors frequently passed Torc Cottage, which sat below the brow of a hill, they could be heard approaching for some distance. Buster would wait by the gate, erupt into a frenzy of barking and race around the rear of the cottage, meeting them as they passed the other side, barking until the tailgate

Buster loved playing in the rich grasslands of the callows bordering the River Shannon

disappeared over the brow of the hill. He would then strut back to us with a satisfied look on his face, one which said, 'I saw it off.' When Buster had a near miss with one of the mechanical beasts, his willingness to 'see it off' diminished. Roger was walking him to the river when a small tractor belonging to a neighbour clattered towards them. Buster lurched at it with such force that his collar gave way. If it had not been for the driver's quick reactions, Buster would have found himself under its huge tyres.

Once a week, the rubbish had to be transported to the church in the centre of Clonown as the dustmen only collected from there. Most locals had rigged up towing gear onto their tractors or cars, enabling their full wheelie bins to be pulled along the uneven lane, but we walked it. This job fell mostly on Roger, who would be accompanied by a bemused Beagle. In the pitch blackness of winter nights, the two of them would head off together, dressed in fluorescent yellow jackets, wheelie bin in tow with Roger sporting his head lamp. Clonown was home to many such whimsical ideas. Another was the post box, which may have been on an undercover mission. Why, in a country where everything was green, were they painted the same colour and hidden in hedgerows? On more than one occasion, I walked right by with an important letter to post, only to slowly retrace my steps to find the box.

As well as a haven for birdlife, the callows were rich in wild flowers, with many rare species. In spring, marsh marigolds emerged, spots of gold that glimmered through the grasses lying flattened by silt from the receding winter floods. As the rains washed this away, the landscape was quickly transformed into a million shades of vibrant green. Tall grasses swayed in the summer breeze, a great, green sea stretching a mile or so inland before meeting the raised bogs. Spikey sedges, frothy cream flowers of meadowsweet and the deep purple of tufted vetch could be found in this swirling sea. Yellow irises lined the ditches amongst ranks of rushes and, above it all, the song of the heaven-bound skylark added its melodious chorus to nature's symphony.

A section of the callows at Clonown was known as the Garavinch. What at first sight appeared to be one continuous area of grassland was divided up into small meadows or strips managed by local farmers. Late summer and harvest time beckoned; tractors trundling across the land cut and gathered the sweet dry grasses for cattle feed as autumn fast approached. As the tall seedheads of the dock turned burnt orange, the landscape basked in a haze of golden hues. In winter, the callows were lost beneath a glistening film of flood water. On cold, frosty mornings, the whole area shimmered as the water-covered fields froze. Thick mists enveloped the landscape in a white blanket, projecting a muted, eerie silence. Migrating whooper swans arrived from their breeding grounds in Iceland; their cries echoed across the Shannon and along the sleepy lanes, creating a mysteriously haunting atmosphere.

Clonown and the callows were a strange place, unassuming yet with an underlying charm. In its own way, the area was unique and, as with other places which had featured in my life, it took leaving to discover this. When we finally prepared to move on a year later, our neighbour, Padraic, said to me, "You'll be reminded of this place when you least expect it and then you'll realise you miss it." His words were true and, although I experienced some of its features elsewhere, when I saw them, it was the callows which came to mind.

We set about creating a daily routine for ourselves in our new home but being in a house seemed alien and lonely; too permanent and fixed for my new-found way of living. *Lily* was back in England and I hankered to be reunited with her. She had become my safe haven; the place where I felt at ease with the world. I was lost without her.

For the next twelve months, we felt boatless and hated it but there was no point moving *Lily* without knowing if we could settle in a new country. Weekends were spent wandering around marinas, seeking availability and moorings prices. The thought of finding a new home for *Lily* was not a problem but all the looking began to get us down and even Buster became depressed. One day, we came across a Dutch barge, used as a hire boat by Riversdale Barge Company, a little shorter perhaps but otherwise almost identical to *Lily*. Buster wasted no time in jumping aboard. Wagging his tail enthusiastically, he dropped onto his side and did his party piece – a sideways shimmy along the side deck – much to the bewildered amusement of the family tucking into their lunch on board.

Discovering the town of Athlone was holding a boating day, we went along and found ourselves in conversation with Gerry from the Heritage Boat Association (HBA). He welcomed us onto his barge and spent hours chatting about the Irish waterways as well as the historical importance of the association and the boats they strived to restore. With a rally coming up at Shannon Harbour on the Grand Canal, Gerry advised us to go along and see more of the fleet.

Shannon Harbour was one of those places instantly loved or hated, a typical canalside settlement where the community was made up of characters as interesting as the motley collection of craft belonging to them. From the dry docks and crumbling outhouses came the noise of tools on steel: banging, reverberating filling the air with a long-forgotten sound of industry. The smell of oily rags, diesel and paint permeated, along with a reminder of pear drops, purchased by the quarter in the corner shop on my way to school, carried back on the scent of cellulose thinners. Roger and I had visited the place on many occasions but never seen it so busy; boats were crammed in, almost filling the cut. The atmosphere was intoxicating and left us wanting more.

Most of our time and money was spent on travelling back and forth to see *Lily* or living apart, as I felt the need to be on board whilst Roger had to return to work. It could not go on; we needed to take *Lily* to Ireland as soon as possible. With the IWA National Festival being held at Redhill on the River Soar, this would make a fitting end to our time on the waterways of the East Midlands. *Lily* could be dressed in all her finery and we could meet up with old friends and go out on a high. With the plan in our heads, thought turned to what the move would entail. We would have liked *Lily* to have reached Ireland under her own steam but, after speaking to some experienced sailors who expressed concerns taking a barge of her size across the Irish Sea and the timescale involved, it was agreed *Lily* was best transported by road.

Having never transported a boat before, we talked to friends and other boat owners with experience of the procedure who could recommend reliable contractors. Several quotes from both English and Irish companies were sourced; it was surprising how much they varied. All-in prices – lift-out, transportation, lift-in by the same company – were higher but resulted in less organisation on our part. However, the money saved by using individual companies for each stage of the operation was worth the extra effort and that was the way we decided to go.

Chapter Two

SETTLING IN

Knowing *Lily* was safe at Farndon Marina, we concentrated on settling in, discovering more of Ireland by car. This suited Buster fine; he loved new experiences and a car ride to one meant it would be more exciting. However, the weather had other ideas and frequently tried its best to dampen our spirits with harsh downpours or constant fine drizzle, known to the Irish as 'soft days'.

With Roger at work, my daily routine revolved around my writing, which was going well. Despite having deadlines to meet, time was my own, which meant there was plenty for Buster. Walks were a major part of the day; most of the week, we stayed local, heading across the callows or along the narrow lanes. At the time, there were hardly any public footpaths in the Republic of Ireland, which was alien to me coming from a country covered in them.

To bring a change to the middle of the week, on Wednesdays I took Buster to Lough Boora Parklands, the remains of a cutaway bog reclaimed and used as a nature reserve and sculpture park. There were many varied sculptures, ranging from a stone pyramid to ornate towers constructed from the remains of the little bog railways which once served the area. The Sky Train, a small diesel locomotive complete with turf trucks standing on a mound, was one of Buster's

favourites. He would climb onto the footplate and, once comfortable, sit and survey the land before him.

Buster on the footplate of the bog train sculpture in Lough Boora Parklands

The parklands were home to the grey partridge. One area was a designated breeding ground where dogs had to be kept on-lead. It made me laugh to see the interpretation board there, which stated: 'Grey Partridge Conversation Area'. I liked the thought of the partridges meeting up for a good old chinwag.

Portumna Forest Park nestled on the edge of Lough Derg, the Shannon's largest lake, and at weekends, with more time on our hands, this was a great place for Roger, Buster and me to visit, although it frequently coincided with a downpour. Walking through the park in heavy rain, it sounded musical as the rain fell through the pines onto the leafy fronds of ferns, thick carpeting of moss and smooth stones in the babbling brooks below. Seeking shelter, the three of us kept to the wooded paths and thoughts of returning home soon sprang to mind. We were about to retreat when a movement caught my eye; in a mossy glade, two red squirrels played. As they leapt and jumped on the springy, water-soaked moss, each one sent up a light spray of rainwater. It was a magical, enchanting scene that held us transfixed until the pair raced off, heading up into the tree tops.

Roger and I soon learnt to take a change of clothes everywhere as Irish rain could quickly penetrate through layers of clothing and we would usually find ourselves struggling with wet gear in a steamed-up car after a walk in the rain. Buster put up with being towelled dry before being able to snuggle down in his faithful old bed. We always seemed to get wet in Ireland.

Chapter Three

CONNEMARA CURIOSITIES

My eyes were drawn upwards, away from the dank darkness, along towering stone walls thickly clad with ivy desperately scrabbling for light, and onwards into the sky above. The brightness made me squint, caused me to refocus, to look again at the scene. I had once stood in the empty chamber of Devil's Hole Lock on the Wey and Arun Canal, long before it was cleared of tree roots and restored to its former glory. At the time, I thought it looked large; now I was sure it would have fitted inside this one at least a couple of times, perhaps more.

The remains of the Cong Canal must be seen to be believed; standing empty, the locks were huge, the chamber walls had gently curved bottoms, the masonry skilfully crafted, smooth and cool to the touch. In the bottom of the lock, I was minuscule, lost and totally in awe. Buster went snuffling in the undergrowth. He was not interested in stonework unless another dog had peed against it or someone had dropped a morsel of food nearby. However, he enjoyed the walk along the canal's former route. Cut through great boulders of rock to create a passage between jagged walls from which a jungle of trees and ferns protruded, it was impressive.

The name of Cong immediately conjured up mystery and intrigue. Despite the spelling being different, the remains of its canal could have been a scene from

The Cong Canal's dry locks towered high into the sky

the great movie *King Kong* because it was truly king-size. I had heard about this failed canal, seen pictures of its waterless locks, but nothing had prepared me for coming face to face with the sheer scale of it. The story of Cong's 'Dry Canal,' built through porous limestone during the worst of the famine years, fascinated me.

The geology was well known to the engineers, who used it to their advantage throughout construction; during winter floods, they worked on the canal near Cong as the upper levels were underwater; in the summer, they used the disappearance of water through the porous limestone to work on the upper reaches, which had dried out. Despite only the lower part of the canal being puddled with clay prior to the abandonment of navigation work, the old story that the canal failed as it would not hold water persisted.

Roger and Buster disappeared into the undergrowth in search of the canal's first lock. From the Cong River, it was possible to gaze into the darkness and make sense of the original structure, now adapted into a boathouse. I heard scrabbling about, a great gasp, followed by silence. Roger must have found it and, by his intake of breath, witnessed proof of its impressiveness. I eagerly awaited his return to find out.

Buster ran out of the undergrowth with a big smile and glint of excitement in his eyes. Tail wagging and tongue hanging out of one side of his mouth, he pulled hard against the lead to reach me; he obviously had something exciting to report. A few seconds behind him, Roger appeared, struggling to hold the extended lead and limping.

"What's happened to you?" Roger bent over to catch his breath and rub the injury.

"I almost broke my neck!" I looked at Buster, who was grinning even wider than before.

"Did you find the lock?"

"Oh yes, I found the lock; it nearly killed me." Whilst pushing through the undergrowth, made up of dark, twisting rhododendrons, Roger had stepped over a large root. As he put his foot down, the ground had given way and his leg disappeared. He had fallen up to his groin. That was when he had made the loud gasp which I had heard. Looking down, Roger could see water and a boat and realised he had found the lock. He had managed to approach from above, putting his foot through the rusty, corrugated roofing placed over the chamber to transform it into a boathouse.

"What did Buster do? Did he help pull you out?" I had visions of my beloved Beagle desperately struggling against the lead, pulling his injured master to safety, saving the day.

"He just sat down, scratched his neck and looked at me."

Connemara was a long drive from our new home but the landscape and its curiosities drew me. Full days were spent exploring the beautiful countryside with its craggy mountains, rock-strewn moors, earthy colours and skies full of big, bold clouds rolling in from the Atlantic. From a distance, the land looked flat, soft and smooth but, on closer inspection, it was full of tiny hillocks, bumps and dips. Having successfully made the first non-stop transatlantic flight in June

Beautiful Connemara landscape vast and full of wildlife

1919, Allcock and Brown crash-landed their Vickers Vimy bomber in this unforgiving terrain, only 3 miles (5km) from the intended landing site at Clifden. I could visualise the cartoon Beagle, Snoopy, in his biplane, swerving at precarious angles, coming in to land in his own adaption of the real-life event.

On the stone pier overlooking Ballyconneely Bay stood the Connemara Smokehouse, a small, family-run business that sold some of the finest smoked fish from the west coast of Ireland, from where Roger purchased a superb pair of smoked salmon steaks.

"These will do nicely for tea and Buster can have the skins; they're good for him, you know." Buzzy appreciated his master's interest in his well-being and gave him a tail wag in anticipation of his evening meal.

The surrounding stone-strewn coastal meadows were dotted with small white horses – Connemara ponies. Some believed that the Connemara developed from Scandinavian ponies brought to Ireland by the Vikings but legend told that galleons from the Armada ran aground in violent storms and the Andalusian horses on board were set loose to breed with the native stock, refining the local ponies.

On the way home, I wanted to find a little-known architectural gem on the eastern side of Lough Corrib at Ballycurrin. Roger turned the car off the main road and headed down a bumpy farm track leading to the lakeshore. As the magnificent vista across the lake opened out, on the end of a rocky promontory sat a quirky stone lighthouse with a millstone as a roof. Leaving the car, Roger and Buster ran along the rocks as if a couple of naughty schoolboys revelling at being out of lessons. There was no way I would get there first; they would be larking about, spoiling my chance for a good photograph.

Ballycurrin Lighthouse on the shores of Lough Corrib

The lighthouse, reputedly the only one of its kind to be found in Ireland, was built under the instruction of Sir Henry Lynch's wife. She was concerned for her husband's well-being when returning inebriated from the hostelries on the Galway shore by rowboat and thought a guiding light would aid his safe return. Having climbed to the top, Roger and Buster passed me on the way back.

"What a lovely place, you should take a picture before you lose the light."

"That's a good idea. Why didn't I think of that?"

Chapter Four

THE HOUSE IN THE WOODS

"Look at this." I thrust the well-thumbed *Inland Waterways News* magazine under Roger's nose. Over the past few months, I had read that the Inland Waterways Association of Ireland (IWAI) was looking for tenants to rent a historical property named Dunrovin and had become intrigued. Time and again, references to this jumped out of the pages at me and, now I had seen a photograph, I knew this was special, somewhere that could no longer be ignored.

"The picture isn't brilliant but I'm sure it has a barrel roof like the lock keeper's cottages on the Stratford-upon-Avon Canal." I could hear excitement building in my voice as I watched Roger scan the page.

"No, it's just shadow on the picture."

"It's at Coosan Point so it can't be far from the water and it'll be closer to work for you. Can we go and look please?"

His eyes met mine from over the rim of his glasses; he knew it was a lost cause. There would not be any peace until I had seen Dunrovin for myself.

"There!" I shouted, as Roger drove by a pair of iron gates set into a hedge. Braking sharply, we came to an abrupt halt. Buster let

The cottage at Dunrovin overlooked Lough Ree's Inner Lakes

out a groan and sat up in his bed, eager to see what the sudden stop was about. Roger reversed until level with the entrance and we peered down the overgrown driveway. "This has to be it, there's no other turning on this side of the road before the lake."

"Are you sure? There's no name on the gate." Roger's tone of voice did not sound very positive.

"No, I'm not but let's look anyway." Roger manoeuvred the car through the narrow entrance into the driveway overhung by hedging. It was a tight fit; the vegetation brushed against the car's bodywork as we bumped along the uneven surface. Mixed feelings of excitement and nervousness crept in. It felt as if we were trespassing, intruding into somewhere we really should not, yet something inside of me urged to go on. I was eager to see more. Peering from the backseat, Buster squeaked in excitement and Roger let the window down for him; he wasted no time in sticking his head into the fresh air and savouring the new scents. After summiting a small rise, the drive turned sharply and plummeted into the darkness of a wood, where birds flitted in and out of the low-lying branches. Through the leafy shade, the shimmering sapphire blue of Lough Ree's Inner Lakes made a tantalising appearance, glinting between the trunks and low branches of alder, beech, macrocarpa, silver birch, spruce and willow trees. Levelling, the driveway entered a clearing, where a small, white-washed cottage peeked out from behind a mask of vegetation and a cluster of rambling pink roses. Its distinctive barrel roof immediately tugged at my heart strings but it was not until later I discovered the true historical value of this ramshackle place.

Damian and Michael from the Dunrovin Trust met us and sowed more seeds of curiosity into my mind.

"Did you know that the cottage was built around an old Nissen hut?" asked Michael.

"Or that it was erected by the late Colonel Harry Rice?" Damian added.

Over the coming months, I discovered much more about this colourful character. After an impressive military career, he had returned to Ireland with his wife, Peggy, and purchased an acre of land at Coosan Point, where he set about creating Dunrovin. A woodland of diverse trees was planted, terraced gardens created and a small dock for his open lake boat excavated. As all this was taking shape, the future of Ireland's inland waterways was in question; it had been proposed that the bridges crossing the River Shannon should have fixed spans, drastically reducing the headroom for navigation. Harry Rice contacted the IWA, recently set up in England, and proposed that an Irish equivalent should be created. Discussions took place at Dunrovin, where groups of like-minded people gathered to air concerns. During one of these meetings, Harry Rice was the first to place a coin on the table and, with these actions, became the founder of the IWAI and Dunrovin its birthplace.

Opening the door to Dunrovin, Roger and I stepped into another world, back to a unique time and place in history, one where people were not afraid to stand up for what they believed in and fought hard to gain what they thought was rightfully theirs. To the waterway enthusiast, the list of people who had regularly visited Dunrovin read like a *Who's Who*; amongst them were Vincent and Ruth Delaney, Sean McBride, Bunny Goodbody and Walter Levinge. This unassuming little place had played host to campaigners, authors, presidents, boat designers and Nobel prizewinners, all brought together for one cause, to fight for the waterways they were **passionate** about.

The acre of ground at Dunrovin was a dog's playground. The dense woods stretched downhill to the water's edge, where Buster could play in the shallows, happily paddling and splashing, pulling out plastic bottles or floating sticks. Clumps of red-stemmed dogwood partially immersed in the water were great places for him to weave through. The boundary needed repairing as the rickety wooden fence between Dunrovin and our next-door neighbour, Rosemary Furlong, the niece of Harry Rice, had gaps all along and was cause for concern. However, Buster never ventured out of his area; he ignored the gaps and the temptation to ease through to discover what was on the other side. Perhaps it was because he was getting older or maybe he was happy and content in the grounds. After all, having the doggy equivalent of an adventure playground on the doorstep was novelty enough.

One of the appeals of Dunrovin was the possibility of having *Lily* moored at the dock. Although far too shallow to get her right in, Roger was confident he could construct a landing stage with scaffolding poles and planks, enabling the bow to be nosed in. From Dunrovin's front door, there was a view straight down to the dock. We would be able to bring *Lily* home, right to the front door!

Renting Dunrovin, we were much more than simply tenants. We became custodians of a historical property. What most people would dismiss as being a rickety old hut sitting in an overgrown wood spilled forth its story to me, almost as if it had been silently waiting for someone to come along and listen. We had found each other and I was soon overwhelmed by the sense of place. Harry Rice had taken over my life; his story captivated my head, my heart and my mind. His book, *Thanks for the Memory*, still considered the definitive guide to Lough Ree, became compulsive reading.

New discoveries were revealed, the house and grounds spoke to me. 'Take this path and you will find a young horse chestnut tree in bloom', or, 'When you reach the water, turn and look up; you will see treecreepers on the rough-textured bark of the spruce.' In just one acre of ground, there was a whole world waiting to be discovered. The bluebells flowering in the spring were one

Winter at Dunrovin   of the greatest surprises. I eagerly awaited the carpet of blue-hazy tones to appear but, when they did, they were mostly white, mutant blooms. Aquilegias spilled over the terraces to give the appearance of water trickling over the mossy rocks, the golden yellow blooms of Himalayan poppies shining as if reflections of sun on water.

The soft golden carpet of leaves left by the trees in autumn made my heart sing when I kicked through them; they provided snuffling material for Buster, bringing him hours of fun. Even as he aged, the opportunity of chasing a crispy, golden leaf blown by a chilly breeze could not be ignored. His tan-and-white coat blended perfectly with the surroundings and it was one of the most difficult times to keep tabs on him.

In the winter, snow fell silently over Dunrovin; the trees broke its fall and left patches of undergrowth free from its frosty covering. Outside, lighting spaced at intervals up the driveway lit the fast-falling flakes perfectly on dark evenings and the curved, old-fashioned style of the lamps gave the place a Dickensian feel. In heavy snowfall, I was reminded of the C. S. Lewis *Narnia* novels; I could clearly picture Mr Tumnus shivering beneath the lamp next to the snow-laden branches of the largest macrocarpa tree.

Goldcrests, with tiny lightning flashes of yellow on their heads, danced through the branches of the smallest shrubs. From behind the bamboo blinds, I could watch them closely as they remained completely unaware of my presence. I adored observing the birds and wildlife at Dunrovin; we were close to civilisation yet, at times, could have been a million miles away. Sometimes, an otter came to call, leaving a tell-tale trail of bubbles in the waters of the dock; playful but ever watchful, he never stayed long. I occasionally saw a fox creeping silently through the grounds, leaving only a trail of paw prints in the snow. I treasured the times when the moorhens left the water and foraged for food close to the house.

As in life, there were also sad times such as when a pair of mallard ducks nesting in a fallen tree had their eggs destroyed. I suspected mink yet could not prove it. The coldest winter in over fifty years left a trail of destruction in the woods. Flocks of redwings, already exhausted from their migration, sought shelter in Dunrovin's grounds but the winter was as harsh as the Scandinavian one they had fled. We awoke to discover many of them frozen to death on the branches or lying dead, circling the tree trunks. I wept for each and every one of those sweet birds with their freckled **breasts** and gentle nature. Life sometimes was so unfair.

Pulling up the blinds one cold and frosty morning, I was greeted by a winter wonderland. A dense hoarfrost coated the trees and wispy wands of the pendulum sage; the lake was frozen and the weak sunrise had washed it in pink streaks so it resembled raspberry-ripple ice cream. There was a movement on the ice, twenty yards or so from the dock. I stared, my mind not registering completely what I saw. It moved, began to speed up, heading for the opposite shore. I ran for the door, stepped out into the bitter coldness of the early morning.

"Buster, get off the ice. Now!" I screamed as loud as I could, sucking in the cold air making my lungs burn in pain. Buster stopped dead, turned and looked at me.

"Now!" I screamed again. He began to run back towards the shore, totally oblivious of the danger. He ran all the way across the ice into the frozen dock and leapt onto dry land, careered up the winding pathway and terrace steps, pushed past me and headed straight for the kitchen, where his breakfast awaited him. I stepped inside, slammed the door and collapsed against the back of it. From that day on, I checked the lake was not frozen before letting Buster out each morning.

When Harry Rice died in 1964, he bequeathed Dunrovin to the IWAI in the hope it would be used as a meeting place. Long before Roger and I had come to Ireland, the IWAI had looked into making this work but it was complicated and they let it out to tenants instead of addressing the situation. Now the new president of the association, Dave McCabe, wanted to tackle the issue and, with a team of committed members, he set about it with great gusto.

Buster was not too sure about the sudden influx. His first reaction was to bark, to warn them they were on his turf, but this was all bravado and, after a few moments, he quietened down. I first met the author Brian Cassells at Dunrovin, when he came to look around with Dave and a group of other IWAI members. In waterway terms, he was a legend, having received the OBE for his work on them. A series of visits by architects, council members and various authorities followed. Finally, Dunrovin was receiving some attention but, as time passed, in our quest to try and save it, we sealed its doom. Reports showed that my little house in the woods was far from stable, not worth restoring in its current state and would be better demolished and a new building erected on the site. I was devastated, as were other IWAI members, although there were some who agreed with the proposals. The association was divided and it became clear why the topic had so often been avoided in the past. Plans for a new building were generated and a long, drawn-out process began, one which resulted in Roger and me being Dunrovin's last tenants.

I had felt guilty about moving Buster away from his doggy playmates at Farndon. He was never to have such a close relationship with a group of dogs again

Buster loved the acre of lake front grounds at Dunrovin

and, although he did make other friends, those playful years had passed. As time marched on, I was to crave the company of our small group and I was sure Buster felt that way too but he made one special friend at Dunrovin, who we called the 'old boy'.

The old boy lived about a mile along the road from Dunrovin, towards the town of Athlone, and, whenever Buster and I passed his home, he would peer through the iron gates and get excited at our approach. I would talk to him and Buster would pull to rub noses with him through the bars. Then, one day, the old boy jumped the stone wall and followed us all the way home. From then on, he almost always accompanied us on our walks, sometimes out but mostly back, returning us safely to the front door, staying for a drink and biscuit. Once safely in the grounds of Dunrovin, I would let Buster off-lead and they would play together. When he had enough, the old boy would quietly slip away. I never saw him leave.

I suspected the old boy to be a long-legged, black, Collie–Labrador cross, getting on in years as his muzzle was beautifully freckled with fine grey hairs. He was always kind and gentle and never barked or growled, despite Buster's constant attempts to try and raise a sound from him. When we left Ireland, I never expected to see him again but, when we returned three years later to support the launch of Brian Cassells' new book, Roger and I drove down to Coosan Point and, as we passed the old boy's house, there he was, sitting at the gate. It appeared time had stood still for him.

Chapter Five

CÉAD MÍLE FÁILTE FOR LILY

The small marina chosen as *Lily*'s new home had no launching facilities so an alternative site enabling her safe return to the water needed to be found. Rinn Marina was only an hour's cruise away and had a twenty-five-ton travelling crane on-site. Although appearing to fulfil our requirements, closer inspection revealed that the launching area for the crane was still under construction. With assurances work would be completed by the time we needed to use the crane, some four months away, we made a booking.

In early July, Buster and I returned to Farndon. There were loose ends to tie up, packing to be done and *Lily*'s safety certificate to renew. During this time, I registered *Lily* with Waterways Ireland, the governing body for the majority of the country's inland waterways. Whilst there was no licence fee for registering *Lily* on the Shannon Navigation, failure to do so could result in hefty fines so it was vital this was all done prior to her departure. Other Irish navigations varied but there was no need to worry about them at this stage; *Lily* would be solely on the Shannon.

Back in Ireland, Roger continually checked on progress at Rinn Marina but, by early August, it was obvious work would not be completed in time, leaving us with the task of finding another crane. Rinn Marina recommended McNally Crane Hire, specialists in the installation and maintenance of wind turbines.

At the end of August, Roger joined Buster and me in England to attend the IWA National Festival, travelling along the Trent and through Nottingham, braving the bridge of pigeons Roger so hated, to reach the Soar. *Lily* was visited by many friends who came to say their goodbyes and wish us good luck. It was an emotional weekend and participating in the event on home waters made it extra special. Buster was briefly reunited with Bosun, the Beagle he had met previously at the St Ives Festival, and made some new friends, Jim and Jess, Whippets belonging to Terry and Monica.

Terry had written a bestseller about their narrowboat travels from England to Carcassonne in France and was at the show promoting his next book. This covered an adventurous journey to America's Indian River. We spent an entertaining evening in their company, talking dogs, boats and books. The two Whippets retired early for the evening, probably just as well as Buster would not have taken lightly to being upstaged by Jim. As far as Buster was concerned, he was the only boating dog in the world, unique and quite beyond comparison, especially to such a thin, wiry-looking creature. He sat close to my legs and eyed Terry carefully, listening to his every word and developing a deepening frown. Every now and then he caught my eye as if saying, 'So, this is the man who doesn't feed his dog'. I am sure Buster was convinced Jim needed a good square meal and, if he was not careful, a strong puff of wind would see him off that narrowboat and into the cut!

A few days later, we were all packed, loose furniture chocked and anything moveable securely tied down ready for the beginning of our new adventure. Whilst Terry talked about taking his narrow dog to the Indian River, we prepared to take our podgy puppy to the Shannon.

On the day of the lift, we were up early and blessed with late summer sunshine, perfect weather for dismantling the wheelhouse and stowing the loose panels. It was a short, downriver cruise to Newark Marina on a mist-shrouded Trent and with it hung a sense of anticipation. We arrived at the same time as the

transportation booked from Hutchinson's Engineering Company and motored straight into the lift which was already prepared. Buster liked Paul, the lorry

Lily on the lorry and ready to begin her journey to Ireland

driver, which helped us click with him and made the process of leaving *Lily* in his capable hands easier. Newark Marina staff worked efficiently, jet-washing *Lily* and lowering her onto the lorry.

Lily was placed onto blocks, then chocked into position and secured to the lorry by heavy chains, a process which looked brutal but was skilfully carried out to avoid damage to the paintwork. Paul constantly checked we were happy with what he was doing and *Lily* was soon secured. Finally, the open wheelhouse area was covered with a tarpaulin for protection against the elements. Perched on the lorry, high and dry, *Lily* was a fish out of water, which made me uneasy.

Paul and *Lily* soon departed, heading off slowly towards Birkenhead to board the overnight ferry to Dublin whilst we headed to Holyhead to catch the last fast-cat crossing of the day. This route was more favourable for Buster as it only took two hours and he could remain safely in the car. We followed the lorry through Nottingham and out towards the M6 before breaking away to keep to schedule, hoping to see *Lily* safe and sound the next morning in the Emerald Isle.

We had no sooner parked the car at Rinn Marina when *Lily* arrived, with a bright and cheery Paul grinning from ear to ear, obviously pleased with the trouble-free run. Just a few minutes later, the crane arrived and, lastly, the marina staff to oversee procedures. All appeared to be going to plan until some boats on trailers blocking the crane site required moving. The trailers were locked and the owner was in England attending the Southampton Boat Show, almost the exact spot I had driven up from the day before after visiting my parents. Roger and I looked at each other; surely this could not be happening? Tony, the marina's appointed overseer, produced a length of baler twine and proceeded to tie the boats to the back of his car and, with a little man-handling, set about forcibly dragging them away.

With space cleared, the crane driver, Dermot, and his assistant began setting up. *Lily* was moved into place and the task of strapping her to the crane began. Walking back from the Rinn River bridge with Buster, there seemed to be a lot of discussion going on, resulting in Dermot climbing into his cab and pulling out the instruction manual, at which point I set about having a silent coronary. After a lot more talking and plenty of adjusting of the strapping, *Lily* was set for the lift and the lorry restraints released. As the crane took the strain, Paul moved the lorry away and there was *Lily*, suspended in the air, looking as weightless, though unfortunately not as graceful, as a bird. A gentle turn was made to position her, followed by a slow descent. As *Lily* finally touched the water, I let out a sigh of relief and shed a tear of joy; it was good to see her back in the environment she was built for.

As the task of clearing up and packing away began, Dermot thought it was now fine to share with us the fact that, despite the company having lifted boats before, *he* never had. In true British fashion, I beat a hasty retreat, popped on board and made a brew, which finally calmed the nerves and reduced my thumping headache into dullness. Looking around, I was amazed nothing had moved on the boat throughout the journey. Paul stayed on and, above the call of duty, helped to reconstruct *Lily*'s wheelhouse before climbing back into his lorry and bidding us a fond farewell. A few minutes later, we too were underway and could not have wished for better weather as we cruised down the little Rinn River to meet the mighty Shannon.

The Rooskey lock keeper already knew of our arrival; the jungle drums worked well in rural Ireland. After negotiating a lift bridge which did not need opening despite over two foot of fresh being on the river, we began the final leg of our journey to the Waterside Marina at Dromod: *Lily*'s new home.

Once safely in our moorings, we were rewarded with a weekend of blazing sunshine and spectacular sunsets. We were instantly made to feel at home, receiving many warm welcomes.

"*Céad míle fáilte*," someone shouted from a sports cruiser as they negotiated their way out of the marina. We must have looked puzzled as they called, "A hundred thousand welcomes," and, with huge waves, motored off into the peaty waters of the Shannon.

Dermot cranes Lily into the waters of the Rinn River

The marina manager, Brian Thornton, would be the first to admit he was a petrolhead, a speed freak who was

instantly likeable despite his dislike for barges. In the evenings, when his day's work was done, his antics would amuse us. Fascinated, we would watch the cool moves and nifty tricks he could do with his jet ski, joking about making score cards to show our appreciation for each routine. As marina manager, we had a lot of dealings with him and he was always pleasant; however, Buster was not so sure. Despite Brian sharing a bacon butty with him, our dog would still curl his top lip and give Brian a growl from time to time. Perhaps it was because he only shared his bacon butty instead of giving him the whole thing.

Lily, moored like a gatekeeper at the marina's entrance, looked out across Lough Bofin towards distant, low-rising hills; the setting was stunning. Reaching our new home for *Lily* would not have been possible without all the colourful characters who had helped and I knew they would be a feature in our memories for many years to come.

Having *Lily* based at Dromod enabled the occasional trip over the border into Northern Ireland. We would drive to her on Friday evening and sleep on board, first thing Saturday driving onto Enniskillen. It was like going home; there were familiar chainstores and cheaper-priced wines than in the Republic so we usually motored back with a car full of goodies. Buster became popular with the local butcher. After we had purchased our products, Buster would wiggle and tail wag in excitement as the butcher handed us a complimentary bag containing two generous cuts of marrowbone.

Whilst in Northern Ireland, we took the chance to visit some favourite places from previous holidays, such as the National Trust's Crom Castle and Castle Archdale. The latter, along with Lower Lough Erne, had been used extensively by the RAF during WWII when a base for Coastal Command and the flying boats patrolling the Atlantic shipping lanes from attack by German U-boats was established. Lough Erne challenged pilots; flat, calm and glassy conditions made it difficult to judge the aircraft's height above water and crashes sometimes sadly ended with fatalities. The place oozed history and, with much of it forming a country park, met with great approval from Buster. Finding places such as these where we could share in history and provide an exciting environment for Buster were welcomed and much sought after.

Chapter Six

CARNADOE AND ICE

We met Daniel, a work colleague of Roger's, in the car park of the out-of-town shopping centre in Carrick-on-Shannon. It was freezing; thick fog hung in the air and the car park glistened. It looked more like a skating rink than a parking area. Buster looked snug and warm wrapped in his fleece coat but underfoot it was treacherous. Wishing to show off with his cocky, look-at-me strut, he failed miserably. Instead, he resembled a cartoon character, his legs flying and sliding in all directions, out of control and terribly unsightly for a Beagle.

Back at the marina, we untied *Lily* and headed off for a winter cruise. Daniel, in the true spirit of Christmas, wore a Santa hat; it offered little protection against the cold but looked the part. The heavy frost had coated the landscape in a beautiful dusting of silver and white; despite the heavily leaden sky, it sparkled on the treetops as we passed through the Derrycairn Narrows and on to Lough Boderg. In the distance, the domed peaks of the mountains surrounding Lough Allen were covered in snow. Entering the narrow, winding channel into the Carnadoe Waters, each stem of the reeds was encircled in its own small disc of ice, watery diamonds which chinked and chimed as *Lily*'s wash passed them. We were cruising to a self-made, musical interlude. Swans ran on water, trying

"LILY" EDITH GELIN 2014

Lily on Lough Boderg, ink and watercolour by Edith Gelin

to take to the wing and escape *Lily's* encroaching bow wave whilst Buster occasionally barked, telling them to be quick about it.

Heading across Kilglass Lough, a stillness descended. The sky was the colour of the soft breast feathers of a greylag goose, creating a monochromatic landscape which seemed to echo and cry about its past in the dull coldness of the day. As one of the most badly affected areas of the Great Famine, its lakeside graveyard had become the final resting place for many. Local legend told how it was the responsibility of the most-recently buried to guard the graveyard until the next soul arrived. Solemn tales for such a pretty place.

Lying offshore from the graveyard was a crannóg, an artificial island and defence dwelling dating from the Iron Age. Here we ran into ice, at first a light coating which dispersed with a musical shattering as *Lily's* bow disturbed it – high-pitched string instrumentals. As chunks skidded off in all directions, the tone became deeper – more bass-like. *Lily* slowed; the ice was getting thicker. Despite the clearly visible public moorings, the trip had to be abandoned. Roger backed *Lily* out of the path she had forged through the ice and turned her when in clear water. Marvelling at winter's beauty, we sadly retreated.

A few days later, the weather had warmed slightly so Roger and I tried again to reach the moorings on Kilglass Lough. It was New Year's Eve when I motored *Lily* into the public moorings. Roger fastened her and, as soon as the boat was safe, retrieved Buster from the chart table. He was pleased to have arrived; despite the cold, he shimmied and shuffled along *Lily*'s decks, swiftly jumping off and running along the pontoon and onto the frosty grass to roll on his back, legs in the air, tail wagging. It felt good to have finally reached our festive-season goal.

That evening, there was a full moon and a deep chill in the air. We toasted the new year with champagne at midnight, popping the cork from the edge of the pontoon. *Lily*'s bodywork was already covered in a glistening coat of frost and her wheelhouse windows were beginning to freeze. Inside, it was a different world; the wood burner doing its job of heating the whole boat, we stripped off layers of clothes, basking in drying heat and opened windows. Buster slept contently, curled up in his bed, soon becoming warm enough to slump out of it, his body lying beached over its soft, fleecy edge.

By the time Buster woke me the next morning, the sun was shining through the portholes. It was warm, the stove still heating *Lily* despite neither of us adding more fuel overnight. Roger dressed and took Buster for his first walk of the day. He was only gone a few seconds when I heard him return.

"You're never going to believe this. We're frozen in!" I jumped out of bed and peeled back a curtain to be greeted by a winter wonderland. The lake had frozen and, on top of it, lay a light dusting of snow. The sun was shining and the sky was a clear blue, the backcloth broken only by a few carelessly slashed vapour trails. It was beautiful; the uninterrupted views from the pontoon the perfect setting to enjoy a pre-breakfast glass of Buck's Fizz. Slowly, reality kicked in: Roger needed to return to work and the car was miles away along icy country lanes. We would have to ice-break our way out of the Carnadoe Waters.

Luckily the ice was not too thick and it soon began to break up under the drive of *Lily*'s hefty weight. Icebreaking was special, the noise alone quite magical. Watching shards of ice tear off, sliding at speed across the remaining icy surface

or plopping into the cold depths of the wintery water, was mesmerising. Buster remained safely in the wheelhouse, watching in amazement through the window. Mute swans struggled to keep

Icebreaking out of the Carnadoe Waters

upright on the ice, using their wings to help balance their plump bodies whilst their large, webbed feet offered little grip on the shiny, smooth surface. We continued to encounter ice for some distance, even the large expanse of Lough Boderg had a good coating but, steaming towards the Derrycairn Narrows, it finally melted away.

Lily was moored at Carnadoe Quay. We had been based there for a few days, having struggled with winter conditions at Dromod, which had left the town without mains water. There was a knock on the wheelhouse door. Buster erupted into a chorus of howling barks; Roger and I looked at each other in amazement.

"Who on earth can that be in the middle of nowhere, in the depths of winter?" Roger, followed hot on the heels by Buster, went up to open the door.

I caught muffled conversation which began with the words, "Are you Roger?" The door closed and Roger was gone. Buster came back downstairs,

Buster acting the circus dog at Carnadoe Quay

not impressed at having been left behind. About ten minutes later, Roger returned, holding an envelope. It was addressed to Alison and Roger, Dutch Barge *Lily*, Carnadoe Quay, Republic of Ireland.

It contained a Christmas card that had come all the way from Canada. It had been delivered to the owner of Carnadoe Marina a few weeks previously and he had promised the postman he would keep hold of it until he next saw us.

"Only in Ireland!" we both exclaimed, before erupting into laughter.

Even the largest of the lakes froze, including Lough Ree. In scenes reminiscent of Scott at the Antarctic, roped-together men struggled to pull a small boat against the wind, which drove snaking streamers of snow across the plains of ice, to reach the last remaining islander, John Connell, and see if he required assistance. Arriving at the island of Inchbofin on Lough Ree, the inhabitant was found well but voiced concern over his herd of cattle. The army was called in to airlift fodder by helicopter for his hungry herd. I had read in Harry Rice's book of a group of men who did the same in the 1950s. They pushed a lake boat in front of them, the theory being if the ice was weak and gave way, they could get into the boat. The plan had one major flaw – whilst they may have saved themselves from an icy drenching, there was no guaranteed way out of the remaining ice.

Once the weather warmed, the ice had to go somewhere and we were soon facing problems with flooding. Water streamed into the grounds of Dunrovin and brought with it all manner of flotsam and jetsam, including a vast tree trunk. Roger, not one to miss an opportunity, launched the dinghy and rowed across the garden to lasso it, with Buster overseeing operations from the bow. Towed back, the wood was left to dry before being sawn up for firewood.

The rising waters caused no end of other problems. At Dromod, Brian arranged for the floating pontoon uprights to be extended. Men arrived in miserable weather to weld extensions on; it was a similar story all over the country. *Lily* had to be moved further into the marina; it was feared that the chains and weights of the breakwater pontoon at which she was berthed had dangerously reached their length limit.

It was not long after these floods that the Dunrovin Duckling arrived. Buster was having a barking frenzy down by the dock. I assumed he had seen a mink and was

Frozen in at Dromod during Ireland's coldest winter in over fifty years

busy seeing it off but the noise continued for such a long time that my curiosity sent me out to him. Hackles up, he bounced up and down on the edge of the dock. I called but he refused to either come or calm down. When I reached him, I looked out across the water. There, in the middle of the dock, bobbing up and down with what could only be described as a cheeky look, was a tiny, yellow rubber duck. Using a long stick, I cautiously leant out and coaxed it towards the shore. Buster was beside himself with excitement, racing up and down, barking madly. Once the duck was out of the water, I threw it for Buster. Catching the duck in his mouth, he raced manically round the grounds. The game lasted most of the morning and, when it finally subsided, I retrieved the duck and placed it on a rock which sat in the middle of the lawn. The Dunrovin Duckling remained there until the day we departed.

We had witnessed Ireland's coldest winter in over fifty years, gone icebreaking, endured flooding and lived to tell the tale but something that lurked unseen was to shake our complacency and toll an ominous bell.

At Derrycairn, Roger and I walked hand in hand; Buster ran carelessly in and out of the thickets. He was happy to be off-lead and loved the damp smells of decaying leaves and unseen woodland creatures. We laughed at his escapades; every now and then, one of us would give chase, which would send him scurrying back into the undergrowth, where we could not follow. Emerging ahead of us, he returned to the gravel pathway to trot briskly along, leading the way. I noticed clearly the smooth roundness of his hindquarters on one side was interrupted by a protruding lump.

"Can you see that?" I asked Roger, pointing to Buster's hind leg.

"See what?"

"The lump on his back leg. I noticed it the other day but I'm sure it's bigger now."

"We're going back to England next week; let's get it checked out by the vet whilst we're at your parents'."

The loud shrill ring of the telephone rudely shattered the peace and my heart sank. Deep down, I knew the outcome, was prepared for bad news and that is what the vet delivered. My eyes met my father's and, in that instant, I realised he already knew but I mouthed the words all the same. "It's cancer." Somewhere in the background amidst my thoughts, single words punctuated them – cancer, tumour, reoccurrence, recovery and radiotherapy – and hit hard, penetrating deep into the pit of my stomach.

It was not all doom and gloom. A mast cell tumour grade two did not signal the end, although, not knowing that then, it may as well have done.

"Can I come and get him now?" I asked the vet urgently, keen to have Buster close to me after the operation.

Back at home, Buster had an uncomfortable night. He was sleepy, confused and wobbly from the anaesthetic. Whining pitifully, he stared directly into my eyes, asking for an explanation I could not give. I held him close and felt his comforting warmth through my clothes. Leaning in with all his weight, he slowly fell into a fitful sleep.

Chapter Seven

SHANNON, TOP TO TAIL

T he Shannon, Ireland's longest river, constantly flowed in and out of lakes, twisting and turning from its source at a small pool on the slopes of the Cuilcagh Mountain in County Cavan to the sea below Limerick.

Lough Allen was the first of the Shannon's great lakes; wild and unspoilt.

"I can't believe we're here." Roger spoke quietly, not wishing to break the spell. It was magical; a clear sky and a still Lough Allen stretched out to meet the surrounding, steely grey mountains.

"I think we must be dreaming," I whispered. Between us sat Buster, recovering well from his tumour-removal operation. He was totally engrossed in the view and only a fool would not have been for this was true beauty.

"I suppose we've come full circle?"

"Yes, I suppose we have, thanks to that old girl." I nodded towards *Lily*, who was sitting proudly in Spencer Harbour.

We had first visited Spencer Harbour many years earlier in a small, glass-fibre cruiser hired from Belturbet on the River Erne. Gifted with wall-to-wall sunshine for the whole week of the holiday, our new waterproof jackets never came out of their bags. We made the most of it, exploring the recently opened Shannon-Erne Waterway (SEW), the Shannon as far south as Tarmonberry,

Lily at Spencer Harbour on Lough Allen, a special place of ours

Clondara and the start of the Royal Canal as well as the Boyle Waters, Lough Key and Lough Allen. I had been instantly smitten by Lough Allen's raw beauty and sense of wildness. Spencer Harbour consisted of an isolated pontoon; there was no land access at that time although we had sat, mesmerised by the view.

"When we get a boat of our own, we must come back here," Roger had said.

"Yes, we must," I had agreed and we had laughed about the fantasy of it all. Even thinking of having a boat of our own was a pipe dream then. Of course, Buster was not around at the time and neither was the thought of having a dog of our own. Our lives had changed dramatically over the intervening years; we had experienced heartache and failures but, with love, support and respect for one another, we had come through. Now, with our dog and our boat, we were living again; a team and force to be reckoned with.

From the Lough Allen Canal, the Shannon gently meandered towards Carrick-on-Shannon. There was a small café with a handy undercover seating area outside where we enjoyed coffee and cake with Buster. It became a treat and, despite Ireland's frequent 'soft days', a visit would rarely be missed. If we happened to bypass the café, Buster would pull as hard as he could on the lead in a desperate attempt to get through the doorway. One of the town's other delights was the secondhand book shop, somewhere we tried to avoid as, once inside, it became fatal, with vast amounts of time and money dwindled away.

A sweeping loop in the Shannon, south of Carrick, was severed by the Jamestown Canal and Albert Lock. At its northern end, the natural river could be navigated as far as Jamestown and, at its southern end, as far as Drumsna. Being off the main navigation, we favoured these quiet and attractive dead-end routes; especially Drumsna, as it was a lock-free cruise from Dromod.

"Lucky, Lucky," the sing-song call rang out in the stillness of the morning. I looked out to see a Spaniel sauntering by, his nose on the ground having picked up a whiff of our boat's dog. Buster heard the call too and was eager to

The peaceful Lough Allen Canal

see what was going on outside. From his seat, Buster made eye contact briefly with the Spaniel before it ran off into the dew-coated grass. Keen to follow, Buster gave a bark and I opened the door to ask the owner if they could play. "Not a problem," came the reply in a thick Cornish accent and we were soon in deep conversation. From that day on, whenever we moored there, Buster would look out for Lucky.

Drumsna was once the home of the English novelist Anthony Trollope. At the time, he was a senior civil servant, sent to the town to investigate the financial affairs of the postmaster. When I told Roger it was Trollope who had recommended use of the post box, Roger replied, "Was he the bright spark who decided to paint them green?"

We were delighted when David and Wendy came to visit. They arrived in their huge, six-wheeled motorhome, which eventually squeezed along the narrow driveway down to the clearing at Dunrovin. Buster was pleased to see Chloe and Millie and the two girls danced and skipped around him in excitement. Chloe was a West Highland Terrier. I would like to say her coat was as white as the driven snow but she was a bundle of mischief and, if there was dirt and muck to be found, she would home in on it. David and Wendy would rush after her, following her down ditches and steep inclines into water courses so she was usually kept securely on her lead. Millie, a little Scottie, was more sensible. She resembled a great black rabbit with her upward-pointing ears and was instantly adorable.

After a few days at Dunrovin, we took our guests to the marina at Dromod. It was a beautiful warm day when we all headed out on board *Lily*. Whilst Chloe and Millie sat at the bow, Buster played the role of Admiral; his personality immediately changed when he knew a cruise was about to start. At Carnadoe Quay, we enjoyed a barbecue; those we had had together on the Trent were legendary. We all ate and drank far too much but laughed plenty. Good times.

Just before the Shannon opened up to form the wide expanse of Lough Ree, it passed through the twin towns of Lanesborough-

Chloe and Millie came to visit and joined us for a cruise on the Shannon

Ballyleague, home to Len and June, fellow IWAI members who had quickly become friends. Having retired from England and moved to Ireland several years before, neither of them had done much boating but, finding themselves living a stone's throw from the Shannon, had become captivated by its beauty and soon discovered watching passing boats was not enough. Wanting to be on the water, they purchased a boat of their own – a fast, high-powered sports boat named *Polecat*, a totally different beast to *Lily*. Being on the water created strong bonds between people no matter what walks of life they came from or what type of vessel they chose to boat in, and so it was with us.

June was well named for, like the first, welcoming, warm days of summer, she was bright and cheerful, a bit of a butterfly who happily flitted about, spreading joy and happiness, adding a splash of intense colour to even the dullest of

197

flowerbeds. June worked a crowd as a butterfly would a garden, picking not necessarily the brightest or prettiest plant but the one containing the sweetest nectar. She had a knack of drawing out the special, and often hidden, qualities in people, would show an interest in them and, by doing so, unknowingly make them feel appreciated and important. It was a rare gift.

Usually, June was found with her camera in hand, busily clicking away no matter what the occasion. That was how we first met, at an IWAI meeting where June was doing her butterfly routine and snapping pictures of the president's regalia. Len was the counterbalancing, calming effect, more methodical in his approach but just as talented a people-person as June. We spent many hours in their company both on and off boats and they became the closest friends we made in Ireland, a friendship which continues to this day.

Although *Lily* was based at Dromod, she was frequently on Lough Ree. Rosemary, our neighbour, had kindly offered us a floating mooring buoy close to Dunrovin. If Roger was feeling energetic, he would row and, if there was loading to be done, Buster accompanied him, sitting perched at the bow, looking as if he were giving the orders whilst Roger puffed and panted at the oars.

When there was enough water in Lough Ree, *Lily* could be moored in Dunrovin's dock. Roger acquired some scaffolding from a work colleague and spent a couple of weekends erecting a substantial landing stage above the remains of the previous one. I had a car number plate made up with *Lily*'s name and added a pot of summer bedding plants and a lifebuoy. It looked rather smart by the time we had finished. Buster loved it; even if *Lily* was not there, he would march up and down the staging, very much an admiral on the poop deck.

Clonmacnoise monastic site, with its tall, round towers and richly engraved stone Celtic crosses, was one of Ireland's treasures. It was usually busy with coachloads of tourists bustling and chattering around the key attractions.

"Can the dog come in with us?" Roger cagily asked the man at the ticket office.

"Yes, of course, as long as he's well-behaved." We had become experts at filling the person who asked that question with unbounding confidence in our hound.

Another man behind the counter peered over and, addressing Buster, casually asked,

"Now then, young lad, what is your interest in archaeology?"

From out of nowhere came a response which had the whole reception area rolling about with laughter. "Bones, of course." Roger beamed and tipped me a wink.

In complete contrast to the monastic ruins came the flat, black Bord na Móna landscape, or perhaps moonscape would be a better description. It was broken only by the distant mountains and the billowing steam from the towers of the power station. Bog trains rattled across the black peat fields on rickety tracks, carrying the valuable commodity or tourists eager to see the alien landscape which Bord na Móna had successfully created. Vast quantities of milled peat fed the Shannon's power stations each year whilst still more was compressed into blocks and briquettes for burning on open fires and stoves. The wide-open spaces still attracted wildlife, birds of prey hovered weightlessly above it and tufty cotton grass swayed to the wind's whistle. Stunted trees and shrubs bordered the black land, home for many a small bird. When we first arrived in Ireland, the red-and-white-striped chimney of Shannonbridge power station was a landmark long used by boaters on the river. By the time *Lily* arrived, the prominent structure had been demolished.

Shannonbridge was a typical Irish town with one main street, bordered each side by shops and public houses. Running down to the waterfront, it crossed the Shannon on an impressive, seventeen-arched stone bridge, dominated at its western end by an imposing Napoleonic fortress. Downstream began an interesting section of the Shannon; joined by the River Suck, a little further south was the entrance to the Grand Canal and, opposite, the former canal which once led to the town of Ballinasloe, famous for its horse fairs.

Beyond Banagher, the Shannon changed character; becoming narrower and beginning to twist and wind, there were numerous backwaters, small islands and then the huge, thundering Meelick Weir sitting to one side of Victoria Lock. Ahead was the Shannon's largest lake, Lough Derg. Both Ree and

The impressive bridge and fortress at Shannonbridge

Derg were referred to as inland seas; large, unpredictable and capable of rapidly changing conditions, they demanded respect. To reach the lake, there was usually a wait at Portumna, where a low-lying swing bridge opened at designated times. There was frequently a backlog of boats but, if we were not in a hurry, it was a good opportunity to catch up with fellow boaters.

"Why does it always rain when we come here?" I strained to see through the wet windscreen. We had entered Lough Derg and, right on cue, the rainclouds rolled in from the Atlantic and spilled their contents. Buster had been on deck, sitting at the bow, but, when the rain started, had sped back inside and now sat in the wheelhouse, looking disheartened. Roger was on holiday from work and we had decided to give Derg the exploration it deserved; however, the weather had other ideas. With the clouds growing increasingly darker, we headed into the harbour of Terryglass to seek shelter. Terryglass was once the home of the great Shannon boatman John Weaver, who, like Harry Rice, campaigned for the waterways of Ireland, becoming a well-known and respected figure amongst fellow boaters.

Rain clouds over Lough Derg

Zigzagging back and forth across the lake, port to port, was a boater's delight. Leaving Terryglass, we headed across to Rossmore Quay, where, in a brief fit of sunshine, we watched an elderly man collecting mayflies in a wooden box to dap for trout. Roger, who was a rather good fly-fisherman, chatted enthusiastically to the elderly man, discovering he had been doing it every year since a small boy. 'Duffers Fortnight' was the celebrated period when, due to the huge numbers of mayfly hatching on the Irish loughs, the trout allegedly threw caution to the wind and greedily gorged on this manna from heaven.

We passed Benjamin Rocks, with its stone cairn topped by a bust, reputedly placed there by a bargee on a dark misty night, then, later that evening at Dromaan, with its winding, stone-bordered harbour entrance, were entertained by tinkers who arrived with their horses to give them a swim. Buster was not at all impressed and growled as they made their way into the water. It was unusual for him; having been brought up with horses, he was normally much friendlier but he always took a dislike to any animal or human who went swimming. He would run up and down the shore or bankside, complaining furiously – about

201

what, I am really not sure – maybe envious that he was not in there with them or warning them of deep water; I would never know.

Entering Garrykennedy in worsening weather, we ended up stuck for three days due to high winds and heavy rain but Buster appreciated the trails through the woods. Eventually, when conditions subsided, we headed across to Mountshannon before turning south to Killaloe and down to Parteen Weir, where Roger turned *Lily* in front of the huge structure. This was the furthest south we were to venture with *Lily*. Beyond Parteen Weir, the navigation entered the headrace of the hydroelectric dam at Ardnacrusha. This magnificent feat of engineering was created in the 1920s by German firm Siemens-Schuckert, and handled 523 cubic yards (400m³) of water per second. Unfortunately, we never got to descend the 100 foot (30.5m) deep, double-chambered lock situated within the structure or cruise to Limerick but later visited by car.

Our trip on Lough Derg was good but the weather had let us down.

"Ireland will be grand when they finish the roof," laughed Roger, struggling out of his wet coat. Buster shook himself furiously, covering the wheelhouse in rainwater, then sulked beneath the towel as I rubbed him dry. After passing through Portumna swing bridge, we made our way northwards towards Victoria Lock. Before we reached it, the clouds had dispersed and the sun was shining, just in time for Roger's return to work.

Chapter Eight

RALLYING AROUND

Approaching Iskeraulin Shoal, Buster started, twisted around in his bed on the chart table and stared across the vastness of Lough Ree.

"What's wrong, Buzz?" He whimpered, turned his head slightly and listened. I could hear it too – the increasing noise of rotating helicopter blades. Stepping out of the wheelhouse, the Coastguard Rescue helicopter swept low and fast over *Lily*; the sight of the mechanical bird made me shiver. "Someone must be in trouble. Turn on the radio."

At the helm, Roger reached for the VHF and flicked through the channels, the radio crackling with static until he found the right one. The words were difficult to decipher but I made out the name of a boat, *Callisto*. In the distance, the helicopter was descending.

"Here, have a look." Roger thrust the binoculars into my hands. As he did so, the boat's name rang a bell.

"Oh no, it's Dave's boat."

Roger met my gaze; a feeling of dread set in. He speeded *Lily* up; our help may be needed. Through the binoculars, I could make out the boat's name. Above it, the down force of the helicopter disturbed the water, sending up misty sprays.

"They must be going to airlift someone off." The thought of a friend being hurt or in danger made me feel sick. Roger turned up the radio and, as we anxiously listened, our panic eased. It was a practice session. Dave was trying to reach a certain speed in his cruiser to allow a crew member to be winched from the moving boat – part of the events planned for the following week's Shannon Boat Rally.

On the day marking the start of the 50th Shannon Boat Rally, the Inner Lakes of Lough Ree were still and reflective; not a breath of wind to ripple the surface. Roger and I had been looking forward to the prestigious event for months but, before ferrying supplies to *Lily*, bobbing on her mooring buoy, there was much to do. Buster sensed there was something special about the day. He jumped into his camping chair in the kitchen doorway, watching every move I made. There was apple and cinnamon cake to bake, salmon fillets to poach, eggs to boil and a chilli con carne to prepare; enough to last the first few days of the rally.

By afternoon, a south-westerly had sprung up but it was not strong enough to hinder hoisting the bunting before departure. Emotions were running high as we slowly slipped our mooring and headed to Lanesborough for the unofficial opening night. Passing Dunrovin, I thought of the late Harry Rice and how proud he would have been knowing so many boaters were excitedly preparing for the event he created.

Reaching Lanesborough, we slowly eased into harbour, aware *Lily* was heavy metal in amongst more fragile glass-fibre and wooden craft. The HBA had taken up residence in one corner and we headed towards them. There was a free mooring against the harbour wall; perfect, Buster could easily be lifted ashore whilst more fragile craft could moor against *Lily*'s offside. Greeted by friends from the Athlone branch of the IWAI along with our temporary neighbours, Cliff and Eunice, in their former turf-carrying barge, 4B, they welcomed us in for tea and cake. The kindness of strangers on the waterways never ceased to amaze me.

The official opening of the rally took place in Carrick-on-Shannon. Organisers had laid on coach transportation but no one had mentioned whether dogs could attend. In the rush of people, we guided Buster onto the coach and sat him comfortably between our legs. As an Irishman once said, 'It's better to seek forgiveness after the event than to ask permission before and be refused.' Everything went well until the coach stopped and Buster let out a chorus of barks, attracting attention; hundreds of eyes were upon us but nobody said a word.

It was a grey, dismal day but the weather was unable to dampen the spirits of those involved. Traditional Irish music played and a small crowd gathered on the quayside. The Irish president, Mary McAleese, arrived to officially open the rally amidst much applause. Later that evening, Lanesborough town put on a special barbecue, a fantastic gesture from an unassuming Shannon port. Throughout the rally, this became a theme: people were pleased that the ralliers were in their town, welcomed us with open arms and greeted us as if heroes of Celtic legend. The atmosphere was like no other rally we had attended.

Whilst the IWA annual National Festival stayed in one location over a bank holiday weekend, in Ireland the whole group moved to different ports over the ten-day-long event. It was an awesome undertaking, more so that year as over 100 boats were expected to attend. Releasing the large and heavy heritage boats from the confines of the harbour at Lanesborough was a slow process but it was a thrill to be on the water amongst such historic vessels. *Lily*'s bunting twisted and curled in the stiff breeze, making weird noises that sent Buster's head tilting and us into fits of laughter.

Port Runny was the first destination. Despite leaving early, *Lily*'s slow speed meant faster, lighter vessels overtook but, as everyone had to wait for instruction on the VHF to be moored, this did not matter. One by one, all the barges were called in to form a sturdy raft off the harbour wall. From this, the lighter-weight vessels were moored. The fleet soon filled and overflowed Port Runny; rumours went around that 133 craft were taking part.

The Coastguard Rescue helicopter arrived the next morning, performing the display we had seen them practising. Dave sped along in his cruiser with the winchman dangling a few feet above the rear deck, the helicopter blades madly whirling overhead. Many had taken their tenders out to join in and they raced back alongside; it really was a spectacle. In the afternoon, we joined forces with the HBA who opened their boats to the public. People had shown interest in the heritage boats and were eager to look inside and learn more about them.

*Coastguard Rescue helicopter winching
a crew member from Callisto*

Visitors flooded in and Buster loved all the attention. We were later joined by the crew of *4B* and friends living close by. Time flew by; rally days were quickly merging together. Exhausted, we retired to bed early to regenerate for the following day's events.

The next move did not go quite so well. We had walked Buster and gone along to the skippers' meeting, which brought everyone up to speed on the day's events, and we were eager to get underway. The next port of call was the Lough Ree Yacht Club (LRYC) at the southern end of the lake.

Lily headed off slowly as a plan had been hatched by the HBA to create a floating raft of barges by breasting them up to each other. An HBA friend, Beth, with her lovely barge, *Aqualegia*, was going to take us under her wing, tying to *Lily* first. She gently bumped alongside and we fastened our barges together. The stability was amazing. We throttled back and waited for the others to catch up. Buster was amused, glancing over to Beth one moment and watching passing boats the next. After a while, there was a call on the radio – the plan was being abandoned. We were disappointed but it was not the end of our fun. An aerial film crew wanted the boats to form a procession the length of the lake; we would still feature in a highlight of the rally. It was a fantastic sight, not only the HBA fleet but the whole rally fleet in one long line, cruising down the centre of Lough Ree on a blustery summer's day.

Waiting patiently for *Lily*'s name to be called to moor at LRYC, we pottered back and forth or drifted in the flow of the Shannon. Buster grew anxious; he wanted to get off the barge and roamed miserably around the decks looking longingly at the meadows beyond. At 7:30 that evening, we finally moored on the outside of a vast raft of vessels, more than six hours after leaving Port Runny. Buster was desperate to reach dry land but, unable to find a route across the moored boats, began to panic. I reached down to pick him up but he cowered and gave a shudder, becoming distressed, which only made matters worse because I began to worry for him. Tired and hungry, we

Following Aqualegia down Lough Ree with bunting flying

found ourselves in a fractious situation. Roger came to the rescue and I carefully lowered Buster down to him from the deck of a high vessel. The boys quickly reached dry land where Buster could relieve himself but this situation clearly was not going to work. It was only four months since Buster's operation and we needed another mooring. Finally, we moved to a more suitable place, too emotionally drained to take part in that evening's event.

Whilst the fleet rested at LRYC, it was decided to open the doors of Dunrovin to fellow IWAI members. Amongst the visitors was David Kileen, who, in 1962, had attended the Shannon Rally, dropping the mast of his yacht at each bridge. Roger fetched and carried people back and forth in his car and took David and his wife next door to Rosemary. They were delighted to see each other after a long spell apart and their smiling faces enabled Dunrovin's open day to end on a high. Taking time out had allowed Buster the opportunity to roam freely in the grounds, having time away from the busy activities. Best of all, though, it provided an opportunity to share with others our love of Dunrovin, which was as much a part of the Shannon Rally as the boats themselves.

When we returned to LRYC, the fancy dress contest was underway. A warm, happy atmosphere penetrated the air and the boats decked in multi-coloured fairy lights sparkled in the darkness of the July night. We did not enter the contest; I knew it was going to be a non-starter from the conversation a few days previously. "Come on, Rog, it will be a laugh."

"And what do you expect me to go as?"

"Look, I've thought it all through and it's easy; everything we need is on board. You can go as Jacques Cousteau; just wear your wetsuit, flippers, snorkel and mask." I could see Roger was not buying the idea so quickly added, "Buster can go with you." My hound gave a double take and, with his eyes fixed firmly on me, began to frown.

"How can Buster come as well?" Finally, I had Roger's attention.

"This is the best bit. I'll make Buster a fin out of cardboard and attach it to either his life jacket or car harness and he can be ... wait for it ..." I dragged it out as long as possible before erupting into, "a Porbeagle shark! Get it? You can be Jacques Cousteau diving with a Poor-Beagle-shark; it will be brilliant!" I finished with an enthusiastic, ear-to-ear grin.

Buster's frown had now grown into a deep sagging above his eyes; he was not impressed. He glanced over at Roger as if to say, 'Don't you even *think* of getting me involved in this one,' then promptly turned his back on us, heading into the wheelhouse.

"See, Buzz doesn't want to do it **and** neither do I." And off Roger went to join Buster.

It was my birthday and we rose early to go shopping in Athlone. I walked Buster around Burgess Park and Roger shopped for the surprise birthday meal he had planned before rushing back for the skippers' meeting. I could not understand what the fuss was about but it all became embarrassingly clear when my birthday was mentioned amongst the more important matters of the day. We found ourselves racing back to *Lily* for a quick departure as the rafting-up and forming a pirouette in the centre of Lough Ree was going ahead.

A total of seventeen barges took part; the line was created by placing the heaviest and largest barges in the centre, with the remainder of the fleet descending in size and weight from each side. *Lily* was nearly on the outside with *Johanna* inboard and the little *Rud Eile* on the very end. Once the barges were all joined up, the two centre barges engaged forward and reverse gear respectively and, slowly, almost 800 tons of steel began to turn like a giant cartwheel. Circling around the outside of the rotating line were smaller cruisers, amongst them *Tsunami* and *Marlou*, who skilfully manoeuvred around each other, their crew engaged in a water pistol fight. Overhead we were buzzed by a low-flying seaplane filming the event for that day's television news bulletin. Roger gently lifted Buster onto the roof of the wheelhouse. Huddled together on *Lily*'s roof, we cheered and waved along with everyone else. Caught up in the electric atmosphere, tingly goosebumps ran up and down my arms as the boats performed and the seaplane filmed.

Later that evening, moored alongside *Bona Spes* at Lakeside Marina, Roger cooked as Buster, stretched out on the sofa, snored

During the pirouette Buster watched from Lily's roof

deeply. We ate and enjoyed a bottle of wine in the candlelit wheelhouse and, as the sun set across the tranquil Inner Lakes, a member of the crew alongside broke into spontaneous song. It was a perfect end to a perfect day, truly a birthday and rally to remember and treasure.

The exhaustion of the rally was overpowering but we had an easy couple of days ahead; a skippers' meeting, a browse around the well-stocked chandlery, land sports and dinghy sailing for those who still had plenty of energy and an auction in aid of the Royal National Lifeboat Institution (RNLI). It had been left up to the ralliers to decorate the Lakeside outbuilding for the evening's events. The whole place was transformed, decorated with fairy lights, candles in all kinds of different holders and colours; it was haphazard but created a beautiful backdrop. Lakeside provided a barbecue evening meal and the drink flowed. It was a lovely evening and Buster came along too, although he was not keen on the accordion music; he **though**t it sounded like a wailing alley cat.

The final move was to Athlone. Leaving the Inner Lakes, we circled Hare Island before rejoining the other barges. Slotting between *Chang-Sha* and *Aqualegia*, the fleet passed LRYC, who were holding their regatta, before arriving in the town. The Irish Army brass band played and children were kept entertained by an assortment of exotic animals, including an iguana. As evening approached, growing anticipation filled the air as crews prepared for the prize-giving and end-of-rally dinner. The Shannon Rally was not just a fun

Even Buster found the 50th
Shannon Rally exhausting

event; it had a serious side too as boaters could take part in various on-water safety exercises where points were gained, the winning crew receiving the Premier Award.

Lily amongst the rally fleet as it rests in Athlone

We chose not to attend as Buster was not permitted in the hotel hosting the event; instead, we arranged a special evening meal of our own on board. Once everyone had vacated their boats, a silence descended. Although their fairy lights still sparkled in the dark, they appeared forlorn, their vibrancy lost, totally overawed by the floodlights illuminating the church on the opposite riverbank.

We enjoyed the peacefulness, watching over the fleet and offering cups of tea to the security men on duty. The quiet did not last, however, as we were woken in the small hours by returning revellers negotiating the way to their boats. Our annoyance at having our sleep disturbed was forgotten the next morning on discovering our neighbours in 4B had won the Premier Award. We were pleased for them; they were a happy, boisterous family who had made us so very welcome during the rally that we could not possibly stay cross at them for long.

Chapter Nine

A ROYAL AFFAIR

During the Shannon Rally, there had been talk of the HBA boycotting the official reopening of the Royal Canal; some considered the opening a farce. Not all the route was fully operational; maintaining a constant water supply throughout the canal and problems with lift bridges at the Dublin end allowing access onto the River Liffey were major issues still to be addressed. These thoughts were foremost in my mind as, on a heavy, grey morning blighted by a cold, northerly wind rippling the high-water levels of the Shannon, we made the leisurely cruise downstream towards Clondara. Would anyone else turn up or would *Lily* be the only boat to make a show?

To reach Clondara meant branching off the windswept Shannon and joining the pretty little Camlin River. *Lily*'s arrival was heralded by a pair of kingfishers, who ducked and dived at high speed in front of her bow, escorting her onwards. Room was tight and I was instantly drawn back to time spent on the River Wissey, forging a way through the narrow, reed-lined river, praying not to meet oncoming craft. Smaller waterways always attracted Buster on deck and he was soon padding around, drinking in passing scents.

Arrival at Clondara came all too soon; it had been a joy to be out on the water, despite the chill, and the sight of some heritage boats was enough to warm my heart. The newly installed Camlin River pontoon sitting below the Royal Canal's entrance lock into Richmond Harbour was full of small craft. The only available space was too short but the friendly crew of a small Springer narrowboat moved their dinghy and *Lily* was quickly secured.

The reopening celebrations were a week away. I was looking forward to spending time with Buster, exploring the area, which had changed since my first visit. Back then, Roger and I had tied our hire boat to the lockside and clambered ashore to view the sleepy harbour. Jam-packed with tatty boats, the way through the bridge at the far end of Richmond Harbour had been blocked; the route beyond, derelict. The old mill on the Camlin River had been little more than a ruin, the whole place appearing lost in time. Now it was hardly recognisable. A major restoration had been carried out; landscaped grounds and gardens, new facilities for boaters and a children's playground installed. The mill had been renovated into apartments; although not fully occupied, the transformation was amazing.

The following few days brought a mixture of weather, which did little to stop our explorations. A damp, misty morning, which the sun fought hard to push through, cast an eerie light across the still, quiet waters of Richmond Harbour; empty of craft, it looked more forlorn than all those years ago when I had first discovered it. Delicate spider webs glistening with dewdrops drooped between the new planting; all was silent but for the rushing waters tipping over the weir. Whilst Richmond Harbour slumbered, there was no rest for the busy little Camlin River. Buster and I set off early for our morning walk. As we did, the sun rose to cast golden hues on the treetops and restored mill buildings. Buster relished the freedom of being off-lead on fresh ground. As we walked, his nose busily worked the towpath, snuffling and sniffing, leading us to the newly installed automated lift bridge: a state-of-the-art device which automatically operated when sensors detected an approaching boat, the first of its kind installed in Ireland.

Throughout the week, with final preparations, the atmosphere grew. Bunting fluttered in the breeze and boats began to arrive. Damian and his wife, Bridie, in their cruiser had been chosen to lock onto the Royal Canal along with a few other craft and travel to Killashee before returning on Friday in the procession of official craft. *Lily* remained on the Camlin River; she

had not been chosen but was there representing Great Britain and we had gone to town, dressing her all over in colourful bunting. In the evenings, her

Rainbow over the lock keeper's cottage at Richmond Harbour

solar-powered fairy lights strung around the wheelhouse twinkled brightly, the glass reflecting them and making them shimmer to create an indoor, artificial night sky.

Buster was excited and I knew I would struggle to take photographs and keep him under control. A kind gentleman from a neighbouring boat offered to look after him and, to my surprise, Buster seemed quite keen on the idea. As the crowds gathered to watch the boats, goosebumps quickly spread over my body. I was part of history in the making; it was an honour and privilege to be at such a landmark event. The reopening of the Royal Canal would create Ireland's only looped inland waterways circuit, later becoming known as the Green and Silver Route after the classic book by Tom Rolt covering his voyage in 1946 prior to the Royal's closure.

On the lockside, new friendships were forged as locals, boaters, journalists and waterways workers celebrated together. As all the excitement built, the heavens opened and spilled forth a sharp shower, rewarding the crowd with a rainbow over the lock keeper's squat cottage – a magical moment born out of a drenching.

When all the fuss had subsided, I gathered Buster in my arms for a huge hug. He had been such a good boy during the locking procedures; sitting still and watching, he knew I was working and needed him to behave. As a reward, we headed off for a nice walk. Later that evening, we were joined by Len and June, who arrived in speedy *Polecat*. It had **been** a while since we had entertained on *Lily* and it was a pleasure to have **company on** board.

Strolling around Richmond Harbour, Roger's mobile phone rang. It was a call from an employment agency wanting to know if he would consider a job in Denmark. The call lasted some time. When it was finally over, he was full of talk. Denmark was not a country known for its inland waterways but a job there would allow us to move *Lily* into Europe. It was difficult containing the excitement of what could be a new chapter in our lives. Pushing the idea from the forefront of our minds, we tried to concentrate on the events unfolding but I was already mentally preparing. Thinking there may not be much time, the pet passport procedure for Buster should **be** started. To cruise in Europe, we would also need to update our boating **certificates**.

The official reopening day rushed by in a blur of activity with much talk, laughter and celebration. Throughout the morning, craft lined up along the canal in readiness for the procession. IWAI friends gathered on Damian's boat and held a music session, filling the air with cheery song, Michael grinning broadly as he strummed on his guitar. The procession was led by *Royal Canal Float No. 3*, an original working barge transformed into a smart passenger boat. We watched all the boats arrive in Richmond Harbour and gave an especially loud cheer when the tiny Wilderness boat, *Toad Hall*, trailed over from England, arrived. This was one of the group of Wilderness boats I had taken care of years previously

Procession of boats into Richmond Harbour marking the reopening of the Royal Canal

at the IWA National Festival held in St Ives; even for boaters, it was sometimes a small world.

A press pass allowed me access into the marquee where speeches were made, drinks and canapés served. It was a great honour meeting Ruth Delaney, one of the original IWAI founder members and author of numerous books on the Irish waterways. We spoke of Harry Rice, his home at Dunrovin and what a wonderful day the official opening was turning out to be – treasured memories.

The celebrations continued the next day with more craft arriving. In the afternoon, we watched the local scouts canoeing on the Camlin River. Len and June had the best views from *Polecat* and invited us aboard. It was not long before the drink began to flow and we were joined by Dave. He entertained us with tales of stormy seas, battles with boats as they tumbled off raging waves into deep, dark troughs as, high above, dolphins jumped out of the water. We were mesmerised, staring with gaping jaws, but Buster, not wanting his title of Admiral undermined, tried his best to look bored. It was a great evening; caught up in the atmosphere, all of us drank far too much Tullamore Dew, the local Irish whiskey, and it was midnight when we realised we had not eaten and the bottle was dry. June whizzed about the galley, quickly preparing a pasta dish to which we contributed a spicy sauce. We ate rapidly, famished to the core. Shortly after, Roger and I, along with a sleepy Buster, retired to *Lily*, happy, content and exhausted.

Despite hitting the whiskey the previous night, I somehow escaped a much-expected thick head, for which I was most grateful. The morning passed slowly as we said goodbye to friends and walked Buster before finally motoring along the Camlin River to rejoin the wide waters of the Shannon. I was sad to leave; the ending of boat gatherings always had an emotional effect but, as rain was falling, it was easier to bring the events to a conclusion.

Sunshine and showers were the order of the day as I steered *Lily* back to base at Dromod. Arriving, I was surprised to find the place deserted; even the public harbour, usually bustling with boats, was quiet. It was a sure sign autumn had arrived; hot on her heels, winter. For many, the boating season was drawing to a close; for us, it was only just beginning.

Chapter Ten

AUTUMN ON THE BOYLE WATERS

Nights were drawing in; it was chilly but still great to be on the move, and we were not alone. We fell in behind a beautiful, old, wooden launch, *Lady-be-good*, and together forged across Lough Bofin, through the Derrycairn Narrows and onto the wider waters of Lough Boderg. Approaching Lough Tap, the light was fading fast but we hoped to reach the moorings below Jamestown Lock before darkness fell.

With no sign of life at the lock and a red light showing, we assumed it closed for the night and moored up accordingly. Buster made no attempt to move; instead, he tilted his head to one side and stared into the evening's growing darkness. The crew in *Lady-be-good* had knocked for the lock keeper and, to our surprise, a few minutes later, both our boats were inside the lock chamber being raised to the canal cut, now cloaked in the gloom of evening.

Exiting, the blackness of night had fallen. Slowly, we made our way along the cut, which had been created to sever a great loop in the Shannon. Hewn out of solid rock, its sides high and topped by trees and shrubs, during daylight it was an impressive sight; at night, it seemed to have absorbed all the darkness of the sky and, even with *Lily*'s lights aglow, it was eerie, silent and still. I prayed there would be room to moor at the end of the cut and my prayers were answered; *Lady-be-good* motored on, mooring in front of a cruiser which had taken up the centre of the available quay wall, a pet hate of mine, whilst we were left to try and squeeze *Lily* between the cruiser and the stone bridge crossing the cut. Not easy in the darkness, we sighed with relief when finally safe and secure. It was an exciting start to our autumn adventure.

Up early the next morning, darkness held up departure. Not that Buster minded; it was our first stop at this mooring and he was keen to take a look, roaming through the damp grass, above which hung a light mist. Finally slipping our moorings, the sun crept above the treetops, illuminating them in a golden glow. No crew were stirring on *Lady-be-good*. *Lily* was extremely quiet for a large barge; we glided by without disturbing them.

Out on the river, away from the cosseting canal cut, a cool chill descended. Buster gave a shiver, rearranging his bedding before settling down to sleep. Below decks, the stove was gently ticking over but Buster, being very much the Admiral, refused to leave the helm and take up a more comfortable position on the sofa. With Buster settled, I went out on deck. The clear, crisp, early-morning light was perfect to capture some stunning photographs. I did not feel the chill.

Carrick-on-Shannon looked beautiful bathed in golden light. The public moorings were full but quiet; everyone still in the Land of Nod. On the far side of the town's bridge, *Lily* slipped into another world. Everywhere was a hive of activity as the hire-fleet bases prepared their craft for new arrivals; it was change-over day. Buster groaned as the sound of voices filtered through the open window to disturb his slumber. The quiet waters had vanished. There were boats everywhere – being cleaned, filled with fuel or having supplies taken aboard.

"D'you remember how excited we used to be when we hired boats?" asked Roger. Memories came flooding back as we talked about our boating holidays – the best-liked, the friends made but, most of all, Buster: his crazy, early-day antics, how all the time and patience spent on him during his early years had paid off and how we had turned our hound into a seasoned boater.

Leaving the Shannon to turn onto the Boyle Waters, *Lily*'s bow sent dabchicks diving for cover. Crossing the small lake of Drumharlow, with the island of Inishatirra at its centre, the trees and woodland were in full autumnal colours. To the north-east, the steely grey Arigna Mountains were a sight to

Perfect early morning reflections on the Boyle Waters

behold and I felt lucky to be alive. Onwards, passing Woodbrook, the mansion immortalised in the eponymous memoir of author David Thomson, I did not want to break the peacefulness, the spell of the day gifted upon us, and *Lily* carried us on in silent contemplation.

At Cootehall, the multi-arched stone bridge with its mirror-like reflections provided perfect circles to cruise through – miniature tunnels of sheer delight – and then we were treated to the same again at the next bridge. A gentle curve in the waterway led to Clarendon Lock with its pretty, tree-fringed banks and constantly chattering weir. In my opinion, this was one of the loveliest locks in Ireland. It was also the only one on the Boyle, a kind of gatekeeper, guardian to a beauty which caused my heart to leap and sing, for beyond lay Lough Key, a lake of magic and mystery, a place to happily become lost in. The lock gates stood open; as if eagerly awaiting our arrival, they invited us to enter and *Lily* slid silently in, giving the lock keeper a surprise. Within the warmth of his control room, he had been so engrossed in the morning's newspaper that he had not heard our approach.

Lough Key was even more beautiful than I remembered: bright blue waters dotted with tree-covered islands in shades of gold and bronze, mute swans gliding effortlessly beneath the low-hanging branches of wiry willows against a backdrop of the Curlew Mountains. We cruised by Bullock Island then turned southwards, passing Sally Island, Orchard Island and Green Island to our east and Drumman's Island to the west. Castle Island, with its turreted folly, turned the already delightful scene into a fairy tale. Irish poet William Butler Yeats had been captivated by Castle Island when he visited in 1895 and wished to create a centre for artistic endeavours on the site. Although it never happened, many believed his visit to this magical place enhanced his mystical style of writing.

Roger moored *Lily* opposite Castle Island. Fortunate with fine weather and uninterrupted views, the days passed quickly and Buster had a fine time, galloping along wooded paths and over ornamental bridges, returning to *Lily* ready for slumber, happy and content. The best times were the evenings, when the Lough Key Country Park day-trippers began to disperse and a hush fell over the former Rockingham Estate. One evening, we enjoyed a barbecue, knowing it would possibly be the last of the season as nights were beginning to cool. Inside, *Lily* was warm and cosy; the perfect place to sit back and ponder the glory of this place.

Autumnal colours on beautiful Lough Key

There was nothing better than rising early in the morning when all the world slumbered, sitting peacefully taking in the surroundings, listening to birdsong and feeling the gradual warmth of the day bloom as if an opening flower. I had woken early and, with my camera in hand, was hoping to take some misty-morning shots of Castle Island, capturing the essence of a world William Butler Yeats would have been happy to reside in forever. Alas, the clear skies of the previous few nights had been replaced by a blanket of grey cloud, quite out of keeping with the romanticism I had hoped to find. Many years ago, on a previous visit to Lough Key, Roger had risen early and been mesmerised by the dawn. Gently, he had awoken me to go on deck to watch the rising sun paint Castle Island a rich golden glow. It was a perfect sunrise, never recaptured; we had already experienced the best.

Beyond Lough Key, the town of Boyle was reached by a short canal, which terminated in a new harbour. Buster was soon scanning both banks, eager to be out on the towpath and snuffling around. There were a few hire boats in the harbour along with some Waterways Ireland craft, a tug and the *Inis Cealtra*, a-state-of-the-art work boat which was undertaking the upgrading of navigation markers.

Bushes of delicate wild fuchsias brightened up the walk into town alongside the unnavigable Boyle River. The abbey was closed for winter and under restoration but still looked impressive, despite the swathes of protective plastic sheeting. Crossing the road and heading into town, we were met by a breeze which sent a crisp, golden carpet of fallen leaves dancing to greet us. Buster played in them, chasing odd ones about as they twisted and fell. At the railway station, we grabbed a bite to eat then boarded a train to Dromod to collect Roger's car. Buster, as always, enjoyed being on the train and, followed by a walk, was in his element. By the time we reached the car, he was glad to sit down and rest, taking the opportunity to sleep on the journey back to *Lily*.

Roger had to leave by 6:30 a.m. for work next day and the morning was dark, a cold, grey blanket enveloping the landscape. I stayed in bed for a couple more hours until Buster finally woke, eager to go out and explore his new surroundings. We walked along the canal towards the Boyle River but, with no bridge across the cut, had to retrace our steps. Buster hung back at the turnaround, looking at me in dismay; he much preferred a circular walk.

One by the one, the hire boats left and, by the time we arrived back, *Lily* was the only craft apart from the work boat. Having the harbour to ourselves was great. I let Buster roam freely around the well-kept grounds whilst I went about my chores, cleaning and emptying the stove. I ran the engine to generate some hot water, mopped down the roof and did the washing up; time passed quickly.

It was 6:30 p.m. by the time Roger arrived home. Buster went mad, barking and jumping up at him, pleased to have his dad home. And that was how the week passed; the days drifted by, Boyle began to feel like home. Being on the water late in the season was a special time; with the masses gone and places quietening down, their true characters were revealed. Gone was the false pretence of long, hot summer days and all that they brought: blousy bedding plants, coachloads of tourists, noisy events. Stripped back to the bare bones, it was possible to honestly judge a place. This was the same with the waterways themselves; to be fully appreciated, they needed to be experienced throughout all seasons.

Lily's roof was covered with ice; it sparkled and twinkled. A mist swirled off the water's surface but soon dispersed as the sun rose and, with it, the temperature. Buster and I set off on our walk and were joined by a local lady, Regina, and her ex-guide dog, Jack. We relished their company and covered several topics including husbands, the Royal Family, the future of the economy and the notorious Dublin criminal the 'Monk', who had reputedly started his nefarious career when a small boy, throwing stones at barges.

Jack was elderly and walked slowly. He and Buster made friends and were soon strolling along side by side, engrossed in doggy banter. When we arrived back at the harbour, I was bid a fond farewell and received a hug from Regina, a surprising and meaningful gesture from a lovely lady and new-found friend.

"I know we will see each other again," she said, stepping back from the hug. But we were due to leave the next day and probably would not be back until the spring.

"I'm not sure this is a good idea," I said to Roger as we struggled uphill in thick mist. Before leaving Boyle Harbour, I wanted to see the Gaelic Chieftain, a modern sculpture overlooking Lough Key, but it seemed a waste of time going in such conditions.

"Look, we may not get another chance. Let's push on; besides, Buzz is enjoying the walk." Looking down at our nose-on-the-ground hound, he was busy grunting away in a world of his own.

I was glad we had continued because, arriving at the site, looming out of the mist and backlit by the rising sun, stood the impressive and somewhat disturbing statue of the Gaelic Chieftain; looking down menacingly, his head slightly tilted, he was fearsome. Buster growled and pulled back on his lead, did a couple of sideways jumps and raised his hackles then paused. A couple of seconds passed then he ran forwards and erupted into one of the loudest 'barooos' I had ever heard him utter. Reminiscent of a battle cry, it reverberated around the Curlew Mountains.

The Gaelic Chieftain represented one of the fiercest battles ever fought and the only one lost by the English. It was 1599, the Irish were in revolt and under the leadership of Chieftain O'Neill. Elizabeth I's General, Sir Conyers Clifford, divided his troops, sending out an advance party who were besieged in Colooney Castle on the far side of the Curlew Mountains. Clifford set out to relieve the men with the remainder of his troops but, by the time they reached the foothills, they were tired and hungry. Keen to get through the Pass of Ballaghboy, Clifford advanced. Lying in wait were the Irish forces, acting under the orders of their commander,

The Gaelic Chieftain

Red Hugh O'Donnell. The English troops were quickly massacred, the head of Clifford sent to the English garrison at Coloney as proof of the defeat and his body for burial on Trinity Island, Lough Key.

We spent a few more days back on Lough Key; gusty breezes, sharp showers and double rainbows accompanied us on a circuit of the lake, where, as far as I could tell, *Lily* was the only boat. The morning of departure, a mist twisted and writhed around Castle Island, allowing me to finally take the shots I had desired. At the lock, we said our farewells to the same lock keeper, who had seen us through not only on the way up but also all those years ago when we had hired a boat. He was part of the fixtures and fittings.

"We'll be back in the spring; see you then," I called to him as Roger guided *Lily* out of the chamber.

"God willing, you will," came his reply as he waved us off.

We never returned to Lough Key with *Lily* as Roger accepted the exciting new position with the company in Denmark and it was with sadness that we read of the lock keeper's passing a short time later.

Mystical Castle Island

Chapter Eleven

LOUGH REE EXPLORATION

Nothing prepared Roger and me for our amazement at seeing Lough Ree for the first time. It may have been the Shannon's second largest lake but, in my opinion, it was the most impressive. Its waters, littered with islands, stretched 16 miles (26km) in length and 7 miles (11km) at the widest point and we came to know them intimately, seeing the lake throughout the ever-changing seasons. We learnt to respect it and became totally spellbound by the so-called Lake of Kings.

Cruising Lough Ree's centrally marked channel, the tree-covered islands provokingly offered fleeting glimpses of crumbling ruined homesteads, churches and monasteries but, with rocky approaches and no marked routes, they were frustratingly unobtainable. I would throttle back and strain to see further into the undergrowth, imagining what architectural wonders were hidden from sight. Buster gave the occasional squeak, thinking the prospect of landing was imminent. In fear of the consequences should we steer *Lily* away from the designated channels, we stuck to them religiously. However, Dunrovin had an ace to play and, through her connections, the lake's hidden gems were revealed.

Lough Ree had several 'secret' routes, anchorages and moorings; some, not even marked on the charts, remained a mystery unless you were lucky enough to have been shown them by a local lakes-man. The marked navigation channel in the northern part of Lough Ree ran to the east of Inchenagh Island. Few people knew an unmarked route, known as the Steamer Channel, ran to the west or that there was a good anchorage in Clooneigh Bay.

The loughs of Killinure, Ballykeeran and Coosan were collectively known as Lough Ree's Inner Lakes. Bordering Dunrovin's grounds, a lot of time was spent on these smaller, calmer waters. Entering Coosan Lough through Levinge's Cut, we would access the hidden anchorage of Gibraltar or, on Killinure, squeeze through the covert, reed-fringed channel behind Temple Island to secretly emerge near Glasson Golf Club. A labyrinth of clandestine opportunities for intrepid boaters, it was also a nose-whirling experience for a scent hound.

Despite an earlier visit to Barley Harbour on Ree's eastern shore by car, we had yet to go there with *Lily*. The harbour, out of bounds to boat hirers for many years, was excluded from some hire-fleet operators' charts as the approach through rocky shoals was considered too dangerous. Dave McCabe and Noel Griffen of the IWAI

Sunrise over Lough Ree's tranquil Inner Lakes

Lily at Barley Harbour

had developed electronic charts for the whole of the Shannon system and we were asked to trial them prior to general release through Garmin, a GPS system. With their assistance, we were finally able to navigate many of Ree's secrets with confidence.

Accessing Barley Harbour was not as difficult as some had led us to believe. Over the years, the mystery surrounding it had grown and the sceptics delighted in warning off any who might attempt to do so. Within the harbour, there was a large, flat-topped rock. When water levels were normal or high, it was not a problem but, if they were low, some craft had been known to catch a prop blade on it. I had seen pictures of youngsters standing on the rock in the middle of the harbour in a particularly dry summer, using it as a diving platform.

Roger navigated *Lily* into the harbour easily with the aid of the trial charts. I marvelled at Lough Ree from the newly seen angle; its waters were smooth and silent, a blue vastness. Buster roamed carelessly around the stone harbour, paddled in the water lapping the wide ramp and rolled on the newly mown lawns. We had entered without problem and left using the infamous rock as a roundabout, skirting its edge to pick up deeper water leading out of the bay. The notorious Barley Harbour had been finally crossed off our list.

IWAI events were often held at Lough Ree Sailing Club. On one occasion, Roger had the opportunity to go sailing for the first time. Buster watched him depart and whimpered soulfully. Two hours later, Roger returned with flushed cheeks and a broad smile.

"How did you get on?"

"I like the idea of travelling without burning diesel but at one point we were going so slow I thought I'd have to get out and push!"

A few weeks later, we were back, joining an IWAI Cruise in Company (CIC) to Nun's Island. There were fifty-two named islands on Lough Ree, many more nameless. Nun's Island, situated close to the centre of the lake, apparently received its name when the Poor Clare nuns from nearby Bethlehem sought refuge there in 1642, whilst their convent was plundered by Roundheads. The owner of the island had agreed to the CIC landing to picnic there before continuing to Lecarrow. We joined a small flotilla of boats and headed straight up the lake to the island where we took up an anchorage. We were the last to access shore by dinghy; although our eight-foot Walker Bay sported a reliable Yamaha outboard, it was not the steadiest of platforms.

"Buster, for goodness' sake, sit still; you'll have the boat over." Already holding on so tight my knuckles were white, the last thing I needed was Buster rocking the boat.

"Will you two stop mucking about? It's difficult enough to steer this damn thing." Roger was taking an erratic course to the beach.

"It's not me; it's your dog moving around." With that, Buster barged by me, upsetting the equilibrium, and we veered to one side.

"Come here, Buster, and sit with me." Buster wobbled over to Roger and finally sat still, allowing Roger to guide the dinghy safely to the gravel beach.

I was eager to view the scant ruins of the island's church but never got the chance. The sky darkened and the wind whipped up, backing to the north quickly and becoming a ferocious squall. As rain started to lash down,

we sheltered in an old landing craft next to the gravel beach. Joking at our predicament, Damian suddenly realised his cruiser, along with the one fastened to it, were being driven by the winds towards the inshore shoal. Rushing to his tender, he raced through the waves and narrowly managed to avert disaster. Cheering from the shelter, several others realised they too were dragging anchor, resulting in a mass exodus from the island. One poor chap, unable to start his outboard, asked Roger to ferry him out to his boat. With *Lily* holding anchor in the deeper water, Roger agreed and was soon bouncing through the waves, delivering him to his boat. Roger returned after a nasty trip and we waited for the squall to blow itself out.

Within ten minutes, the conditions had improved enough to return to *Lily*. Retrieving the anchor, we followed Damian up the lake, turning into Blackbrink Bay to enter the Lecarrow Canal. Constructed in the 1840s to transport stone from the local quarry to the navigation works at Athlone, its narrow channel led to Lecarrow Quay, where there was only one slot available for *Lily*. Boats were packed four deep across the canal, blocking it completely.

The ruined castle of Rinn Dúin was situated close by. The site was occupied by the Normans, who built the castle and the small settlement which had grown up in the shadow of its walls. Considered one of the most important medieval monuments in the country, it was a good place to visit with Buster as there were looped walks of varying lengths in the vicinity.

Later that evening, after my third pint of Guinness in the local pub, with the time well past midnight, I could hardly keep my eyes open. We left the pub as more people arrived and, the following morning, were first up. It was well past noon before the others began to stir.

The Inny River, also known as the Owenacharra River, flowed into Lough Ree at its widest point. We ventured into the river late one afternoon and carefully followed its winding course to a footbridge marking the end of navigation. Roger moored *Lily* on the grassy bank of a field; it was the first time in many years that the mooring pins and mallet were

Buster walking the plank as the sun sets over the Inny River

needed. The gangplank was essential for accessing the field and Buster had not forgotten how to use it, trotting up and down with great confidence. After the wide water of the lake, the river was an oasis of calm; we had the place to ourselves and a sunset to cherish.

I would miss this truly impressive lake. It was the place where we had experienced many firsts: navigating to secret harbours, rallying with the IWAI, pirouetting with the HBA and cruising in company. We had made our home on the shores of Lough Ree, seen it through its many moods and revelled in its beauty. For us, it was second to none.

Chapter Twelve

A GRAND DEPARTURE

Without the need for a pet passport, travelling back and forth to Ireland with Buster had been easy. Moving to Europe, however, involved more stringent conditions. Buster was already microchipped but now needed to be vaccinated against rabies and have all the details of his annual inoculations officially recorded. Our vet in England carried out the procedures, which were straightforward, and Buster was soon ready to travel the world.

"Have dog, will travel," Roger chuckled when I waved Buster's new passport under his nose.

"We always said we would; now we really are." I reached down, gave Buster a gentle ear tug. "Now we're going places. What have you got to say about that?"

Buster gave me one of his snoring-awake impressions, which usually meant he was bored, and dragged me towards the nearest shrub for a wee.

"There's a place in the passport for a photo," I shouted to Roger from the nearby herbaceous border. "Think I know just the one." I giggled as I watched Roger trying to thumb through the pages of the passport whilst wrestling with a handful of paperwork. Our vet had been efficient, printing off Buster's medical records, ready for registration with a new vet in Denmark.

The job Roger had accepted in Denmark was with an English-speaking international company. Although cutting short our time in Ireland, it was an opportunity not to be missed. With Roger having a few months of time on his hands before the new job started, after a lot of discussion we decided to cruise *Lily* back to England. This would involve a trip down the Shannon to join the Grand Canal to Dublin and a sea crossing: firstly, to Holyhead and then Liverpool to join the English canal system, heading back to our beloved River Trent. *Lily* would overwinter there whilst we settled into our new lives in Denmark. With a mixture of fear and excitement, we prepared for a 'Grand' departure.

Leaving Dromod, we headed south, entering Lough Ree in blustery conditions.

"We'll have to divert into Port Runny." Roger was checking the chart. *Lily* had developed a fault and something was seriously wrong; it would have been foolish to push on. Lough Ree could be unforgiving in rough weather and attempting a crossing in a boat with mechanical problems could end in disaster. *Lily* coughed and spluttered her way through the choppy conditions to reach port. Occasionally, her engine died without warning then would suddenly kick back into life as if the whole episode had been imagined.

Thinking the problem was an air lock, Roger spent ages re-bleeding the fuel system; it was temperamental and, by the time the task was completed, it was late evening. Next morning, following a couple of test runs in the sheltered bay, we set off to complete the crossing of Lough Ree. *Lily* ploughed through the waves but, with Dunrovin in sight, the same coughing and spluttering returned.

"She almost appears to be shuddering, like she's frightened of something." I stared at Roger as *Lily* broke into another series of violent lurches.

"Maybe she's trying to tell us something."

"Like what?" I already knew what Roger was going to say.

"Like 'don't go'."

"More like 'please don't take me across the Irish Sea; I'm only a little barge'." Deep down, I had the same fears. Were we doing the right thing? Heading into

Europe was a big move but attempting to cross the Irish Sea in a barge was even bigger, perhaps madness?

Roger carefully nursed *Lily* into the dock at Dunrovin and spent the next week sorting the problem, which he discovered was diesel bug. Having to dispose of the diesel was heartbreaking; flushing and cleaning the tanks time-consuming but the only way to ensure the nasty organism was out of the fuel system. With additives and lots of love and attention, we made a series of trials across the Inner Lakes and, later, further afield, taking emotional farewell trips to favourite places on Lough Ree. When all was satisfactory, we cast off, already a couple of weeks behind schedule.

Departing Dunrovin, I savoured the last glimpses of my little house in the woods until *Lily* finally carried us out of the Inner Lake's sheltered waters into the wide expanse of Lough Ree. We had left part of our hearts behind but took some comfort in knowing that the IWAI were joining forces with the RNLI, putting forward plans to use the grounds in an exciting joint venture consisting of a modern, new building with a meeting room and lifeboat station. Harry Rice had said the Shannon's motto should be 'Resurgam', meaning 'I shall come into my own again.' It was thanks to his creation of the IWAI that it did; not to water-borne trade but to holidaymakers and leisure boaters. I was hopeful that, in time, this name could also be applied to Dunrovin and that Harry would have approved.

The day was rough and the strong wind created little white horses which bucked hard against *Lily*'s steelwork, making the last trip on Lough Ree uncomfortable. Perhaps the lake did not want us to leave either, I thought to myself, as Roger steered her around the headland, passing the southern tip of Hare Island and Pott's Shallow.

Penning down in Athlone Lock, Roger shouted from the wheelhouse, "Take a good look around; this will be our last time through here with *Lily*." From the bow, I slowly scanned the view; it had become a familiar sight over the past few years and I would miss it. The left bank with Sean's Bar, the brightly coloured shop and house fronts, the looming stone walls of the castle and, above, keeping a careful watch, the stunning, twin-towered church. Buster sensed there was something different about this trip. Instead of relaxing in his bed, he too was taking in the surroundings. I am sure he knew we were leaving; that there would be no more walks in Burgess Park, along the riverside promenade or down by the abandoned Athlone Canal.

Boating with Buster

Our last night on the mighty Shannon was spent at Clonmacnoise, which I had many fond memories of: farmer Jimmy Curly walking bold as brass towards *Lily* across the lush, green meadows bordered by the peaty Shannon waters, a bag of his mother's delicious homemade scones in hand; still summer nights lying on *Lily*'s roof, watching millions of stars twinkling in the night sky, the steel work cool on our bare limbs; Buster's frenzied barking at cows gathered around the pontoon, barring access to land. They were as vivid and bright as when they happened, gems caught in sunlight, forever planted in my mind.

The night was not peaceful as, outside, a storm raged, creating waves on the Shannon that dashed against *Lily*'s hull, keeping me awake for hours. Was the Shannon vying for attention; did the river not want us to leave either? Roger and I spent the next morning with Buster, walking the narrow lanes and meadows. Finally, we climbed up to the castle ruins and drank in the view of the river's twisting course through the callows.

Later that afternoon, with passage into Shannon Harbour already booked, *Lily* battled through the windy conditions to join the Grand Canal. Getting to grips with the locks was going to take some patience; the small landing stage was already occupied, all glass-fibre craft. Mooring to them even temporarily was not wise.

Castle ruins at Clonmacnoise

"The gates are open; drive her in and I'll climb off," Roger instructed but there were no ladders set into the walls; it was impossible for him to get off. Gazing upwards, scratching heads and wondering how best to tackle the problem, the lock keeper appeared.

"Thank goodness for that," I said to Buzzy. "I didn't fancy trying to reverse out of here in this weather." With the lock keeper's assistance, we were soon through the first two locks, leading to the centre of Shannon Harbour, where passage was paid and departure times arranged. A leisurely walk around the harbour followed, passing the ivy-clad ruins of the former Grand Canal Company's hotel, which remained the main focal point, despite the last tourist having long since checked out. We sat outside the pub and supped pints of Guinness before heading back to *Lily,* where Buster made friends with several dogs and enjoyed their company for the remainder of the afternoon.

At 9:30 a.m. the next morning, it was time to begin our 82 mile (132km) journey across Ireland on what was once the country's major commercial route, linking the hinterland surrounding the Shannon with the sea ports at Dublin. Slowly, *Lily* carried us past the forlorn ruins, newly installed residential moorings and motley collection of craft lining the banks towards the next lock where Alan, the lock keeper, met us. On the Grand, lock keepers were responsible for their own designated areas and would phone ahead to the next keeper when boaters left their section. If all went well, there should be a constant stream of assistance; in reality, it was quite different.

At Belmont, we encountered our first double lock. In Ireland, these were counted as one and, when rising, both chambers were filled at once. When Alan explained the procedure, it sounded harsh but, with *Lily* situated so far back, the turbulence was not too bad and she was soon steadily rising. Alan saw us safely and efficiently through his section but told us we would not get much further without a lock key. We had read the locks at Tullamore were kept padlocked through the town as vandals opened them in the depths of night, draining the pounds, but we had not expected to find ones in rural areas locked. We later discovered the rural locks were not padlocked. The Irish name for a windlass, the device used to work the paddles on a lock, was a lock key. They were available from Shannon Harbour, by then several hours behind us. Luckily, our EA windlass fitted and, although not really man enough for the job, saw us through until the absent lock keeper finally made a show.

Approaching a familiar stretch of canal not far from Lough Boora Parklands, I walked the towpath with Buster. He raced ahead of *Lily*, as if guiding her. I liked to think he was saying, 'Come on, *Lily* old girl, this is the way. I've done this bit of the canal before. Follow me!'

Weed growth was a major problem on the Grand, which Waterways Ireland were attempting to address by trialling jute matting on one section, laid and weighted down on the canal bed to stem growth. Weed cutters were out in force but their hard work did little to help *Lily*, who struggled through the thick growth. Roger spent more time with his arms down the inspection hatch than in the wheelhouse; it was a constant stop-start trip for miles. I lost count of all the buckets full of shredded weed that Roger collected.

Mooring bankside proved difficult as the edges were very shallow but, when we did, it was worth the effort. The land was diverse: areas of wild, open peatbog and lush meadows where hares playfully bounded and caused Buster to tremble with excitement. Spotting them from the boat, he would race to the bow to sit transfixed until they disappeared, returning to me sweet-smelling from brushing against the herb pot; a mixture of lemon balm, rosemary, parsley and thyme.

At Tullamore, lock keepers met and guided us through the vandal-proof locks. Roger replenished our whiskey supplies at the Tullamore Dew Whiskey Centre and we walked Buster along the towpath to Boland's Lock, the turreted, lock keeper's house sparking reminiscence of previous holidays in quirky properties.

At Edenderry, we enjoyed an overnight stop, a take-away supper and some entertainment by local campanologists.

"There's a fish and chip shop over there," Roger almost screamed in delight. He had missed his favourite take-away supper since leaving England and we had not come across many in Ireland.

*Buster sitting next to the herb pot
at Lily's bow watching for hares*

"I suppose that means you'd like fish and chips for supper?" I knew the answer but played innocent. I looked down at Buster, who was grinning madly and doing a strange continuous half-sitting-down and half-standing-up routine. *Go on, go on, say yes*, his movements encouraged. Buster was partial to fish, especially the skin. I could take it or leave it but, looking at the pair of them, I thought refusal may result in mutiny.

"Alright, but go now; there are school kids about and I don't want to be here alone in case there's trouble." Roger grabbed his wallet and rushed across the road; it was the fastest he had moved in weeks. Buster watched from the wheelhouse, leant his chin on the open window sill and licked his lips in anticipation. I nestled onto the seat alongside him. "You're looking forward to supper, aren't you, Buzzy boy?"

I became aware of children's voices from behind and could sense a group approaching. Once alongside the wheelhouse, the three boys stopped. Buster sniffed the air, sighed at them for blocking his view and strained his neck to see beyond, eager to spot Roger returning with food.

"Nice dog," one of them commented.

"Nice boat," said another.

"Where you going?" asked the third. I stood up, placed an arm around Buster, leant out of the wheelhouse slightly and answered.

"Thanks, we're heading for Dublin. What about you, have you finished school for the day?"

"Yeah, but got homework to do." The answer was accompanied by groans, huffs and puffs, scuffing of shoes on gravel. They had all been given what they considered excessive after-school tasks to complete. One of them noticed the brass bell on the side of the wheelhouse.

"What's the bell for?"

"That's if someone comes to call and I'm downstairs; they can ring it like a doorbell and then I can come up and see who it is."

The boy stepped forwards with a grin, grasped the plaited rope on the bell and rattled the brass clanger as hard as he could. The bell rang out and people in the street turned to see what all the commotion was about.

"You mean like this?" Laughing, all his mates were soon joining in, taking it in turns to ring *Lily*'s brass bell. When Roger returned with our supper, the boys were long gone but I related the story for him.

"Oh great," he said with a huge sigh. "You know what will happen now, don't you?"

"What?"

"They'll be back in the middle of the night, ringing that bell; we won't get a moment's peace." With that, he headed off to the engine room to find a screwdriver and removed the bell.

At Lowtown, we reached the junction to the Barrow Line of the Grand. The area bustled with craft crowded around the small boat yard approaching the lock, allowing entry to the Grand's beautiful summit level. The clear waters, marking the highest point of our journey, revealed a forest of weed. Despite all the problems that this caused *Lily*, the swaying aquatic vegetation was somehow magical. Approaching the town of Sallins, we moored near Digby Bridge. There were many aqueducts along the canal, the Leinester Aqueduct over the River

Liffey the most impressive. Stopping here gave us an opportunity to walk Buster and take a closer look.

A tranquil mooring on the Grand Canal

We had secured *Lily* on her mooring pins when the mobile rang; it was the lock keeper informing us not to go any further as a car had been driven into the canal, blocking passage through Sallins. The entire bank holiday weekend was spent waiting for the go-ahead but this was not a bad thing. The constant wrapping of weed around *Lily's* propeller had caused violent shuddering and, on closer inspection, Roger found that some of the fuel pipes had been damaged. Luckily, in nearby Naas there was an Aladdin's cave of a hardware shop to which he cycled and purchased new pipe fittings.

Over the following days, some familiar boats and crew appeared: members of the HBA returning to the Shannon after attending the Dublin Rally, amongst them *Nieuwe Zorgen*, which slowly emerged through a shroud of misty dampness as if a ghostly apparition, delivering cheerful greetings from her crew. By the time we arrived at Sallins, the offending car had been removed. All that remained was a swathe of police tape where the vehicle had left the quayside.

Unable to fill up in Edenderry as the tap had been disconnected, *Lily* was short on water. At Sallins, the cut was jam-packed with boats; reaching a tap did not look promising. Roger slowed alongside a narrowboat; there was no sign of anyone on board but, putting *Lily* in reverse, the doors opened and out stepped an elderly gentleman.

"Hello, do you mind if we fasten alongside; we need to top up with water?"

"That'll be fine. Pass me the line." We were quickly secure and topping up the tanks. The kind gentleman did not implant comfort in our minds about heading into Dublin. "You won't get me venturing down there but good luck to you." We prepared to set off. "If you come back this way, be sure to look me up," he added as I waved him farewell.

"Did he ask you to bring him back a parrot?" asked Roger when I returned to the wheelhouse. During the times when the canal was a thriving trade route, Dublin had appeared to many as being an exotic location and the question had become a regularly asked one of the bargees.

"No, you fool, of course he didn't!" We both laughed; Buster frowned and turned his back on us.

<h1 style="text-align:center">Chapter Thirteen</h1>

<h1 style="text-align:center">BANDIT COUNTRY AND BEYOND</h1>

Boaters were not permitted beyond Hazelhatch without assistance from Waterways Ireland. The village was considered the last safe place before heading into Dublin's city suburbs or what locals termed Bandit Country. As the area approached, a feeling of dread loomed. We had been subjected to tales of tinkers riding horses with muffled hooves along the towpaths at night, searching out vulnerable boaters, and gypsy children jumping on board for a ride along the cut. Fearing the worst, we took every precaution, locking windows and doors, removing the red ensign as advised by the lock keepers, although, as *Lily* had Nottingham in block capitals emblazoned across her rear, it seemed ridiculous, and covered the rigid-inflatable boat (RIB) with tatty old tarpaulins and chicken-feed sacks to disguise it.

The recent purchase of the RIB had caused some concern. Unlike our little tender, which fitted snugly on *Lily*'s back cabin roof and the roof rack of the car, this was a bit of a beast and had to be towed everywhere. It had already proved a good investment, being much more stable than the little tender Roger called 'the death trap' due to the way it wobbled when all three of us were in it. Buster could move around in the RIB without upsetting the balance; stepping on the soft surrounding tubes to gain access was easy for him. It also handled well, especially in rougher conditions, and its speed enabled quick crossings of large expanses of water.

In the event, all our precautions were to no avail as we were, at one point, ambushed by a group of youths who hurled stones at us. *Lily* took a couple of nasty hits but by far the more concerning problem was lack of water in the circle line around Dublin city centre, which caused her to run aground on more than one occasion. The amount of rubbish which was ultimately picked up by her prop was shocking. Waterways Ireland staff laughed it off and said we were lucky not to have picked up a mattress …

Standing at the bow, I peered into the clear waters of the Grand Canal. They were a treasure trove of rubbish: carrier bags filled with litter, bricks, shopping trolleys, old clothing, bicycles – all manner of items that had nothing in common save that they were surplus to the requirements of their owners. Every now and then, I raised my arm and called to Roger, signalling him to knock *Lily* into neutral, hoping she would glide over the offending items. With daylight fading, I noticed a white oval shape ahead in the water. As *Lily* slowly approached, the shape gradually materialised into the pale ivory face of a child, its open, staring eyes gazing at me through a mass of long blonde hair. My heart sank, I shuddered and, without taking my eyes off the face, raised an arm to alert Roger but no sound would come from my dry mouth. Then I realised the face belonged to a doll not a child and, with a sense of relief, turned to Roger, who leant out of the wheelhouse.

"Are you alright? You look like you've seen a ghost."

"It doesn't matter, it's nothing." I shook my head but I had seen a ghost and the haunting image remained with me for weeks.

The strangest items received courtesy of *Lily*'s inspection hatch included a large black umbrella, fully opened of course, and an artificial Christmas tree, complete with baubles and tinsel, which left me wondering what type of Christmas its owners must have had to warrant the tree ending up in the cut. Unfortunately, by this stage of the trip, I no longer had either the inspiration to photograph our finds or, with Roger's speedy slinging of the tree across the cut accompanied by a chorus of blue language, the speed to reach for the camera. Suddenly buckets of weed seemed appealing.

Waterways Ireland staff worked late into the evening to see us to safety, for which we were grateful. Despite setting out early in the morning, the problems encountered had put us over six hours behind. Approaching the entrance to the Grand Canal Basin, there was one last bridge to negotiate, the lowest on the system. We hoped *Lily* would slip beneath but, in a wicked twist of fate, she was a few centimetres too high. Exhausted and in darkness, we had to dismantle the wheelhouse. After years of practice, Roger and I usually worked well together; in a matter of minutes, we could have everything neatly stowed away but, tired and hungry, it was an unwelcome chore and I was surprised nothing was lost overboard during the process. Finally – and long overdue – we silently slid into the basin, moored up at the first available spot and slept like logs.

The next morning, Joe, who had been introduced to us at the HBA rally and was now the HBA chairman, headed along the pontoon, greeting us with a wide grin and plenty of well wishes. It was difficult to stop myself from flinging my arms around his neck and bursting into tears, such was the overwhelming sensation of discovering a familiar, friendly face after all the upset of the previous day. Buster eyed Joe suspiciously, perhaps wondering where his young Beagle puppy was. Joe was one of only a handful of people I knew brave enough to boat with a Beagle. Mick, moored a few yards away in his heritage barge *31B*, joined us. His barge was affectionately known as 'the jam boat' as it had once traded in preserves and confectionery. Not hearing *Lily* arrive, he had been surprised to discover us at first light. Eileen arrived later, having locked up from the Liffey in her 1890s River Barrow barge, *Rud Eile*; she was halfway around the Green and Silver Route. Warm greetings and cups of strong tea on board followed and, surrounded by the warmth and hospitality we had grown used to receiving on the Irish waterways, we felt calmer, safer and could finally appreciate what we had achieved.

The Basin complex at Ringsend was large, consisting of an inner and outer basin with graving docks. The smaller of the two, the Grand Canal Basin, where we were based, had excellent moorings surrounding the cube-shaped building of the Waterways Museum, known as the 'box in the docks'. One of the most striking buildings within this complex was the Grand Canal Theatre, best viewed after dark when the Urban Forest sculptures in front of it were fully illuminated. We whiled away twelve days waiting for a weather window, taking walks through Dublin, exploring parks and the shady tree-lined towpaths, but eventually city living began taking its toll. Buster had grown

Stormy skies over the Grand Canal Basin, Dublin

bored with the hard landscape and took to lying on the concrete pontoon, looking as if he had been robbed of his last Bonio. With a spell of good weather forecast, we decided to leave for Poolbeg Marina on the tidal Liffey, from where Dublin Bay could be accessed at any state of the tide.

Dropping down through the locks to join the River Liffey, I felt reborn; escaping the confines of the canal and finding myself in a wide expanse of water was rejuvenating. Upstream, the entrance to the reopened Royal Canal was visible. Despite the hard work of the Grand, we were tempted to head back and complete the Green and Silver Route, which many of our friends and colleagues were undertaking. Our trip downstream on the Liffey was short; black guillemots raced by *Lily*, their bright red legs almost lighting the way, guiding us into Poolbeg Marina.

Buster lay recumbent on *Lily*'s deck and snored loudly. It was a beautiful day. The seagulls glided by, complaining every now and then with a shrill cry, interrupting the gentle, musical lapping of the tidal River Liffey. The great white hulk of cruise ship *Azura* berthed in the docks opposite dwarfed *Lily*, its hundreds of tiny cabin windows catching the sunlight; glinting and glimmering, dancing metallic specks. It was a scene more reminiscent of a Mediterranean port: hot, humid, lazy days and sangria – not at all what one would expect of Ireland.

Poolbeg Marina was one of the most amazing places we had ever stayed; the constant coming and going of cruise liners, ferries, container vessels, cargo ships and fuel tankers kept us entertained and frequently up into the small hours. In wonder, we watched the little tugs push and pull to manoeuvre gargantuan vessels into their berths, performing a finely tuned, water-based dance every evening for which we had the best seats in the house.

A few days later, Roger and Buster prepared to take the fast-cat across the Irish Sea. Buster was going to stay with my parents whilst we attempted the sea voyage with *Lily*. In hindsight, this was perhaps the wrong decision. We had never embarked on a journey without Buster and maybe this would be a bad omen. I

Buster chilling out at Poolbeg Marina on the tidal River Liffey

hugged them both goodbye, asking Buster to be a good boy. Roger would be away overnight, driving Buster down to the South Coast before returning to the Midlands and collecting David, who had offered to be the third crew member our insurance company stipulated to undertake the crossing. *Lily* was not the same without Buster on board; it was very quiet. There was no gentle sound of his breathing, no muffled barks from his dreaming or gentle tap of his paw on my leg when he wanted to go outside. From the moment he walked out of the wheelhouse, I missed him dreadfully and my heart ached for his return.

David arrived wearing his familiar, wide smile and carrying a case, full of enthusiasm despite being almost arrested on charges of terrorism when the gas cylinder for inflating his life jacket was discovered in his bag. Roger had delivered Buster safely to animal farm. The journey had gone well and they had enjoyed a long walk on Buster's favourite beach in Wales so I could rest assured my boy was happy and content. We were all set, chomping at the bit to get underway, but the fickle Irish weather had other ideas and promptly slammed shut the weather window.

Whilst waiting for the next window of opportunity, Norwegian-born Kenneth sailed into Poolbeg in the battered *Johanna*, her weather-worn ensign in tatters. Kenneth had sailed *Johanna* to the Caribbean, for the most part single-handed, and was returning home to Oslo. Having reached Ireland via the Azores, he was taking a well-earned rest whilst waiting for his parents to join him. Together, they were going to sail *Johanna* home, heading back through Scotland's Caledonian Canal. "Taking a shortcut home," Kenneth called it. To us, it sounded a trip full of wonder and we delighted in listening to his plans for the voyage.

How we laughed and enjoyed Kenneth's company during our prolonged stay in Poolbeg; the stories of his sailing adventures entertained us for days, as did bottles of wine from his onboard cellar and the boxes of sweet, sticky, homemade cakes Shirley had given to Roger for the journey home. Without doubt, one of the wonders of boating was chance meetings with people; boaters often touched each other's lives briefly yet left memories that lasted a lifetime.

A few days later, an opportunity to depart arose and, after informing Dublin Port Authority and the coastguard of our intentions, we eagerly set off. Passing familiar landmarks and navigation aids that, from the fast-cat or ferry looked tiny but which towered above *Lily*, she seemed small and vulnerable. Some distance off Howth Head, in fading light and a nasty rolling sea which *Lily* was not riding well, a unanimous decision to abandon the attempt was made as the prospect of battling through rough seas for hours on end was not appealing. Retreating with tails between our legs, we found ourselves swiftly running out of time. With no foreseeable spell of calm weather ahead, we had to resort to road transport. Roger was bitterly disappointed — it was not the end to our time in Ireland that he had planned — but secretly I was glad as the sea crossing held no appeal for me. It was the journey across the Pennines on the English canals that had captured my imagination.

MGM Boats at Dún Laoghaire on the far side of Dublin Bay had a suitable lift and the transport company we had previously used were free at short notice to rescue us. With everything booked, we enjoyed a beautiful morning cruise down the Liffey and across Dublin Bay. Gifted with warm sunshine and calm waters added to the frustration at not being able to complete the voyage home. The few days spent at Dún Laoghaire Marina were fantastic; the facilities were good and there was the added attraction of resident seals. The huge harbour was designed by

A Dún Laoghaire Harbour seal

Scottish engineer John Rennie and constructed in 1817 using local stone from Dalkey Quarry. Considered one of the finest artificial harbours in the world, I could not help thinking how much Buster would have enjoyed barking at the seals, taking leisurely strolls along the promenade and indulging in the odd ice cream.

A soft drizzle fell as we retrieved the RIB from the waters of Dún Laoghaire harbour. The seals gathered to bid us farewell, appearing melancholy as if they knew our departure was tugging at heartstrings. We had unknowingly chosen a day with one of the lowest spring tides, making the lift to the quayside for *Lily* substantial. As Hutchinson's lorry pulled into place and *Lily* was lowered onto it, the sun broke through, giving us the chance to dry off the dismantled wheelhouse before she was covered with a tarpaulin for the journey. *Lily* may not have crossed the Irish Sea under her own steam but she travelled home in style on the Dún Laoghaire fast-cat service – no ordinary ferry for her.

For the last time, we made the journey along the North Wales coast, passing familiar places: favourite dog walks, hotels and restaurants we had occupied to and from Ireland. As Roger drove, I drifted in and out of sleep until billowing clouds of steam from the Trent Valley's power stations welcomed us home. We never ventured down the Barrow or along the SEW with *Lily* but we had had a fantastic three years in Ireland, during which time we learnt many lessons: to take tales with a pinch of salt and to enjoy the craic, go with the flow. For us, Ireland's truly amazing waterways and laid-back way of life remained unfinished business.

We never embarked on another sea trip or, indeed, any other kind of waterway wandering without having the Admiral on board. He and *Lily* had become one; almost unable to function without each other. Both Roger and I were scolded harshly when we arrived to collect him from animal farm. Rushing up to us, he let out an ear-rattling 'barooo', leaning back and refusing to be stroked or hugged. His doggy dialect translated as, 'Did you two seriously think you'd be able to take that boat across the Irish Sea without me? Had you forgotten I'm the Admiral of the ship?'

Section Three

EUROPE

Buster's travels in Europe

DENMARK

GERMANY

THE NETHERLANDS

BALTIC SEA

NORTH SEA

Gilleleje
Helsingør
Rungsted
Ven
Hundsted
Jyllinge
Orø
Roskilde
Copenhagen
Rødvig
Stege
Præstø
Vordingborg
Nykøbing
Gedser
Bergstaaken
Lübeck
Schwerin
Lauenberg
Domitz
Plau
Waren
Mirow
Fürstenberg
Rheinsberg
Obere-Havel
Oder-Havel
Spree
Berlin
Schmöckwitz
Potsdam
Brandenburg
Magdeburg
Hanover
Osnabruck
Mittellandkanal
Dortmund-Ems
Groningen
Meppel
Dokkum
Harlingen
Makkum
Amsterdam

Elbe-Muritz
Muritz-Havel
Stör
Elbe
Elbe
Havel
Elbe-Havel
Mittellandkanal

Chapter One

TIME MACHINE TO DENMARK

We did not have much time to waste at the Channel Tunnel. It was a hot day and Buster lapped up a bowl of cool water with grateful appreciation in the little shade the towed RIB provided before trotting off with Roger.

I looked around the car park and wondered where people were heading; were they on holidays, visiting family or on business matters? Buster's time machine was loaded to bursting point, on top a new silver roof box. We were moving and the anticipation of what lay ahead caused my stomach to flutter nervously.

When the boys returned, it was time to board. I scooped Buster up and placed him into the car, fastening his harness.

"What adventures await the puppy today?" I whispered into his ear whilst reaching over to click the final fastening into place. His wet nose nuzzled my ear and the sweet scent of summer warmth from his fur filled my nostrils.

"All set?" asked Roger as I climbed into the passenger seat. I took one last look around, scanned the view of my homeland and wondered what life had in store for us in Europe. I took a deep breath.

Buster eagerly awaits the opening of the picnic bag at the service station in Belgium

"Yeah, all set. Now let's get out of here."

On the train, Buster slept in the car as if on the road; as there was no need for him to get out, he knew no different but, without the car's air-conditioning, it was hot and stuffy. In less than thirty minutes, we were through. Emerging from the darkness of the tunnel into France, Buster stirred and woke. Roger opened the window, allowing Buster to drink in new scents and get some much-needed fresh air.

"Does it smell different, Buzzy?" He was busy snorting and sniffing; I guessed it must. The first part of the journey had gone well. Buster had left his homeland; now I prayed all the procedures had been carried out correctly and his pet passport would allow him to cross borders without problems. More importantly, I hoped returning would go smoothly. I would not find out until the spring.

With the air-conditioning in full swing, we settled down for the long journey ahead. Blurring images of crop fields, small villages, sweeping wind turbines and speeding cars accompanied us. The day was beginning to cool when Roger pulled over at a service station in Belgium. Setting out a blanket to enjoy a picnic supper courtesy of Shirley, I wondered how long it would be before I again tasted her delicious homemade Scotch eggs and quiche. Buster seemed bemused. He sat on the grass after eating his dinner and watched the trucks pull in and out, hissing air brakes and mechanical vibration. He was not interested in snuffling or walking, only watching, as if he needed to concentrate in case questions were asked later.

The drive through France, Belgium and the Netherlands passed quickly but Germany was a large country; the almost endless fields of maize and towering wind turbines went on and on, long into the evening. It was late and we were tired; diversions at roadworks on the motorway near Essen had led into the town. Confused and lost, we sat quietly in the car, emotions flooding over us, the only noise Buster's gentle snoring.

The next day, we entered Denmark, drove up the Jutland peninsula, crossed onto the island of Funen and headed for the 9.3 mile (15km) long Storebælt Bridge. This spectacular piece of engineering linked Funen to the island of Sjælland, our new home, and was the highlight of the journey.

We had rented a house perched on a slope; with a spectacular garden divided into several terraces, it stretched down to the shores of Lake Buresø. A stream trickled from top to bottom, flowing in and out of pools as it went. There were areas of low-growing ground elder and lady's mantle for Buster to wade through, hedgerows for him to duck beneath and grassy lawns to lounge upon. Whilst Roger started his new job, I set about making the place feel homely. To help us settle in Denmark and deal with any red tape, we had Gita, a relocation specialist. She found Buster a local vet, recorded him on the Danish dog register and helped Roger and me apply for residency. We all laughed when Buster was accepted into the country before us mere humans.

Just a few weeks later, devastating news reached us: Roger's father had passed away. Les had in so many ways been the root for our inspiration to explore the waterways. As a young boy, Roger had been taken on narrowboat holidays and, later, he and his father had delighted in discovering lost canal routes. He was our greatest advocate, always encouraging, eager to hear where we had been or what we had planned. We were all hit hard by the loss.

Les had always had a soft spot for Buster and had loved to see him but his frail, translucent skin, a result of old age and diabetes, had meant Buster's stubby claws sometimes tore so, despite the urge to give him a hug, a gentle pat on the head was all we could allow. Buster had loved the visits just as much. To him, Les's house was an Aladdin's cave; he never knew what he would find. Roaming through the rooms of Les's house, Buster would occasionally find a delectable treat; if lucky, the large, white, chalky disc of a peppermint, one of Les's naughty treats. During one visit, Buster could be heard in the bedroom, snuffling about, groaning and obviously trying to reach something.

"What are you up to, Buster?" Roger had called.

"There's nothing in there to hurt him; he's alright," Les had replied.

A few minutes later, Buster had emerged from the bedroom, his mouth bubbling and oozing as if a mad, rabid dog. He was smacking his chops as bubbles emerged to froth and dribble down his chin. We had all sat and watched in disbelief, then Les had begun to chuckle. "I dropped that and it rolled under the bed. I'd been meaning to ask someone to reach it." Buster had picked up a well-known brand of antacid tablet, looking similar to the brand of peppermint he so liked.

Roger returned to England alone for the funeral as the journey was too much for us all to undertake. On the day he arrived home, I drove to the airport to collect him. From the rearview mirror, he looked like a little school boy, lost and forlorn.

"Here he is, Buzzy."

I jumped out of the car and ran into Roger's arms. I held him tight but it was not enough to stop tears from falling. Buster erupted into a series of barks; he had twisted himself around on the back seat and was gazing out of the window, eagerly awaiting to be reunited with Roger.

"For goodness' sake, listen to that fuss. You'd best go and give him a hug. He's really missed you." I planted a kiss on his wet cheek. Roger rushed to the car and flung open the door. Sounds of barking and laughter filled the Danish streets, carrying some of the heartache away with them.

With the RIB in Denmark, there was the opportunity to explore local waters. At weekends, we would pack a picnic and launch the RIB on Roskilde Fjord. It was not the same without *Lily* but at least we were afloat. Buster loved having the wind beneath his ears as the boat zipped over the water at high speed, then delighted even more in a walk and a picnic lunch at a new location.

Along with the house came the use of a small boat and electric motor. Most evenings when Roger returned from work, we pootled around the lake, each with a halo of midges hovering above our heads.

"If we get *Lily* put in the water somewhere around the Hook of Holland, we can take our time travelling through the country, visit Amsterdam and cross the Ijsselmeer. It will be the trip of a lifetime." Roger was in full flow, enthusiastic and keen as he steered the little boat by the elegant homes bordering the lake. "I think it's called the mast-up route; it's a way for yachts to reach the Baltic without having to de-mast or sail all the way around the coast."

I began researching, gathering maps and guides, reading up as much as time would allow. Buster, by my side on the sofa as I clunked away on the laptop, snored heavily and occasionally gave me a swift jab in the ribs with his back leg.

Being away from *Lily* was hard but it was not going to be forever. In the early days, we were busy finding our feet in Denmark so it was not something to dwell on. I was occupied writing articles and had offered *Roger and Buster enjoy a spin in the RIB*

to help boaters heading to Ireland. This had triggered quite a response; people were hungry for information and a special friendship with fellow barge owners Steve and Della soon developed. They were about to embark on their own Irish adventure and regular correspondence with them became a welcome part of my day. Putting time into researching new waterways for *Lily* helped ease the separation; Roger and I talked about the trip and started to research marinas. I set about purchasing items to collect from England in the spring: courtesy flags, new filters, various engine spares. My parents would telephone almost daily saying they had received a parcel, small package, a pallet of hull paint. Preparing for our new adventure afloat was exciting. We were eagerly looking forward to it but then things went wrong …

Chapter Two

IN HOT PURSUIT

The mature beech woods surrounding our new home stretched for miles; they were full of walks, tracks and trails and home to deer by the hundreds. When Buster fancied a change, there was different terrain around the lake or across nearby crop fields. At the end of our gravel lane, there were meadows where horses grazed. I would talk to them, pulling up handfuls of lush grass rich in buttercups and red clover for them to munch on.

Most days, Buster and I were on our main walk for two hours but, on this day, I was clock-watching; the chimney sweep was due. We had rushed our walk, the same circuit but in less time, and were both tired. I returned with time to spare and let us in through the back door, taking off Buster's collar and lead. He headed into the garden, where we would usually sit together for a short while before getting on with the day's chores. I flicked on the coffee machine and joined Buster, who was lying on the patio doing an excellent snoring-awake impression.

"Are you alright, Buzz?" There was a loud rustle in the undergrowth. It was a deer and a deer spelt disaster.

Buster went from exhausted, flopped-out pooch to a hunter on a mission. He pulled back his head and erupted into a full-blown 'barooo'. The deer began

259

to run and Buster followed in full cry, delighted to be on the hunt. Together, they hurtled up and down the terraces, the deer unable to find a way out. I was terrified it was going to break its spindly legs on the stone terracing as it leapt from one stone to another, desperately looking for an exit.

Reaching the lawn at the bottom of the garden, the deer was suddenly fully exposed. Buster raced towards it, thundering across the short grass.

"Barooo, barooo, barooo," he cried, driven on by uncontrollable instinct. The deer turned and headed back up the terraces, leaping in great bounds whilst Buster tore through everything, the trail left behind making the garden look as if it had been flattened by a tornado. When the deer appeared by the house, I saw my chance to capture Buster. If the deer ran past me and jumped the low fence, it could escape down the wooded footpath and I could head off Buster. Perfect.

The deer prepared to jump but, at the last moment, spotted me and promptly turned, leaping over Buster and

Buster relaxing in the garden of our new Danish home

continuing back down the terraces. I ran at Buster but he was too quick and had already turned to follow. After years of living with a Beagle, I knew it was useless but shouted nonetheless, "Buster, leave it." I tried lowering my voice in a desperate attempt to sound demanding, but it was no good. I waited on the top terrace but this time they did not return. I heard Buster's cry from some distance away; they had somehow fled the garden and were racing through the woods.

Grabbing my mobile, I ran across the driveway and knocked on the door of my landlady's house, thrust the keys in her hand and explained about the chimney sweep. I ran along the lanes, picking up the footpath through the woods and around the lake. Everything was a blur but Buster's cry could still be heard. I followed as best I could. As deer and dogs do not stick to footpaths, they could be some distance from where the paths would lead me. There was no sign of Buster in the woods although I thought I glimpsed his tail, whipping back and forth like a battle flag on the brow of a grassy meadow. By then, his cries had stopped and I could not be sure. I called but there was no response. There was a road a short distance ahead and panic was building. Sick with worry, I phoned Roger, disturbing him at work, and asked if he could slowly drive around to see if he could find Buster. Over two hours had passed and there was no sight or sound of him.

Reluctantly, I began walking back to the house, beside myself, hardly able to catch my breath. Roger phoned to say he had driven around the lake and seen nothing so was going to head home. I was to meet him there. My feet were finding it difficult to move; after our walk that morning and two hours searching for Buster, I was exhausted, my mind full of dire scenarios. I was not sure Buster would find his way home; the habitat was new to him and he did not have his collar on so, if someone found him, they would have no contact details. We would only be reunited if a vet or local authority traced us through his microchip. I felt light-headed, as if in a dream; this could not be happening …

I dragged myself up the steep footpath leading away from the lake and reached the top as the mobile rang. It was Roger.

"I've got him, he's alright."

I collapsed onto my knees and howled like a baby, watched over by curious horses which, up until that moment, had been happily grazing.

"Thank goodness, is he really alright?"

"Well, he's totally exhausted and looks a mess but, yeah, he's OK. I found him collapsed in a heap by the front door. I'd only been in a couple of minutes and heard a thud, went to look and there he was. I'm going to get him in the shower. You take it easy; make your way back slowly."

Mustering the last of my strength, I raced home to find Roger drying Buster, who was wrapped in towels and still damp when I flung my arms around him.

"Come on, Al, let me finish drying the poor old boy." But I could not let go. I thought I had lost him for sure. I tried to explain to Roger but the words would not come; instead, I blabbed and gasped through big, salty tears.

"I know," Roger put an arm around me. I looked up into his eyes; they too were full of tears. "Look at him, he's alright now."

Wrapped in damp towels, Buster wore a deep frown and looked thoroughly fed up but I could not help smiling at him; he was such a funny old boy and I loved him deeply. As Roger finished towelling Buster, he grumbled under his breath but sat and dozed between us once the hairdryer was warming his fur. He was soon asleep.

For the next few days, Buster and I took it easy. Our walks were short, he appeared tired and his legs were stiff but he was bright and cheerful. At the weekend, we took the RIB out for a spin on Roskilde Fjord but Buster was not his usual self; the water was a little choppy and he did not relax as normal. I slowly increased the length of Buster's walks over the next few days and he seemed to be enjoying them but, as we climbed out of a wooded valley to join a farm track, he sat down in the long wayside grass, looked at me with sad eyes and refused to go on.

Despite encouragement, I could not get Buster to move, not even for a treat. I attempted to carry him but he was far too heavy. I struggled with him in my arms for a few hundred yards then gently placed him back down but he would not stand; he would only sit. With Roger overseas on business, I could not telephone him to collect us in the car. I was running out of ideas but had one trick left. Turning my back on Buster, I walked away. Very slowly and stiffly, Buster raised his plump bottom off the ground and began walking after me but he was struggling and I was worried for him. He took a few more steps, stopped and sat down.

"What is it, old chap?" I walked back to him and leant down to rub his neck. Buster turned his head and pushed the back of his neck into my hand, enjoying the rub. "You take it easy, there's no hurry." I sat on the ground beside him, wrapped one arm around his shoulders and listened to the skylarks whilst he rested.

When Buster was ready, he rose to his feet and slowly began making his way back home. From somewhere, he had found inner strength, for which I was grateful. It was a long, slow walk back. Every now and then, I lifted him into my arms, carrying him as far as I could, then he would walk a little further by himself. Eventually, we made it home and, after a restful afternoon, he was back to his normal self.

When Roger telephoned that evening, I explained what had happened and we agreed to get Buster to the vet as soon as Roger arrived home the following day. After dinner, Buster and I settled down in front of the television but, an hour or so later, he wanted to get up. Walking across the room, he collapsed in a heap on the floor; his legs had given out beneath him. I rushed to him and slid down on my knees. He wagged his tail and looked at me. He was bright and alert but, when I tried to lift him onto his legs, he had no power to stand; he just went limp. I remembered his life jacket was in the house. It was a struggle getting him into it but, once on, with its strong handle on the back, I could lift him and move him into his bed. At least there he was more comfortable. Later that evening, he tried to get up and go outside but again his legs could hardly take his weight. Carrying him outside by supporting him in his lifejacket, he squatted and relieved himself then almost collapsed again under his own weight. There was something seriously wrong with his legs.

Charlotte, our local vet, checked Buster out and, suspecting cruciate ligament damage, referred him to a colleague based on the outskirts of Copenhagen. Claus, a specialist in orthopaedic disorders, diagnosed ligament damage but, after taking fluid samples from Buster's knees, found a more serious underlying problem aggravating it: Idiopathic Immune-Mediated Polyarthritis (IIMP) — an auto-immune disease whereby the immune system attacks the body, in Buster's case, the fluid sacks surrounding the knee joints. If not detected, this could quickly lead to broken bones as, without fluid, these were vulnerable to damage and infection.

The only way to suppress the disease was with steroids. The treatment was intense to begin with and Buster practically rattled with all the drugs inside him. Cod liver oil capsules and multi-vitamins also became part of Buster's drug regime, which was complicated. Roger devised a spreadsheet, making it easier to mark off daily doses and keep check on the slow reduction of the steroid treatment. The drugs made Buster extremely thirsty; he would drink a lot and need to go outside every hour or so. We took it in turns to sleep downstairs with him although it was Roger who took the lion's share. Buster came to rely on and trust him completely throughout this episode as Roger became his carer, carrying him in and out of the house, up and down stairs until, slowly, he began to heal.

Buster already had a few fatty lumps on his body. They were not a major cause for concern and we had been monitoring them but, with the steroid treatment, they began increasing in size. One in particular was becoming much larger; although unsightly, it was harmless. Buster was not well enough to face an operation and putting in a drain was a risk with the immune system disease, so the lumps had to be left for the time being.

Our first Christmas in Denmark was not a happy one; there was no *Lily* and Buster was poorly but we tried to make the best of it. Buster was unable to walk as far as the woods he loved. One chilly December day, as Christmas fast approached, I knelt beside him and, with tears in my eyes, whispered in his ear, "Don't worry, Buzzy, if you can't make it to the woods, we'll bring the woods to you." The following day, Roger and I went out and purchased a real Christmas tree, which Buster dozed happily beneath throughout the festive season.

As Buster slowly recovered, he managed to walk further in the garden. I patiently waited for him, come rain or shine, as he snuffled or sat and gazed at the view. The terraces became our goals; one by one, as the weeks passed, we gradually made our way further and further down the garden. The walk back was steep; it had to be taken slowly and, if Buster could not manage, I would lift him into my arms and struggle back to the house with him. One day, instead of going to the next terrace, Buster walked straight by and, with determination, headed down onto the main lawn, along the

wooden jetty and sat by the lake. I crouched beside him and hugged him tightly to my body. Through my tears, I whispered to him, "Do you know what you have just done, Buzzy boy?" He wriggled to escape my grasp and

Buster was unwell during our first Christmas in Denmark but that did not stop him making a mess with the wrapping paper!

peered up into my wet eyes. "You made it to the bottom of the garden, all by yourself. My super, super boy, my super one!"

From that day on, Buster walked to the jetty almost every day, even when the snow fell and it was bitterly cold. I would make myself a mug of hot chocolate, sprinkle it with marshmallows and carry it with me. When we reached the jetty, I lifted Buster onto the wooden seat and he would tuck himself under my arm, push his body into mine and there we would sit, cuddled together, loving and supporting each other. In my pocket, there would be one or two of his favourite treats and, when I had finished my drink, he would eagerly nuzzle me for them. Side by side, we would then make the long, slow climb back to the house.

Chapter Three

LILY GOES DUTCH

I t was a long drive back to England but, with Buster still recovering, lazy days of sleeping in his time machine were a good way of restricting his movement. There was no need to have worried about re-entering the country with him; the procedure at the Channel Tunnel was as straightforward as buying groceries at a supermarket. One bleep of the scanner and all his information was there for the staff to check against his pet passport – the wonders of modern technology. Buster gazed up at me in astonishment when the scanner held over the chip inside his body gave out an electronic bleep.

"Look at that – special offer: buy one get one free."

"You want another one?" I joked with Roger. Buster threw us a look of contempt, turned his back on us and sulked.

Heading downriver towards Newark Marina, the towering, shiny, metal chimneys and pipework of Staythorpe Power Station loomed out of the early-morning mist. It had changed a lot since we had been away, the small, red-brick building replaced by a modern, futuristic-looking structure. The waters of the Trent gushed over Averham Weir to wash the webbed feet of the mute swans resting on its narrow ledge as I guided *Lily* into Newark Dyke. Buster gave a whimper as *Lily* glided past Hilary's house; he had met up with Bunty, the love of his life, as well as dear Roxy and, despite not being able to walk far, relished time in their company, as I did in Hilary's. At Newark Marina, the crane was ready for *Lily*, the strops hanging loose in the water. Roger drove her straight in and shut down the engine. Next time *Lily* would be started, she would be on Dutch waterways.

The idea of travelling northwards through the Dutch waterways had been shelved, the plan curtailed to ease the burden on Buster's recovery. Instead, *Lily* was going to be transported directly to Harlingen in the northern province of Friesland, cutting a huge chunk off the original planned journey. Over the next few days, Roger, with help from David, was going to black *Lily*'s lower hull, fit new anodes and give her a general spruce-up so she looked her best for arrival in a new country.

Looking resplendent in new paintwork and sporting her new SSR number – an advised but not essential requirement for cruising in Europe – *Lily* was good to go and finally loaded onto the lorry. Whilst she headed north to Hull for the ferry to the Hook of Holland, we headed south, taking the Channel Tunnel and driving through France, Belgium and on to the Netherlands.

It was 7 a.m. when we arrived at Harlingen. McDonald's had just opened so we headed in and filled our bodies with much-needed strong coffee and a hot breakfast. Buster ate in the car park and, after a walk, we drove the short distance to Scheepsreparatie Friesland (SRF), where we would be reunited with *Lily*. It had been a rough, windswept night. I had worried about the ferry crossing and how *Lily* had fared; I was eager to see her but, on arrival, she was nowhere in sight.

"I hope everything's alright." We both scanned the boatyard in disappointment. A light drizzle was falling, the sky a nondescript grey and lack of sleep beginning to take its toll. Roger's mobile rang; it was the driver saying he would not arrive until 10 a.m. but that everything was fine following the rough ferry crossing. With our minds at ease, we snuggled down in the car outside the main gates of SRF and dozed. Every time I woke, I glanced expectantly up the road, hoping to see the truck on which *Lily* was perched high and dry appear from around the corner.

True to his word, at 10 a.m. the driver turned the truck hauling *Lily* into the approach road.

"Here she is." I leapt out of the car into the dank drizzle. My cry awoke Buster with a start, who sat bolt upright and peered through the rain-spattered glass to see what all the fuss was about. Once Buster saw *Lily*, he let out some happy squeaks; his home had arrived and he was keen to take up residence. As the truck passed, I looked up at *Lily*. Sitting in the galley window, wearing that same cheeky grin, was Dunrovin Duckling. I was surprised to see the duck after the rough journey but there it was, looking ahead, facing the bow.

SRF were quick and efficient; soon *Lily* was lifted by their huge, overhead crane and placed back into the water. The employees chuckled when they saw *Lily*, saying how small she was compared to the usual craft lifted in and out. It was obvious from the other boats in the yard and at the surrounding moorings *Lily* was going to shake off the 'large' reputation she had acquired in England. A few minutes later, the wheelhouse had been erected and we were underway, moving *Lily* into her temporary berth.

Our first encounter with a box mooring resulted in instant dislike. The idea was to drive the bow into the quay, passing between two upright, wooden poles onto which the rear of the boat was secured, after which the front was fastened on the quay so the vessel was left floating in the box-like space. Trying to disembark was almost impossible, especially with a barge. *Lily*'s bow had a blunt point and two large, handmade rope fenders; it was unlikely she would ever be close enough to allow her crew to step off.

Below decks, everything was as we had left it. We were home and all together again, safe in our own little world. One of the things I loved most about *Lily* was having my home constantly with me, a bit like a tortoise. After the hustle and bustle of the day, retreating below, I was instantly at home. I could be in the centre of a bustling city or the open countryside and know everything which made my life comfortable was below decks.

Our first morning on board *Lily* in Friesland and conversation turned to where we should base her long term. SRF had been kind enough to allow us the much-hated box mooring over the Easter period, enough time to find *Lily* a new home. With the time machine it was easy, possible to cover more ground and see some of the countryside and familiarise ourselves with the area.

"There are quite a few marinas around here." I pointed at the waterways chart. It was like a road map. I had never seen so many waterways in one place; it would take a lifetime to navigate them all. "It also looks as if there'll be some good walking places for Buster." Buster perked up at the mention of his name and watched me closely.

"OK, we'll head out that way and see what we find."

Buster was not keen on the Lunegat Marina; he thought it sounded like the sort of place where a mad cat resided so he was pleased when I crossed it off the list. We stumbled upon a small boating club, basic but nice and, more importantly, secure — top priority with us being so far away in Denmark. The village of Westergeest in which it was situated was in the middle of nowhere, surrounded by large, flat meadows where sheep grazed amongst flocks of lapwings and oystercatchers. The wind blew strongly, raced and whistled across the open landscape, disturbing the waters of the little dykes, running along them as if a shiver down the spine. Like the British fens, here was a landscape of big skies and plenty of space. I wondered if it seemed familiar to Buster, *Harlingen in Friesland, The Netherlands*

Buster wearing a broad sometimes-smile at Lily's new mooring in Westergeest

who was born in the rural wilds of Lincolnshire. He certainly loved a view and, as old age approached, would happily spend time gazing into the yonder, perhaps dreaming of fitter days when he chased hares across the wide expanse without a care in the world.

Henk, the harbour master, spoke no English but somehow Roger made himself understood with the help of a few old mariners who were interested in why a British couple would want to rent a berth at their boat club. Buster sat quietly and listened to the conversation; perhaps he understood better than us. I walked him around the small site with its grassy banks separating the main body of the marina from the canal; he paddled and drank the water from the slipway. He liked it and that was good enough for me.

Although Buster was happy to be back on *Lily*, things had changed. He could no longer race up and down the stairs – his back legs did not have sufficient strength – instead, he sat at the top or bottom and waited patiently for one of us to lift him. He could not jump onto our bed at night; now he had to tap the bottom of it with his paw or give a squeak to let us know he needed a Buster Boost. On deck, I was fearful for him, afraid he may stumble and hurt himself, but he made his way around *Lily* as before, only slower and more carefully. It was obvious he knew the limits of his body's capability and adjusted his actions and movements accordingly. In the wheelhouse, he took up his usual position in his bed on the chart table and was his happy old self, surveying the scenes unfolding before him. At times, the change in Buster made me feel sad but seeing him happily playing the Admiral changed that.

Over the years, Buster's long, soft, velvety ears had brushed my cheeks and wiped away many fallen tears. His cool, wet nose had nuzzled into my neck and his warm body had snuggled tightly against me on dark lonely nights. Cocooned in the cosiness of *Lily*, he had lived through some of the darkest of days and some of the happiest with me, always unquestioning, forgiving and loving. He listened without interrupting, knew when I was hurting and realised a brief brush against my leg or hand was all that was needed to bring a smile and some comfort. I owed this Beagle my life and well-being. I was determined to get him through the illness, make him fit and healthy, see him into double figures, support him as he had me and make all our lives as full as possible.

Chapter Four

FROLICKING IN FRIESLAND

The Netherlands: land of tulips, windmills, quaint little houses with neat gardens, dykes, canals and barges, large round cheeses, wooden clogs and flat landscapes dominated by big skies. How I wished I had paid more attention at school during geography lessons when the land reclamations of the Netherlands came across as a bore to a teenager. Now I was hungry for information about this land, whose origins could have been born from a science-fiction novel. Friesland appeared to be a strange place; the coast made up of shifting sands and mud flats, dotted with low-lying islands reached by deep, scoured channels. A region famed for black-and-white cattle, ice skating marathons and polevaulting over dykes.

Lily's first trip on the waterways of Friesland began with a sharp frosty morning that gave way to a beautifully cloudless sky and sunshine strong enough to warm the wheelhouse and allow windows to be opened. It was glorious. Heading eastwards along the huge Van Harinxmakanaal towards *Lily*'s new home, we came face to face with some gigantic commercial vessels. The waterway linked the coast with the Prinses Margrietkanaal, the main inland route for freight travelling across Northern Europe; seeing huge commercial vessels was going to become a regular occurrence. We were also joined by some beautiful Dutch

Traditional Dutch sailing vessel

tjalks and schuitjes; traditional curvy-hulled sailing vessels, broad of beam, majestic – the buxom maiden aunts of the waterways.

In a lush meadow bordering the canal, a farmer was helping a sheep give birth to the second of her twin lambs. Almost immediately, the damp, yellow-coloured lamb was on its feet, nuzzling and attempting to suckle from its mother. Oystercatchers laughed mockingly and lapwings darted and weaved through the sky like kites being constantly tugged back and forth by wind and string. The sails of the windmills – both ancient and modern – turned; large, creaking, wooden sails and modern, super-slim, polycarbon blades, both possessing a beauty of their own. Friesland was already a feast for the eyes and it seemed Buster felt the same, paying close attention to the surroundings as we slipped silently through them. He was recovering well, much better than hoped, and we were sure the time on the boat would further aid his recovery. After all, this was the place he really regarded as home.

Overnight, we moored on a small island in Bergumer Meer. It was ideal for Buster as he could roam unhindered; there were no other boats about and he could not go missing. Sat in the wheelhouse, Roger and I watched the huge commercial craft coming and going across the lake. As it grew dark, a large Dutch barge, no more than a silhouette against the inky-coloured sky, silently eased into the moorings, keeping *Lily* company throughout the night. The commercials kept working; all that was visible were the slow-moving dots of their navigation lights drifting across the darkness.

Springtime in Friesland was breathtakingly beautiful, a kaleidoscopic whirl of colour, with even the smallest hamlet having a display of bulbs ranging from the delicately thin crocuses planted directly into lawns to full-blown, blousy displays in glazed pots, wooden tubs and window boxes. Commercial tulip fields – long striped rows of rainbow colours planted in bulk – were located further south in provinces bordering the North Sea. In Friesland, bulbs were planted for the sheer joy of spring.

Dokkum was the most northerly town there. Compact and close to Westergeest for short trips, it offered a variety of walks for Buster. Its people were friendly and welcoming; the moorings in a wonderful setting nestled beneath the former ramparts, overlooked by two spectacular windmills, one of which housed a pet shop. It was not just old Amsterdam which had mice in windmills. During the spring, the tulips were a spectacle, bursting from the grassy banks of the ramparts to encircle the town in a colourful bangle of blooms.

"I'm going to buy Mum a bag of these tulip bulbs; they're the same as the ones on display along the ramparts." Roger wasn't listening to me as we stepped into the supermarket in Dokkum. He was on a mission – to pick up a loaf of our favourite corn bread; beyond the crust, its bright yellow interior the colour of sunshine, lay a slice of summer there for the taking. It was not until returning to *Lily* and unpacking that I took a closer look at the label on the pack of bulbs.

"Hey, Roger, you're never going to believe this; the packet of bulbs has *Lily* on the label." Sure enough, there was *Lily* moored beneath the windmill on Dokkum's ramparts. We raced back to the supermarket and cleaned them out, the bulbs making wonderful gifts for family and friends back home.

Buster surrounded by colourful tulips in Dokkum

Overseas, things were different and it took a while to get used to how they worked. Payment for opening lift and swing bridges was collected by a bridge keeper, who usually lowered a wooden clog attached to a fishing rod to a crew member of the passing boat. Having a collection of coins on board became a priority. At our first bridge, Buster was at the bow with me when the clog was lowered. He thought it was great fun to snap at it when it dangled in front of his nose. The novelty was short-lived; just as well, given the numerous bridges in Friesland.

No one seemed to get up early and boaters did not get underway until later. Having Buster, we were usually up first thing and preferred to get underway as soon as possible; travelling along deserted waterways as dawn broke was magical. This often resulted in us arriving at a marina or town harbour as it was being vacated, giving us a choice of mooring spaces. It meant our boating routine shifted. We used to travel late into the evenings; now we would be settled before lunch, allowing more time ashore.

Buster's leg problems meant that off-water activities were limited. It was a growing concern that we would go somewhere with Buster only for him to be unable to make the return walk. We adjusted to suit him, the least we could do after all the years of friendship he had given us. It then occurred to me a bike trailer would solve the problem.

Boating with Buster

Purchase of a doggyhut bike trailer opened new doors. On a warm spring day, Roger unpacked the contraption at Dokkum for Buster's first trip. Dozing in the sunshine, Buster became aware something out of the ordinary was happening. He opened one eye and watched Roger speculatively. Buster was soon up and eager to get closer. He had sat in it and been pushed about in the garden at home but this was the first time he had seen it attached to a bicycle.

Buster was desperate to get into the trailer but was unable to muster the strength in his back legs. Roger carefully picked him up and placed him inside where his bed was waiting for him. Buster looked extremely comfy, lying on the new blanket I had placed in his bed, which was now looking very tatty. It had been patched several times but to throw it away was unthinkable; he had had it since the day we got him. With a tickle behind the ears and words of encouragement, the canvas doorway was zipped up and he was ready for his first trip.

"Right then, here goes." Roger pushed on the pedal and they began to move, going slowly along the ramparts to the windmill. Turning, Roger made his way back. "Blimey," he said, pulling up. "That was hard work; this dog weighs a ton." Poor Buster, he was overweight and it was

Buster with his doggyhut bike trailer

something we were working hard on, with limited success. The steroids made him constantly hungry and, combined with a Beagle's desire to always be eating, it was a recipe for disaster. "I'm going to go right around the ramparts with him now."

"OK, be careful and you be a good boy, Buzz." Through the mesh window, I could see him clearly looking back at me. I watched them set off, passing the boats and tulips. I heard Buster bark. I waved at him and realised what he was thinking – he was being taken away from me. As the pair of them faded into the distance, barking rang out. People stopped to see what had caused the dog such distress. We were rarely apart these days and his illness had made him clingy.

About quarter of an hour later, I heard Buster's familiar bark in the distance; the boys were on the final leg. The barking got louder and louder; Buster knew he was almost back. When they arrived, Roger was puffed out and Buster was beside himself at being reunited with me.

"He barked like that all the way round. You'd better come next time."

The Lits-Lauwersmeer Route passed through Drachten and the Âlde Feanen National Park towards Sneek. The Lauwersmeer was once an estuary but was closed to the Waddenzee by the construction of a dam and sluice, part of a flood defence programme in the 1960s. It was now a nature reserve, known for its flocks of spoonbills and herds of Konik ponies. There were quiet islands with free moorings where Egyptian geese with their young waded in the shallow waters: perfect rural retreats for Buster. At Lauwersoog, a small community had built up around the sea lock, an excellent place to enjoy the fresh fish and shrimp dishes of the area. Out on the sea, the flat-bottomed Dutch barges with their towering masts and raggedy rigging eerily crept between the low-lying Frisian Islands. I was reminded of my neighbour Rosemary in Ireland; of our last meeting before leaving Dunrovin, tea on the patio under a July sun, talk of Erskine Childers and *The Riddle of the Sands*.

Popping into the neighbouring province of Groningen to Zoutkamp, the sun was unforgiving. Roger rigged up an umbrella on Buster's camping chair, allowing him to lounge in the shade. Brightly coloured fishermen's huts, moored shrimping vessels, flat fish drying on lines and golden sunsets enthralled us. At Electra, Roger disturbed the

Brightly coloured fishermen's huts in the Groningen port of Zoutkamp

workers during a coffee break and asked if he could possibly look around the large pumping station. It worked tirelessly to keep the land below sea level free from flood, replacing the wind-powered pumps of old.

Walking in the Âlde Feanen Nature Reserve, open and windswept, golden with reeds, Buster stopped dead, stretched his neck forwards, raised a front paw and frowned. He was pointing, but at what? I had not noticed the stork in the long wispy grass, performing a slow-motion walk so as not to disturb its prey. Buster stared at the bird, not sure what he was looking at, shifted his body and sat down, happy to observe rather than chase the strange creature. Since his illness, letting him off-lead was not such a great concern; he never wandered far although I still needed to be vigilant. One of the best places to let him have freedom was along the cycle paths bordering the waterways and fields. On one side, the navigable waterway was a barrier hindering escape; on the other, the low-lying fields where sheep grazed were wired and usually had a narrow dyke in front of the fencing – enough to stop Buster these days.

Walking along the pathway listening to birdsong and the rustle of the breeze through the reeds, a man on a bicycle approached, giving us a shrill 'brrring brrring' on his bell. Moving to one side to let him pass, he cycled into the distance. Arriving at a wooden bridge crossing the waterway, he dismounted and rummaged about in his basket. Buster was watching but only half-heartedly with one eye; the other – and his nose – firmly on the ground.

From out of the basket, the man pulled a large banana and began peeling it. Immediately, Buster lifted his head, sniffed the air and sauntered off along the cycle path.

"Where's he going? Oh no, he's got a scent." Roger quickened his pace.

"No, he hasn't; it's alright. Look." Next to the front wheel sat Buster, watching the man tuck into his banana.

"I don't believe this," laughed Roger. "He's begging for a piece of banana."

"It looks like it. He hasn't had one for ages." My dad had started giving Buster the occasional piece of banana as a treat. Buster barked; the man was coming to the end of the banana and Buster was fearful he would not get a piece. He barked again. We were close enough to see Buster was dribbling; that was enough to make the man quickly finish his snack. Placing the peel back into the basket, he cycled off, leaving Buster looking totally bewildered and without a taste of his favourite fruit.

Chapter Five

TO THE LIGHTHOUSE

We were humbled when Len and June visited us in Denmark. They drove all the way from Ireland in their motorhome and spent a week with us. Their arrival coincided with a difficult period. Our landlord had decided to sell the house and we had been forced to look for new accommodation. On top of Roger's father's death and Buster's ongoing health problems, it was hassle we did not need. June's bright outlook on life, combined with Len's practical advice, raised our hopes. The new house we were going to rent had a more suitable garden for Buster; *Lily*, although still some distance away, was now in Europe and Roger's job was going well. But it was a day trip to Stevns Klint, a stunning range of white limestone cliffs south of Copenhagen, which put Buster's life back on track.

"Can we go and look at the lighthouse?" June was as full of enthusiasm as the day was of sunshine.

"It's a long way; I'm not sure Buster will make it." I peered down at him sitting in the long grass; he looked tired and had already managed a nice walk. June looked disappointed. "Tell you what, you go ahead; we'll bring up the rear. If it's too much for him, we'll sit and wait for you to come back." It was a lovely day; boats were speeding by far below and there was a beautiful view of Højerup church so waiting would not be a problem. June was soon striding out along the cliff path, her long locks of hair floating weightlessly on the gentle sea breeze. She was eager to make our wait as short as possible. Len was hot on her heels whilst Roger and I prepared to take a slow stroll with Buster but, realising our guests had left, he wanted to catch up.

"Take it easy, Buzzy." He was pulling on the lead. "There's no rush, old chap." After a few hundred yards, Buster was panting. It was a hot day and, as we had not planned on walking far, we had left his drink in the car.

"Let's stop for a while." I gathered Buster in on his extending lead and Roger tried to make him sit but Buster wanted to catch up and began barking and pulling. Frightened he would damage his legs straining against the tight lead, off we went. He had adopted a bit of a hobble since being diagnosed but was walking extremely well, had plenty of strength and, much to our surprise, made it to the lighthouse.

"That's the furthest he's walked in months," I said to June when we caught her up. We all took turns to climb to the top, taking in the fine views. Buster rested and enjoyed a welcome drink courtesy of the lighthouse keeper. An hour or so later, we walked slowly back along the cliff path. In the car, Buster settled down on the back seat between Len and me, instantly falling asleep.

That evening, Buster snuggled up to June on the sofa. He was not one for sharing his love; the action was totally unexpected and out of character but I was sure he was saying 'thank you'. Len and June's visit, and in particular the walk to the lighthouse, had lifted Buster's spirits as well as our own. He was a different dog following that walk; it had given him back some of the confidence lost through the illness and for that I shall be forever thankful to June and her dogged determination to reach the lighthouse.

Favourite places were not hard to find in Friesland; there were so many locally that there really was no need to travel far but, on occasion, we did venture further. Amongst the places we visited was Sneek and the surrounding area. Roger moored *Lily* opposite the famous Watergate, a medieval city gate straddling a canal into the city. The overnight mooring fee was high but, thinking we may never be that way again, worth paying. Buster was not keen on the city, although he relished snuffling around the cheese stall in the market and prised a huge piece of discarded chewing gum from the pavement, managing to smear the revolting stuff all over one of his ears and along the side of his mouth.

"Urhhh, for goodness' sake, Buster, that's been in someone's germ-ridden mouth!" It was disgusting; there was no way I was going to touch the stuff. Buster was slapping his chops and eyeing me as if he had a prize steak not a nasty old piece of gum. "Roger, get that gum off your dog."

"Why is he always *my* dog when he does something disgusting?"

Whenever Buster endured something he was not overly keen on, I tried to reward him. With the exception of the incident with the chewing gum, he had been extremely good in the city so the reward was a countryside mooring and a nice walk. IJlst was just outside of Sneek yet could not have been more different; quiet and rural, surrounded by fields. On the waterfront stood De Rat, one of only a handful of wind-powered sawmills still in existence. Buster seemed keen to visit; each time I had mentioned the mill's name, he lifted his head and looked around, as if expecting to find a rodent to chase.

At Boswold, a busy road bridge needed to be opened for most craft but *Lily* squeezed

The wind-powered saw mill, De Rat at IJlst

beneath, much to the annoyance of the flybridge cruisers which had to queue, waiting for the designated opening time. Buster always managed to put on a real show in these situations. Playing the role of Admiral to the full, he would ignore the other craft and concentrate solely on the way ahead. I had to admit I was rather keen on these moments too; *Lily* may not have had the speed but she always got there eventually and, in some cases, like this one, she got there first.

Friesland was full of tiny waterways with low bridges branching off the larger ones. With *Lily*'s wheelhouse dismantled, we could easily access most of these. It was great fun inventing circular routes by linking several together. The trips we created were diverse; one minute, *Lily* would be sharing wide thoroughfares with huge, cargo-carrying barges, the next, she would be squeezing down a reed-lined channel with barely room to spare. We could be in open countryside, seemingly miles from anywhere, then slipping unseen and unheard into a city centre just minutes later – delightful, diverse Friesland.

After spending time in the bustling city of Leeuwarden, we took the mast-up route back to the marina. De Zwaluw, the windmill at Burdaard, was impressive and claimed to be the highest in Friesland. Just about to open to visitors, the attendant, wearing stompy, wooden clogs, was eager to invite us in.

"Bring the dog; he can come in too," he boomed as he strode towards us. Fearing he would tread on Buster's feet in the heavy-looking footwear, I kept Buster close. "There's a film show; go in and I'll put it on for you." There was nothing like a film show to lull Buster into a deep sleep. He had fallen asleep so deeply through the one at Clonmacnoise in Ireland when my mum visited that we stayed on to watch the German version but, as it came to an end, Buster began snoring, annoying some cinema-goers. Here we were alone and, as predicted, Buster was soon sprawled on the cobbled floor of the windmill, snoring loud enough to rattle its sails.

It was our first winter in the country and I was eager to get underway. Henk watched the departure and thought us slightly crazy; no one knew when the winter freeze would come. *Lily* was the only boat in Grou; everyone had packed up for the winter except us. After a week away from the marina, our drinking water supply was low but there was nowhere to fill up as taps had been drained down in the public harbours.

"Try the chandlery," suggested a local man. "He's open today." Roger was soon back, wearing a broad grin.

"We can fill the aquaroll and there's no charge." The aquaroll was proving a valuable addition to *Lily*'s onboard equipment. A plastic barrel with two thin rubber tyres around its body, a handle could be attached, allowing easy manoeuvrability. It was great for water, although I knew of other boaters who used them for fuel. "By the way, the guy in the chandlery was surprised to see us. Apparently, the locals are usually ice skating at this time of year where *Lily*'s moored."

Winter skies were full of streaming ribbons of geese; their raucous cries filled the air. At dusk, they left the coastal mud flats and headed inland for overnight shelter. Their numbers competed with the black, swirling murmurations of starlings, which weaved and twisted above the vast open flatlands.

Moored on the edge of the nature reserve late one evening, a solitary candle lit the wheelhouse. The moon was full and had created a slinky, silver pathway on the water and, through the open windows, the sounds of the night filtered in. From high above came the sound of geese.

"I didn't think birds flew at night. Well, not very often anyway," I said to Roger who was leaning out of the window. Buster had heard them and lifted his ears, tuning in on the cries.

"Take a look at this." Roger stepped back from the window with a grin. I walked over and leant out; the sound was instantly louder. Looking up into the night sky, I could see long, twisting ribbons of geese, possibly hundreds of them, illuminated by the light of the moon. I watched spellbound as they kept coming, flying over *Lily* in the dead of night. It was beautiful.

"Isn't there a song about wild geese flying with the moon on their wings?" Roger asked.

"Yes." I replied. "'My Favourite Things'." We both had a little sing-song, much to Buster's disgust. I had never seen geese fly at night before and never have since. Perhaps we were simply in the right place at the right time but it will always remain one of my most special memories of wintertime in Friesland.

Chapter Six

THE TURFROUTE

The Turfroute was a network of narrow waterways in southeast Friesland originally created to transport peat. When trade ceased, many of them were threatened with closure but locals campaigned to save them and succeeded. Looked after by volunteers, they formed a tourist route, open for a limited number of weeks each year. By adding more mainline waterways in the neighbouring provinces of Drenthe and Overijssel, it was possible to create a large looped circuit, known as the Big Turfroute, which formed the main holiday afloat during our second year in the Netherlands.

Buster had taken well to the doggyhut and enjoyed trips in it almost as much as being on *Lily*. Sometimes, he would half-heartedly lift one leg in a vain attempt to get inside and look around at one of us, his deep brown eyes pleading for help. His bed held him in place and buffered him from the sometimes jerky motion. Roger took the lead, pulling Buster's hefty weight, whilst I took up the rear. If I started in front or overtook them, Buster would erupt in a fit of barking, telling Roger to pedal faster and catch up with his mummy.

One of the best off-water excursions involved a bicycle ride from Appelscha to the nearby Drents-Friese Wold National Park, famed for its inland, drifting sand dunes. It was an easy ride to the park; the Dutch were great at providing

Buster at the inland drifting sand dunes

purpose-built bicycle paths, even to the most rural outposts. We sped alongside roads and rattled over cattle grids, before eventually emerging in the open landscape of

Boats on the Drentsche-Hoofdvaart waterway

the national park where cows and sheep grazed. Buster could hardly contain himself, squeaking with excitement and letting us know by barking a few times when he smelt something of interest or fancied a stroll. It was a great day of adventure, his trailer transporting him from one scent to another without the need for exertion.

The landscape was diverse: coniferous forests, open heath and fens. There was lots to see but the drifting sand dunes were the highlight. It seemed strange to come across towering mounds of sand miles away from the sea. The strong winds that fiercely whipped across the flat landscape carried the sand with it, transporting the dunes a little further inland over time. Buster ran around and rolled in the soft golden sand but could not figure out why there was no sea to paddle in. He slammed himself down on all fours, legs splayed wide, and barked for one of us to give chase, skidding and jumping, sending up a fine spray of sand in his wake. He may have been getting on in years but he still enjoyed playing the puppy now and then and sometimes had to be reined in for fear he may injure himself.

The locks along the Turfroute looked odd – they had no balance beams. Luckily, boat crews did not have to operate them. The job looked precarious and had to be done with a long-hooked pole, taking considerable skill and effort from the lock keepers. I am sure if Roger or I had attempted the job we would have ended up in the water. There were many swing bridges along the way, some of which were opened by friendly locals or school children who asked for a few coins in payment. I did not mind paying; it saved a job.

The Drentsche-Hoofdvaart waterway provided fond memories of towering lime kilns, precariously balanced megaliths, open-air Shakespeare theatre, nesting storks, Buster lazily lounging and the delightfully named Dwingaloo. I wanted to sing 'Skip to my Lou, my darlin'' as I followed the boys through the small town on my bicycle. It was bustling with activity; pavements were being briskly swept by women in housecoats, men were putting up orange, blue and white bunting, moving planters of orange flowers and tying orange ribbons to lamp posts.

"What's going on?" Roger had pulled over to watch.

"It looks as if the whole place has been tangoed," I joked (doused in a popular brand of fizzy orangeade). Even the unusual, onion-shaped spire of the church had been draped in vibrant orange cloth. We later discovered it was in anticipation of a visit by the newly appointed king, the first in the Netherlands for over 120 years.

Dwingaloo was dressed in orange, even the church spire

Giethoorn was known as the Venice of the North and, with such an impressive title and given my fondness for the Italian city, it was inevitable our trip on the Turfroute would eventually lead there. *Lily* had to be left on the outskirts; only small boats could gain access into the centre of the former turf village, which, instead of roads, had waterways crossed by numerous timber bridges. Immaculately kept gardens rolled down to the water's edge, where shade-loving plants thrived.

The Tjonger, a canalised river, buzzed and hummed with an armada of insects; *Lily* was escorted by a pair of great green dragonflies, one on either side of her bow. Occasionally, one would break ranks, come to the wheelhouse, hover in mid-air eyeing me before quickly diving away again. Along the bank, delicate damsel flies, butterflies and bees were momentarily disturbed as the lock keeper, travelling parallel to *Lily*, whizzed along the towpath on his electric-powered moped. He accompanied us all the way along this magical waterway, opening locks and bridges as he went.

A bicycle trip to Oranjewoud and the Belvedere Museum of Art was remarkable for an extraordinary encounter. It was a hot day and the going was slow, especially for Roger, pulling Buster in his trailer. We walked through the woods to a viewing tower. After a short break, we made our way back to the bicycles. Buster led the way; his extended lead pulled out as far as it could go as he snuffled and sniffed his way along the path. My eyes caught a low movement to the front and one side of us. It was the longest snake I had ever seen in my life and the shock of seeing it rendered me speechless; despite trying, I could not get the word 'snake' out. Buster was way out in front and I knew as soon as Roger saw it he would panic.

"Don't pull the lead. I don't want him to come back," I shouted, meaning I did not want Buster to cross the snake's path. Roger started pulling Buster back towards us and the snake. I assumed Roger had seen it and could not understand what he was doing. As thick as my forearm, the snake was now almost halfway across the path, the shade from the trees preventing identification.

"What are you doing? Can't you see that bloody great snake?" I cried, instantly regretting it as Roger stepped back in fear and yanked Buster with him. The snake recoiled and I was afraid it was about to strike. "Buzzy, come on; here's a biscuit." Luckily, Buster did not hang about and ran towards me. With a sigh of relief at having him safe, I dug in my pockets for a biscuit. The snake slithered off across the path and vanished into the undergrowth.

"I never saw it," gasped Roger, shaken by the episode.

Making our way back to the bicycles, we realised how lucky we had been, speculated about what we would have done if the worst had happened and how we really should be prepared for such things when out on the bicycles.

We had arranged to meet Roger's cousin, Teresa, and her husband, Peter, at Echtenerbrug. Fortunately, they managed to find a pitch for their campervan next to *Lily,* where Buster and their dog, Pixie, instantly became playmates. Pixie was a beautiful, black, Tibetan Terrier, a landlubber, a motorhome kind of girl, but took to her first boat ride extremely well when they accompanied us on a short cruise up the Helomavaart to Ossenzijl and back. It was a great idea to meet up in the Netherlands, a chance for the dogs to become friends on neutral ground before seeing each other again on our home turf in Denmark a few weeks later.

Buster relished having a doggy friend at home for a few days. Pixie rushed into the house each morning, eager to greet him, and then together they would run around the garden. They shared the car travelling into Copenhagen to visit the Little Mermaid and Nyhavn. We were sitting in a café with Buster sprawled out on the cool pavement when Teresa mentioned how large the lump on his side looked. She was right; it had increased, looked horrid and was also

Buster and Pixie sharing the car

slowing him down. If Buster was well enough to undergo surgery, I promised myself this would be a priority once our guests had left.

On wobbly legs and wearing a fetching, navy-blue, all-in-one bodysuit, Buster was led into the veterinary reception by a young trainee who had obviously taken a shine to our lumpy, bumpy boy. Sleepy and with eyes half-closed, Buster whimpered when he spotted me then sat down with a plop, his unsteady legs no longer able to support his weight under the influence of anaesthesia. Dropping to my knees, I hugged Buster, telling him that everything would be alright. As he whimpered softly in my ear, I could feel his warm breath on the side of my face and the weight of his body as he slumped against me. Feeling safe in my arms, sleep overcame him.

Claus was keen to show us the lumps that had been removed.

"It's just like a tray of meat on display in a butcher's shop," he laughed. Luckily, I was not squeamish but interested to see what he meant so went to look. The bulbous lumps of fatty tissue sat on a sterilised metal tray. They looked huge; Buster had carried their weight for months. No wonder he had slowed down. Little by little, day by day, they had grown and hindered his movement. Now that they had been removed, he could enjoy the summer ahead.

With bills paid and paperwork signed, Roger scooped up Buster in his strong arms.

"I've got you now, my boy." He nuzzled his face deep into Buster's warm neck. We thanked everyone and left, Roger holding Buster tightly to his chest and then carefully placing him into his faithful old bed with its clean, cosy bedding in the back of the car. I sat beside him on the journey home; with his head resting in the palm of my hand, he slept deeply.

Once home, Buster slept for several more hours and, when he finally woke, enjoyed a bowl of warm rice, which he ate with relish. With his hunger satisfied, he went straight back to sleep, not moving again until the morning. Roger remained by his side all night, boys together looking out for one another. Loving and looking after Buster during this time, both Roger and I felt we were giving him back some of the love and loyalty he had shown us over the years but it also made me feel vulnerable to think how awful it would be without him. I thanked my lucky stars on more than one occasion during Buster's recuperation. From that point on, I felt blessed for every day we had together.

The bodysuit was a great way of protecting Buster from damaging the stitches and much better than one of those unsightly plastic cones around his neck but the days were hot and it became uncomfortable for him. I solved the problem by dressing Buster in one of Roger's old T-shirts. The soft cotton fabric was gentle on the scar tissue and loose enough to be airy. Pulling the T-shirt over Buster's head, I placed his front legs in the sleeves. They had to be rolled up a little to prevent him tripping and I gathered the body of the T-shirt up onto his back and tied it in a knot. With his privates free, Buster could wander in and out of the garden to do his business, retaining his dignity.

For a few hours each day, I removed the T-shirt and let Buster sit outside in the warmth, the sun and fresh air working its healing magic on his patchwork body. He sat on the lawn near the sweet-scented lavender bushes and watched the bees buzzing on the purple flowers or dozed in the sun, stretched out with his head resting on his front paws. Soon, his wounds were healing and Buster

Get well cards and gifts arrived for Buster

became puppylike, full of life and mischief. It was as if he knew what he had gone through had helped him, given him a new

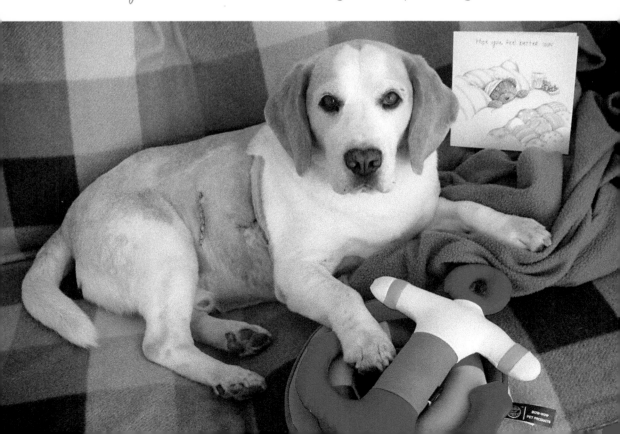

lease of life. Without the lumps, he was lighter, more agile, fitter and brighter. Cards and messages arrived from well-wishers, amongst them a present from my sister containing some soft toys, one the shape of an anchor, which Buster adored. He may have been forced temporarily into the life of a landlubber but his doggy heart remained faithful to his on-water life. In no time at all, we were preparing for his first post-op visit to *Lily*.

It was a long drive to the barge but we were happy to arrive and looked forward to spending our second Christmas on the Dutch waterways. Walking along the jetty to *Lily*, I noticed something worrying.

"Roger," I shouted, "someone's pulled out the electric supply."

He rushed from the car and we all hurriedly shuffled along the icy deck to get to the wheelhouse. Once inside, it was obvious the power had been off for a long time. We had been away from the boat for several months whilst Buster recuperated and inside it was freezing cold. The damp had taken hold; spots of mildew had formed on some of the interior surfaces.

Roger phoned Henk, who almost immediately arrived on the scene and offered what help he could. There was little he could do; the damage had been done. The battery management system had shut everything down before finally giving up the ghost itself. It was strange how, in situations like this, a simple issue could cause more grief than the original problem. In this case, resetting the battery management system took hours. Roger turned things on and off and I turned the boat upside down to find the instruction manual, which had been stowed somewhere 'safe'. Eventually, it came to light and we discovered that reactivating the system was a simple matter of pressing a button. The batteries, however, had other ideas; they had taken a battering and, despite being put on charge overnight, could not be saved.

Throughout the entire drama, Buster remained his usual happy self, glad to be back on board and doing his usual shimmying on the rug and 'telling off' of toys left behind from before his operation. New batteries were eventually sourced from a local car spares shop suggested by Henk and a disastrous Christmas was narrowly averted.

Chapter Seven

CROSSING BORDERS

With Buster making steady progress, we began to visit *Lily* more but, as the drive back and forth was long, I would often remain on board whilst Roger returned to work in Denmark.

Most of the time, I would be marina-based or, whilst Roger was with me, we would find somewhere suitable where I could be left for the week. On other occasions, I would handle *Lily* alone but this needed to be done with caution. Despite having the relevant qualifications, operating twenty tons of steel alone could not be taken lightly. I never tackled anything other than a straightforward cruise; lift bridges and locks were avoided, as were any moorings where space could be tight, but these short and precious trips with Buster brought us even closer together. On one of these trips, Buster became a cover star. Caught relaxing in the camping chair, he appeared on the front cover of DBA The Barge Association's *Blue Flag* journal, reaching a worldwide audience.

Buster was soon well enough to undertake a longer journey. Onboard *Lily*, his home was constantly with him; everything he needed was close to hand. A long cruise would be ideal recuperation, enabling him to take it easy yet still see new and exciting things from the comfort of his bed. Bringing *Lily* closer to Denmark would also enable Roger to spend more time on board and less travelling.

After an overnight stop in Groningen, a full day's cruising had been planned but, on arrival at the first lock on the Oosterdiep at Veendam, our plans were put on hold, though not by choice. Bertus, the harbour master and general harbinger of bad news, said it was impossible to continue; we would have to wait until the following morning.

Roger was holding *Lily* midstream, waiting to be let through the lift bridges and locks leading to the Stadskanaal, Ter Apel and the Haren-Rütenbrock Kanal, which crossed the border into Germany. Bertus had moved us quickly through the first few bridges before he disappeared, claiming, "I'm needed to get another boat through the entrance lock." Being marooned in the middle of the canal for almost an hour, with a Pedro cruiser treading water behind, was trying the patience of all concerned. The only good thing to come out of the delay was making the acquaintance of Thomas and his crew, who were taking the newly purchased Pedro, *Azteca*, home to Germany. Roger had nosed *Lily* into the canal bank and I had managed to get Buster ashore for a short walk before Bertus returned

BLUE FLAG

THE JOURNAL OF DBA -
THE BARGE ASSOCIATION   BF103 DECEMBER 2013

Buster became a Blue Flag cover star, courtesy of DBA The Barge Association

with a suspicious-looking mobile team of waterways workers who resembled a group of mafia gansters.

"Great," said Roger. "Now we should see some action."

Things went well for a while; the bridges were lifted as *Lily* approached and closed as *Azteca* exited, the team leap-frogging each other on mopeds and in vans but, at the next lock, the same thing happened and both boats were left treading water between the lock just exited and the next lift bridge. This was getting ridiculous; the constant delays were a worry. We needed to get *Lily* across the German border before the canal's Easter shut-down otherwise we would not reach Hanover, where Roger had a flight booked back to Denmark.

At the final lock before the Stadskanaal, Roger expressed his concern to the burly team leader, who looked more than odd sporting a full-length overcoat in the warm spring sunshine. From the lockside, he frowned down on us; his glare immediately made me feel guilty, as if we had asked for the earth, moon and stars not simply for him to do his job. Buster growled and I put my arm around him in a vain attempt to calm him down.

"It's alright, old chap, nothing to worry about," but I had an uneasy feeling the same as Buster. I could feel Buster's body begin to tense but, before the growl erupted into a bark, the man swiftly turned and disappeared.

"Well done, Buzz," Roger sighed. "Now we've had it; you've frightened him off."

Away from the boats, there was a conversation between the rest of the workers. It was impossible to hear what was being said but, with neither of us speaking Dutch, we would not have understood it anyway. The team leader went over to Thomas, where another conversation took place, then back to the team before finally striding over to us with a meaningful gait. He told us they would be happy to work through their lunch break to get us to Ter Apel for a 'consideration' – an unofficial surcharge of €20 each boat. Against better judgement, and because of our deadline, we paid but it was worth every penny; the transformation was amazing, as if the team had suddenly woken up. Overcoats came off and shirt sleeves were rolled up; we had a smooth ride and raised bridges all the way to our evening mooring. The pace was apparently too much for our German companions as, somewhere along the way, they were left behind. The last we saw of them, they were pulling in to moor as the lift bridge we passed beneath was promptly closed to bar their way.

"They decided to stop" was all we were told.

Next morning, we were ushered through the final lock by another Dutch team before turning east onto the Haren-Rütenbrock Kanal. The border crossing was seamless, although the difference was obvious; with no team around, we were under the watchful eye of a video camera. Approaching the first lock, the gates magically opened and, once the light turned green, we entered. Whilst *Lily* was in the chamber, Roger changed the courtesy flag; she was ready to cruise in Germany. It was eerie. All the way down the canal, the locks and bridges opened remotely with Teutonic precision – German engineering at its best. At the final lock, lowering craft onto the Dortmund-Ems, it all became clear. The genial lock keeper explained that he remotely controlled the canal's locks and lift bridges.

There was a sudden change of character on entering the Dortmund-Ems. The narrow canals had disappeared, replaced by a major river navigation, wide and sweeping. I wanted to stop at the port of Haren but the wind was wicked. Roger always told people that boating was one of those things when, just as you thought you had got it down to a fine art, it would bite you in the rear. It was my turn to discover that.

I approached the pontoon as slowly as I could in the wind, hoping Roger would jump off quickly and take a turn with a rope. *Lily* was coming alongside nicely but, as Roger prepared to jump and I reduced the revs, a brisk surge of wind swept her away. I circled and tried again. This time, Roger got off before another surge of wind but was unable to hold *Lily*. He teetered about on the very end of the pontoon. It was unstable and he was grasping onto the upright supporting pole so as not to lose his footing.

With Roger trying to tell me how best to tackle the approach, by now we had begun to acquire an audience and I had had enough. I drove *Lily* bow on towards the pontoon, shouting at Roger to get on. The wind was again blowing *Lily* away and to one side; it was useless. Roger leapt onto the bow, using *Lily*'s strong fenders as footholds, and somehow managed to climb on board. I let the wind whisk *Lily* around and, once she was facing the exit back onto the river, steamed away. There was no way I was going to moor there after we had just been the cabaret act for the entire town.

The vast towering gates of the locks on the Dortmund-Ems were unnerving. Meppen Lock was displaying a red light; we waited, *Lily* treading water midstream, almost shuddering. If a boat had a heart or a soul, as I am sure ours did, she was feeling frightened of the unknown. Buster pulled himself up from his reclining position and scanned the scene. He pointed his wet, shiny nose into the air and sniffed. He sensed something we could not.

When the red light flickered to green, Roger slowly eased *Lily* forwards, passing beneath a vast guillotine gate, which dripped and drawled as if a famished mechanical beast. Tied in at the front of the lock was a huge commercial barge; it must have reached the lock shortly before us but had enough time to disappear from view, which explained why the red light was displayed. It was a shock seeing the huge beast sitting there. As the locks were built specifically to take commercial traffic, the bollards were placed a long way apart, making it impossible to secure both *Lily*'s bow and stern. Buster watched in amusement as Roger and I struggled to get the ropes to reach; no doubt he was muttering under his breath what incompetent crew he had.

Lily looked small in the deep Meppen Lock

"We'll have to try a centre rope," yelled Roger from the rear of the boat. I was up front and tied in but could see him struggling. Roger secured a rope around the strong metal roof rail then looped it around the lock's bollard. Once secure, I released the front rope and took my place at the helm with Buster, standing guard over the engine in case the plan failed and the assistance of power was needed.

Poised, Roger gripped the rope tightly and waited for the lock to spring into action. We waited and waited but nothing happened. He loosened his grip and I stepped outside the wheelhouse. It was silent, with only the gentle drip of water from the suspended guillotine gate. Buster sighed and snuggled into his bed, growing bored.

"What d'you think is going on?" I asked.

"I can only assume we're waiting for another boat but it can't be a commercial; they wouldn't have let us in." Commercial craft were generally placed into a lock chamber before any leisure craft, both for safety and business reasons. For them, time was money; they needed to be underway not jostling about with the tourists. After what seemed a lifetime, Buster jumped up in his bed and sniffed the air; peering back along the river, he shifted back and forth, waiting and watching. Something was coming and, whatever it was, he was excited about it.

'Peep peep peeeeep.' The horn was loud; we all jumped with surprise.

'Peep peep peeeeep.' It sounded again and into view steamed our new German friends on *Azteca*, who we had last seen fading into the distance on the Stadskanaal.

"Barooo, barooo," cried Buster in return. A crazy moment of madness followed. The captain on the commercial came out; tucked into his large, muscle-bulging arms was a little Terrier pup, all eyes. We waved and all wore huge grins, a reunion of a friendship hardly begun; this was how life was on the waterways. With a chuckle,

A commercial barge passing through a rainbow on the Dortmund-Ems

the captain, a gentle giant, tickled the Terrier under the chin and raised his hand in a wave before returning to the wheelhouse.

"Barooooo," Buster let out a howl of happiness as *Azteca* breezed into the lock chamber and tied in opposite us. Our new-found friends had suffered a blocked raw water inlet filter and missed out on the race to Ter Apel. They had been hot on our heels all that morning, desperate to catch up and lock share. Finally, the great gate was lowered and we were soon delivered onto another section of this waterway.

As *Lily* carried us up the Dortmund-Ems, sharp showers provided rainbows to cruise through. She was visited by grey wagtails which landed on her roof and picked off insects from my terracotta clogs planted with bedding. The bravest came right up to the wheelhouse and feasted on insects caught in spiders' webs around the roofline. Our first encounter with the German waterways had made an impression: they were big, bold and beautiful. Buster was relaxed and happy, content to be on the move and back to his role of Admiral.

Chapter Eight

FAR, FAR, FAR UP
THE MITTELLAND KANAL

In the 1970s, the German pop group Kraftwerk had a hit with 'Autobahn' and for months Roger had been driving Buster and me mad with his new version of it: *Far, far, far up the Mittelland Kanal, with Woey by my side*. On this motorway for motorboats, there was no let-up in the singing or our big cheesy grins. Motoring through central Germany, with electronic, synthesised music ringing in our ears and memories of our youth in mind, Buster viewed us with complete disdain.

The Mittelland Kanal was an amazing feat of modern engineering. It stretched for over 186 miles (300km) across the centre of Germany, a waterway version of a motorway, with barges carrying thousands of tons of coal, timber, steel, scrap and a variety of manufactured goods. The canal had some impressive aqueducts — the best-known at Minden across the River Weser and at Magdeburg across the Elbe Valley — yet it only had three locks along its entire length. Researching the route, I found it mostly described as dull and boring. It was indeed straight but this made for relaxed cruising, perfect for an elderly Beagle, whilst the pretty, wooded banks thick with flowering cherry trees

and spring flowers made it pleasing on the eye.

Anxiety kicked in each time a water police vessel was spotted as speed

Most skippers of the huge commercial barges were courteous but on occasion gave us little room to manoeuvre

limits were strictly enforced and ships' papers frequently checked, fools not suffered gladly. As they slowly motored by, eyeing *Lily* up and down with stern expressions, I reacted with a huge smile and a wave. This worked well, with the majority returning the gesture. Buster was also a great distraction; they would point and smile at him or perhaps he frightened them a little as he often looked more authoritarian than they did.

Playing cat and mouse with Thomas and his crew on *Azteca* was great fun. Rising early, Roger and I made ground on *Azteca*, slipping by unseen and unheard as they slept. Passing early one morning, Thomas emerged sleepy-eyed in his night clothes and, in disbelief, gave us a wave and laughed. It was late afternoon by the time they caught us up, leaving *Lily* trailing in their frothy wake. By nightfall, they were long gone and we moored alone, only to leapfrog them again the following morning; and so it continued all the way to Hanover.

Boating with Buster

Seelze on the outskirts of Hanover became my home for two weeks. Boating to a deadline, knowing a booked flight awaited Roger, was exhausting but reaching our destination satisfying. I adored my boating life and time alone on the water with Buster was precious. In an ideal world, both Roger and I would have been on board full-time but we did not have the luxury of being rich or able to take early retirement. For Roger especially, holding down a full-time job and trying to combine it with boating was challenging and, at times, stressful. When many boaters were relaxing with sundowners, one of us would usually be trying to retrieve a car or fathom the local transport system. Late flights or long drives home on Sundays were a part of our lives we would have preferred not to have.

It was a short train ride into the city of Hanover, the capital of Lower Saxony, and, with Buster used to train travel, no chore taking him along for sightseeing. It was hard to believe that, during WWII, the city was almost completely destroyed as many of the historical monuments had been sympathetically restored to their former glory and many new vibrant works of art added. Coffee on the terrace of the elegant town hall with its lakeside and garden views, brightly coloured love locks hanging from the ornamental railings and Buster gazing in disbelief at the huge mirror carp in the waters were some of the fond memories I had of Hanover. When

Hanover Town Hall

Roger returned, I was able to share with him the highlights of my finds and Buster delighted at having his pack reunited.

Jan, the harbour master at Yachthafen Seelze, was a true old-school gentleman who took an interest in us and could not do enough to help. Despite growing used to the boating community, I remained wary of strangers and, although his offer to take me shopping in his car was extremely thoughtful, my instincts kicked in and I turned him down. Not one to give up easily, Jan suggested we cycled into the town of Seelze together so he could show me where everything was but I had to turn that offer down too. The doggyhut trailer was too heavy for me to tow; Buster's days of trotting alongside the bike were behind him and, since his illness, he had become stressed when left alone. I felt rather bad afterwards, especially as Buster had taken a shine to our host, but Jan did not take it to heart. Instead, he gave me a map with detailed instructions on where to find all I could possibly need. One of the best discoveries I made was that Germany produced cakes which were every bit as good as French cakes and they quickly became a wicked indulgence.

Jan and I enjoyed many friendly chats. He was a great Charles Dickens fan, his favourite novel being *A Christmas Carol*, and, whenever we talked, sooner or later it would come up. We discussed the characters and storyline as best we could with his broken English. The day we departed, Jan came and saw us off. Out of the blue, he took us by surprise when he said, "Before you go, I wish to apologise for what my country did during the war." Both Roger and I were shocked, taken aback and left feeling sad that Jan felt the need to personally do this. Roger was quick to cut in, to tell him it was in the past; everyone was a victim of war and he had no need to apologise. Jan hung his head and, with watery eyes, told us how, in his younger years, he had sailed around the world, loved life on the water but always felt ashamed to fly his country's ensign because he knew, or thought he knew, what people were thinking when they saw it. My heart ached for him.

That Christmas, I sent Jan a card; inside it a woven Charles Dickens bookmark, ordered especially for him from the Charles Dickens Museum in London. I received a lovely letter back with his best wishes and the hope that we would one day meet again. I will never forget this special man and, even if we never meet again in this lifetime, when I read or see something relating to Charles Dickens, my thoughts recall Jan with much warmth and fondness.

A huge barge from the Czech Republic loomed down on *Lily*. Unsure what to do, Roger was holding her midstream, waiting for communication from the lock keeper or for me to pick out appropriate signage through the binoculars, neither of which was forthcoming. Roger tried the VHF; as his German was not good he spoke in English and waited for a reply. It seemed an age before a gruff voice came back over the VHF and in perfect English said, "Only German is spoken on the radio." With a crackle, the radio went dead.

"Now what?" Roger asked but I had no more idea than him. Hoping for some elaboration on the lock keeper's remark, Roger hung on as long as possible before motoring *Lily* out of the way. As the huge barge passed, a voice shouted from the bow,

"You need to wait there." I looked up to see a man pointing towards the quay. Following his direction, I could make out the signage I had been desperately searching for.

"Thank you," I shouted back. There we found an intercom and were soon in conversation with the lock keeper. He was ecstatic having a British boat to see through his lock, explaining they liked to keep the radio conversations in German and for commercial traffic only. There was a short wait, just enough time to get Buster off for a quick stroll, before the all clear to continue into the lock behind the barge.

The entrance was dark and creepy. It felt as if *Lily* was entering a cave leading into a lost world, the high, tree-lined banks and greyness of the day only adding to the illusion. Inside the chamber, the huge barge was already secure and the same man was now at the stern, waving us forwards. He remained attentive throughout the locking process, constantly asking if all was well. As *Lily* was slowly raised into the daylight, more pleasant surroundings were revealed. When it was time to leave, the man advised us to wait. Already knowing the huge propellers of commercial barges could create turbulent wash, we had no intention of moving until it was out of the way.

Exiting the lock was a test of nerves as the two parallel chambers had been raised together, spilling forth a flotilla of shipping in the middle of which we found ourselves. Backing off to let the workers forge ahead, we were buffeted this way and that as the wash from the gargantuan workhorses of the waterways created a mini Aegir along the canal.

It had been a full day's cruising and, with tiredness creeping in, we decided to moor at the next spot, which happened to be alongside a huge, coal-fired power station where great mounds of the black gold towered. The quayside was littered with fallen nuggets – overspill from the loading process – which was too good an opportunity to miss. With *Lily*'s coal scuttle almost empty, we pulled Buster's poo bags from our pockets and greedily collected the scattered coal. It was amazing what good uses poo bags had been put to in the past, collecting all manner of wild berries and mushrooms, but this was a first for fuel.

Having owned a couple of Volkswagen Golfs during my lifetime, I was looking forward to visiting Wolfsburg, home of the famous car manufacturer. It was a bitter disappointment as, on trying to enter the extensive car plant's village which lined the banks of the Mittelland Kanal, we were turned away – dogs were not permitted. I felt cheated, especially as the company had released an advertising campaign featuring all manner of pooches riding in various models of their cars, their heads stuck out of windows; ears and jowls flapping in the breeze.

The Elbe Aqueduct, also known as the Magdeburg Water Bridge, was the longest in Europe. To gain a better view, I clambered onto *Lily*'s rear cabin, leaving Roger to steer the 3,012 feet (918m) spanning the Elbe Valley and River. Beyond, the Mittelland Kanal joined the Elbe-Havel Kanal at the 61 feet (18.6m) deep Hohenwarthe Lock. This had innovative floating bollards which made the long, dark descent easy but the damp, towering walls stretching high above *Lily* made me feel vulnerable – not surprising, as this was the deepest lock we had ever encountered.

Chapter Nine

ON TO BERLIN

Before reaching Berlin, I wanted to visit Potsdam and one of the world's most beautiful palace complexes. Situated some distance from the waterfront, the trusty doggyhut was called upon. Although dogs were not permitted into the palaces, they were allowed into the wonderful 700 acre (283ha) grounds, which began life as the summer residence for Frederick the Great in 1747. A collection of formal gardens, water features, follies, pavilions and parkland awaited; it was one of the most amazing places I had ever visited. Buster sat proudly in his carriage, for all the world looking like royalty, with Roger and me playing the role of footmen as he was towed through the grounds, people stepping aside to let us pass.

With *Lily* on a good mooring opposite Babelsberg Park, once home to the German film industry, it was an ideal opportunity to take the train into Berlin, a chance to see some sights and get our bearings before taking *Lily* into the city centre on the River Spree. The German public transport system allowed dogs for the price of a child's ticket although owners could be requested to muzzle their pooch. As Buster did not have one, I wore a pair of extra-long socks, the idea being that, if asked, I could use one as a temporary muzzle. Thankfully, it was not needed. Buster behaved well – he always had done on public transport – and

*Visiting the impressive palace
complex at Potsdam*

*Buster and Lily moored
opposite Babel Park*

rode on a double-decker fast train and the underground, where Roger carried him in his arms up and down the escalators. Leaning down, he said, "Come on, my boy." Buzz lifted a front leg, placed his paw on Roger's shoulder and awaited the scoop into the air. He loved being up high, surveying the surroundings, and the sight of him elicited beaming smiles from passersby.

Visits to the Brandenburg Gate and Holocaust Memorial were followed by a doggy break for Buster in the Tiergarten, the Global Stone Project providing a good location in which to relax with our hound. Back on the underground to Checkpoint Charlie, Buster and I posed for a photographic opportunity with American look-alike soldiers. By now, Buster was growing tired; it was time to retreat to the quieter surroundings of Potsdam. Although he had made an amazing recovery, he still needed plenty of rest, care and attention. Whilst he could cope with a full day out, this needed to be followed by one or two quiet ones. Everything we planned took this into consideration.

Leaving Potsdam, we headed beneath Glienicke Bridge, which, during the Cold War, had been a restricted border crossing between the Eastern Bloc and the Western powers. Because of its strategic position, it was used to exchange captured agents and became known as the Bridge of Spies. *Lily* ploughed across glistening lakes bordered by elegant mansions, ornate churches and spellbinding palaces oozing opulence but beneath the façades were the remnants of war, which, as we travelled further east, became more prominent.

Joining the River Spree at Spandau, where a chorus of 'Gold' by Spandau Ballet sung in our best karaoke voices had Buster burying his head in his bed, we entered the main city of Berlin and moored at Tiergarten.

"Shall we risk going through?" asked Roger.

"You heard what they said to the cruiser. I don't think it's worth the risk, especially after all the stories of late. We'll go first thing; it'll be nice to do an early-morning cruise."

The crew of the cruiser in front of us had been told that only those with a VHF radio and a good understanding of the German language were permitted to navigate the River Spree between Tiergarten and the lock at Mühlendamm. During the day, trip boats and commercial barges had priority. Most leisure craft took the early morning or late evening slots, usually travelling in convoy. We had missed that morning's and thought the evening one best avoided, especially as the route ahead was unknown. Despite having a VHF and Roger's schoolboy German getting us by, his knowledge was rusty and my own was non-existent but for a few choice words such as *trockener Weißwein* (dry white wine), an essential when ordering a drink. Several British boats had been boarded by water police in recent months and I did not relish the thought of authorities on board. At the time, boats under 15 metres (49ft) in length generally got away with most things in Europe so I was happy to adhere to this rule. Larger boats faced different regulations and, in Germany, these were strictly enforced and accompanied with hefty fines if broken.

It was a restless night; the small park alongside had attracted people who appeared down on their luck, perhaps homeless. Buster paid them close attention but was not bothered by their presence; he was a good judge of character.

"If there's someone asleep on that bench opposite *Lily* in the morning, I'm going to make them a cup of tea."

"Are you mad?" snapped Roger.

"No, if we wake up and *Lily* has been untouched through the night and we've had a guardian homeless person watching over us, then that's what I'm going to do. Our and *Lily*'s safety are what matters. I may even make them a bacon sandwich." Roger shook his head in disbelief but Buster had heard the word 'bacon' and was licking his lips; he thought the idea rather fine. The bench was empty in the morning and I felt a little sad to find it so but really should not have; I would like to think that perhaps those people who lingered during the day did have homes to go to after all.

"Come on, Buzz, up you go." I placed him next to the helm. He looked at me with concern. "I know what you're thinking, old chap. Perhaps we'll have a bacon butty later."

I had been hoping for a lovely sunny morning; instead, it was grey and overcast but Crew *Lily* were bright, cheerful and ready to see what Berlin had to offer. We had the Spree to ourselves and I could almost feel *Lily* quiver in excitement as she headed into the city centre.

"It's alright, old girl." I patted her superstructure as I made my way to the bow to take photographs. The first of the early-morning commuters were heading into work, *Lily* enough to make them stop and look. Alongside Hauptbahnhof, the modern train station, the homeless were rising, most of them waving, happy despite their situation. Spellbinding scenes of an architectural dreamland unfolded; huge, grey stone buildings loomed alongside modern, glass-fronted structures, an eclectic mix of old and new.

"Slow down," I urged Roger. He throttled back to let *Lily* slowly potter, allowing my eyes to feast on the cityscape, noting the Reichstag building with its glass dome and Museum Island, fronted by the voluptuously curved Bode Museum. Ahead, the Fernsehturm, the rotating TV tower known locally as the Toothpick, its top constantly fading in and out of low-lying cloud; the austere frontage of the Neuer Marstal and, finally, the lock, which was displaying a red light.

There was a short wait as a large commercial barge penned through, the first boat we had encountered all morning. With the lock behind us, the day began to brighten. To complete our circular tour of Berlin, we needed to lock onto the Landwehr Kanal beyond the spectacular red-brick, Gothic, double-decker Oberbaum

Early-morning cruise through Berlin on the Spree passing the Bode Museum

Bridge and close to the impressive Molecule Man sculpture towering proudly midstream in the Spree.

There was time to finally make those bacon butties at the entrance to the Landwehr Kanal; steaming mugs of tea accompanied them and a view like no other. Buster had his own delicious rasher of smoked bacon – a small treat which he wasted no time in wolfing down – after which he went for a wander on the grass alongside the moorings, following an invisible trail towards the lock.

From nowhere a voice boomed, "Hello, your dog." I looked around but could not see anyone. "Your dog, if you please." I swung around; there was no one in sight. I could see Buzz – he was fine – which made it more mysterious. "Can you call your dog please?" I realised the voice was coming from the lock intercom system and, calling Buster, I fumbled for the intercom.

"Sorry," I said, not sure if the person on the other end could hear me.

"That's OK," the voice echoed back, "but please he is not permitted by the lock. Keep him with you." I looked at Buster, who was ambling back, wondering what all the fuss was about.

"Come here. Look what you've done; you've gone and got me into trouble," I mock-scolded. He gazed up into my eyes, throwing me one of his 'I wasn't doing anything' looks.

The Landwehr Kanal was completely different to the Spree: a narrow channel, lined for the most part with sloping concrete sides, and, rather than heading through the main sights of the city, took a one-way route through the parks and suburbs. Whilst there was no need to be concerned about meeting oncoming traffic, whoever was at the helm needed eyes in the back of their head as the fast-moving trip boats had an unnerving way of creeping silently up behind.

The last section passed through the zoological gardens. The cries from the monkey enclosure soon enticed Buster out on deck, where he trotted around, trying to make out where the sounds were coming from and what strange creature was making them.

With *Lily's* circular cruise of Berlin complete, we headed away from the vibrant city to enter a wilder terrain.

Chapter Ten

LAND OF A THOUSAND LAKES

Mecklenburg was known as 'the land of a thousand lakes' – no matter which way one travelled through the region, water courses of some form or another were never far away. With lakes being my thing, I was looking forward to reaching the wider waters and natural beauty Mecklenburg offered. I hoped it was going to be a dream come true; I was not disappointed.

The Obere-Havel was one of the most charming river navigations and, with its semi-automatic locks and pleasant moorings, one of the easiest to use. Diversions could be made onto side routes and interlinked lakes, to spectacular waterside palaces and away-from-it-all anchorages. Its twisting course through small towns and villages, dense woodland and lush water meadows made it a sensory feast, and not just for me. Buster stood at the bow with his feet on the edge, nose high in the air, drinking in the scents. Guiding *Lily* around a sharp bend, lined with thick, swaying reeds, a sudden rustling noise sent Buster into a frenzy. Whimpering and whining, he jogged on the spot when a deer leapt from the undergrowth into the water right in front of *Lily*'s bow and swam across the river.

"What was that, Buzz?" I tried to distract him but need not have bothered as strange echoing noises – the trumpeting call of cranes – had done that.

Spiralling above, birds of prey climbed invisible staircases of thermals; carrying us into the heart of Germany's Lake District, this river was a nature-lover's paradise.

Lily needed a home for the summer season and we thought this was more or less settled after earlier enquires with Kuhnle Tours, a major hire-fleet company, so this was our first destination. To get there meant venturing onto the largest lake in Germany – Lake Müritz. As the biggest lake *Lily* had ever tackled and knowing how weather conditions could change as quickly on large inland lakes as they could at sea, Roger and I prepared accordingly. Lifejackets, of course, but other items too such as a grab bag filled with essentials, including passports, driving licences and a mobile phone.

An early-morning start found *Lily* waiting at Mirow Lock, first in line to pass through. Buster dozed in his bed and paid little attention to the locking process; he had seen it all before. Approaching the lake, the sky turned dark and looked full of rain. The expanse of water was huge, still and grey, a slumbering beast which perhaps would not relish disturbance from early risers. Unlike the Irish loughs, Lake Müritz was without islands; it was a large bowl of water, stretching for as far as the eye could see. Buster sat up and looked all around, scrutinising the great expanse as if checking Roger's course-

Early-morning stillness at Mirow Lock

plotting skills. Once happy, he gave a quiet, under-the-breath mumble and settled down to doze, satisfied that the crew had everything under control.

The journey was straightforward and, on reaching our destination, luck was on our side; a yacht was preparing to leave the only suitably sized mooring so I held *Lily* off and waited patiently for them to vacate the berth.

"The season's already started; we don't have room for you." The receptionist was adamant. Roger had spent a lot of time trying to negotiate but, despite the phone calls and constant returns to plead with them, it appeared nothing could be done to accommodate *Lily*, despite the provisional promise. Sitting in the wheelhouse, telephoning my parents with the news, I caught a movement. It was an eagle, close enough to reach, so close I could clearly see the yellow ring around its eye. Without warning, the bird plummeted to the water, grasping a fish in its talons. This was where I wanted to be, close to nature; it felt right but, before a desperate search for a berth in the local area could ensue, Roger needed to collect the car.

Over the years, Roger had cycled many miles in our harbour-hopping procedures and his trips tended to take place during the early hours of the morning or late at night. Encountering the unusual had become common and I eagerly awaited his return to hear what oddities he had stumbled upon. He once free-wheeled into a town centre in the small hours to discover a car ablaze in the middle of an empty car park. On other occasions, he narrowly missed a group of playful badger cubs emerging at speed from a wooded verge and had the bicycle's handlebars detach themselves from the main frame whilst struggling up an incline in darkness. However, the most frightening experience happened on this trip, when he encountered a fully grown wild boar in the Mürtiz National Park. I sat on the edge of my seat as he recalled hearing strange grunting sounds. Buster eyed him in disbelief as he described how he had stopped the bike to listen and spotted the huge, rough-coated boar watching him through the undergrowth only a couple of feet away. After making eye contact, Roger did not hang around to see the boar's next move. With his legs rotating as fast as possible on the minute-sized pedals of the little boat bike, he sped off, accompanied by the sound of crashing undergrowth and piggy snorts. He never once glanced back over his shoulder and, when the noises ceased, did not relax until he was out of the park and back on the road.

The search for a marina led us to Ferienzentrum Yachthafen in Rechlin.

"Come in. Bring the dog; dogs are welcome. It's fine," said the small, dark-haired lady behind the reception desk. Silvarna gave Buster a welcoming smile then picked up a small plastic bag from a wicker basket and handed it to me. Printed on the label was a picture of a dog and the words '*Herzlich Willkommen*'. Inside were half a dozen dog biscuits. I looked down at Buster, who was nodding his head in approval. We had found our new home in Germany.

I was taken aback when I met Steven, the harbour master. It was the first time *Lily* would be left in the care of someone so young. Suddenly, I felt old. He was dressed all in black, had bleached blond hair, bulging muscles adorned with tattoos, and earrings larger than my own. Could this 'boy' be trusted with my barge? Despite his lack of English, he greeted us warmly, including Buster, who grinned broadly, almost mockingly. I am sure he was thinking, 'This will get the pair of them worried.'

Trying to sort out the details and contract for the berth took a little time as English was not widely spoken in what was the former Eastern Bloc. Steven disappeared into the hotel – the marina let rooms as well as moorings – and returned with Nette. Small and dark, happy and bright, with tattoos of fairies and flowers, she was instantly loveable and her English was not bad either.

As it turned out, Steven was one of the best harbour masters I have had the pleasure to meet. He worked extremely long hours yet was always friendly, helpful and ready to take a line. He was a presence without being intrusive and *Lily* was safe in his care. Buster had Steven in fits of laughter at lunchtimes. After Buster's walk to dry land for his midday wee, a mad dash back to *Lily* ensued, Buster barking non-stop all the way, desperate to get his much-loved Bonio biscuit. If Steven was in the way, Buster would skim by him. 'Watch out, Beagle coming through,' he seemed to shout. Steven would quickly jump to one side out of his

A beautiful Mecklenburg sunset

path and, laughing, watch him disappear along the pontoon.

Dogs were allowed in the office, restaurant and rooms at the Ferienzentrum. It was a home from home and we revelled in going out for meals knowing Buster was welcome too. Nette was there, always attentive and always eager to practise her English. It felt as if we had been adopted by a dog-friendly family; it was perfect.

In the evenings, Mecklenburg bestowed magical sunsets upon us. To miss having a sundowner in *Lily*'s wheelhouse became unthinkable. It was the best part of the day, a time to relax and gently ponder; many plans were hatched from evenings such as these.

"Let's take *Lily* home."

"Back to England? Do you really want to go home?" I was shocked to hear Roger say this but really should not have been as we had considered it on several occasions following Buster's first diagnosis.

"No, not back to England. To Denmark."

"Wow, to Denmark? But there's nowhere for her to go; there are no rivers or canals."

"We could circumnavigate Sjælland, call into Roskilde Fjord on the way round, have a season on the Baltic." I could tell from the excited tone in Roger's voice that he had been thinking about this for a while.

With the Admiral overseeing events, *Lily* had travelled a long way from Friesland in the Netherlands to the Mecklenburg Lakes in Germany. She had covered a total distance of 533 miles (857km) — more if time spent exploring lakes was calculated — worked through fifty-four locks and fifty-five opening bridges. She had done us proud. Safely delivered at our destination, we now had the whole summer before us. It was time to kick back.

The truly beautiful Mecklenburg Lakes had me in their grasp and being on the doorstep to Lake Mürtiz was where we spent most of the summer: lazing on deck, bobbing in quiet anchorages and at the diverse ports found along its shores, such as Klink, with its French-style chateau, Robel, with boathouses on stilts

The colourful port of Waren on Lake Müritz

and Waren, with its colourful, Mediterranean-style waterfront. Buster was allowed into Müritzeum at Waren. With his entrance ticket came a poo bag; very thoughtful. He found the aquarium especially fascinating, becoming mesmerised by the huge sturgeon, pike and carp.

Some days I would motor *Lily* along the Mürtiz Arm, a peaceful dead end with twisting, reed-lined channels and deep pools littered with water lilies leading to the port of Bucholz. Buster would bark at the gaudy, red-crested pochard ducks with their rusty-orange coloured heads and red, beady eyes. Mecklenburg was full of the unusual. Even the craft on its waters were odd: caravans and campervans on motor-driven platforms, shacks on motorised pontoons – known as Bungalow Boats or Bunbos – and giant-sized pedalos. When an energetic feeling grabbed us, we would lock through to Mirow and moor near the palace, have fresh bread rolls delivered by the harbour master to *Lily*'s door at breakfast time and generally bask in laziness. It was an unusual summer – we were not normally ones to lounge about or take in the sun – so it was a welcome change in one of the most amazing destinations a boater could imagine.

The varied boathouses were a feature of the Mecklenburg Lakes region of Germany

Buster peered over the bow of *Lily*. He was wearing his 'I'm not impressed expression' and gazing down on us in the water as a schoolteacher might on a naughty pupil, eyebrows raised above bifocals in disgust. He was alone on *Lily*, abandoned by his crew. Mutiny on our part was a serious crime and I knew he would be sulky for the remainder of the day. After a swim around the boat, I was ready to get back on board and shower off. There was no sign of Buster on deck so I quietly walked into the wheelhouse and looked down the steps into the saloon, where, curled up in a little ball on the sofa, fast asleep, was Buster.

The summer slipped by effortlessly, relaxing and peaceful. Travel to and from Denmark was easy; on the Rostock to Gedser ferry, Buster was allowed out of the car and up on deck with us. On warm sunny days, we sat outside together, where he could watch the tiny boats far below, gaze at people along the quayside and, once out on the open sea, lie down and relax. On the odd days when the wind was chilly, we sat inside and Buster dozed on his blanket at our feet.

Buster and I were going to spend a week on board *Lily* in Rechlin; we were looking forward to it. Roger was preparing to head home when I noticed a few spots of blood on the steps.

"Buster must have hurt himself," I said as Roger struggled through the doorway with a mountain of items to take home. I gave Buster a check-over and discovered between his pads a small, bloody lump. My heart plummeted as, together, Roger and I bathed it and took a closer look. Once cleaned up, it seemed very small and my panic subsided.

I kept close tabs on Buster's foot all week knowing that, if veterinary assistance was required, the wonderful marina staff would do all they could. By the end of the week, despite having a lovely time, I was growing concerned; the lump had increased in size and was bleeding frequently. It was time to call Claus. I made the call to Roger and that weekend he drove over and collected us.

*Alison and Buster on board
Lily crossing Lake Müritz*

"You did the right thing; it's a tumour and needs to come out before it gets any larger," said Claus. "It's in a nasty place; there's not a lot of flesh there so I'm not going to be able to take away as much as I would like." Roger and I glanced at each other, fear and concern written all over our faces. When I looked back at Claus, he was gently stroking Buster's head. Looking at me, he said, "I think we owe him this chance." I thought, *I owe him my life*. Over the years, Claus had always been honest with us; we felt comfortable with him, knowing he would do his best for Buster.

Roger drove Buster to the veterinary clinic early the next morning then went straight on to work. The house was empty without Buster but I was glad to be there rather than the boat, which would have been even worse without his presence. Buster had had operations before but this time I felt terrified for him; I could not shake the feeling. As well as removing the tumour, Claus was going to remove a further two lumps. One was a real concern as it was close to where the original tumour had been over four years previously.

Following surgery, there was no cute little bodysuit on this occasion; instead, one of those horrid cones which not only Buster but all dogs seemed to hate. Claus had removed as much as he could on Buster's foot but the stitches were tight as hardly any spare flesh was left. The other lumps were all fatty tissue and the operation had gone well. Back home, Buster was slow to get up on his feet; he seemed exhausted and the recovery time was longer than for previous operations.

A few days after his return, I was making myself a cup of coffee when I heard a noise, so familiar that I did not even think much of it. But then it clicked; it was Buster getting up into his camping chair. I whizzed round and there, sitting in the sun, was my chin-strap-woey. He seemed fine so I left him to doze and, when he awoke, gently lifted him down onto the cool tile floor. A few days later, he was too quick for me and red spots of blood trailing across the floor sent alarm bells ringing. Buster had jumped down from the camping chair and split the stitches in the bottom of his foot.

It was a setback but Claus was positive and gave us some antiseptic cream and words of advice. He could put a staple in the foot but that seemed a little severe and the wound had begun to heal. In a few days' time, the remaining stitches would be removed. We agreed to restrict his movement and leave things as they were.

It was time to face facts. Roger and I spent many evenings discussing Buster's health and, in the end, decided to give him time out. He had undergone some major operations over the past couple of years, was still struggling with the underlying problem of IIMP and was now eleven years old. We did not know how much longer we had with him and wanted to enjoy what was left. His recovery time was eating into his quality of life.

"No operations for the next twelve months; agreed?" asked Roger.

"Agreed … unless of course it's an emergency."

Chapter Eleven

EASTERN BLOC WINTER

The cranes were beginning to leave, their noisy cries echoing over Lake Müritz. Early mornings and evenings, swallows swirled around the boats in the marina, darkening the sky with their vast numbers. I had never witnessed such an intense migration as that in the Mecklenburg Lakes and, as the birds prepared to head south, so did we. There were no facilities open to boaters throughout winter in this region of Germany but, thanks to a couple I had met through the internet, a winter berth in Berlin had been secured. Alison and Roger, our namesakes, had a beautiful barge, *Iron Lady*. Built in the Czech Republic, they had cruised her through Europe, spending the previous winter in Köpenick, part of the former Eastern Bloc, and the marina came highly recommended.

We bid a sad farewell to Steven and Nette and all the friends we had made but there was something special about saying, "See you in the spring." The autumn journey back through the Obere-Havel was stunningly beautiful. Early mornings began with misty shrouds and a refreshing chill to the air. As the day progressed and the sun rose into clear skies, it created perfect, mirror-like reflections for *Lily's* bow to distort. She glided almost silently through them, causing the dew-heavy reed heads to nod in approval of their

autumnal visitor. As far as I was concerned, the beautiful Obere-Havel could go on forever; it was perfect.

Rustic style Bunbos on the Obere-Havel

At Lehnitz Lock, a queue of traffic waited. Commercial barges were plentiful and having priority relegated the leisure craft undertaking their autumnal exodus. A large white cruiser pulled alongside and the couple asked if they could moor to *Lily*; there was no room remaining on the waiting jetty. They had a dog on board and Buster was keen to meet his new four-legged shipmate.

When the green light was finally given, there was a great rush of activity and boats everywhere as they hurriedly streamed towards the lock. Poor *Lily* fought desperately to keep up with them but the lightweight glass-fibre craft with powerful engines left our hefty barge standing. By the time *Lily* entered the lock, every other boat was tied in, their crews staring at us as if we were to blame for keeping them waiting all afternoon.

It was growing dark by the time the descent was over so Roger and I decided to stop for the night. Other boats, whose crew knew the river, continued but the couple who had moored to us also decided to stay and kindly guided us into a spot below the lock where turbulence was slight.

Buster played with their dog whilst we chatted together. The man fetched two pig's ears and the dogs settled down, crunching contentedly on their treats.

"We're leaving early in the morning. We still have a long way to go but we'll try not to disturb you." The man gathered his dog and prepared to go back on board.

"It was nice meeting you." I offered my outstretched hand but he could not take it. An industrial accident had resulted in limited movement in his right arm so instead we shook left hands and laughed together.

"Have a Happy Christmas," he said with a broad grin.

"Happy Christmas! Bit early, isn't it?"

"Yes, but it's what we do at the end of the season because we don't see each other again until the spring."

"Well, you have a Happy Christmas too and a safe journey home." I leant down and gave his dog a pat.

"Thank you and maybe we'll see you next year. We're often on Lake Müritz. Come find us; you are welcome."

To reach Köpenick, we had the same routine to go through in Berlin. This time, we were adventurous and joined the night convoy. Buster knew we were waiting for something – there was never any pulling the wool over his eyes – and he, like us, felt anticipation in the air. It was dark by 10 p.m. A couple of other boats had joined us throughout the afternoon and, as the departure time arrived, engines fired up. Roger and I had not done much night cruising and what we had was on waters we knew well; consequently, we proceeded cautiously along the Spree. Buster was sleepy and kept yawning, fighting his tiredness. The first few miles were uneventful; lights were being turned on in buildings and slowly the city was coming to life. From behind, a trip boat slid by, music thumping, laser-beam lights reaching high into the night sky. Buster watched it pass and grumbled under his breath.

Approaching Hauptbahnhof, it became hectic. A huge commercial barge slowly edged out of a side water into the river, causing all traffic to stop; even the trip boat had to give way, causing a concertina effect. The boats which had been neatly spaced out were now squashed together, sitting midstream in darkness, projected images and lights flashed around the city's main buildings. Slowly the traffic sorted itself out and moved on. One boat headed into the city's main moorings, doing the Berlin Shuffle, a routine where boaters headed from one city mooring to the next each day. As the bridges came thick and fast, so did the trip and disco boats. Their bright lights and music kept Buster interested but their selfish attitude towards other boaters kept Roger and me on our toes.

"I'm going to put the mast down. This next bridge is tight and these trip boats keep trying to push us over. If we're not careful, *Lily*'s going to take a hit." Roger made his way to the bow to access the roof. The river was getting choppy from the wash; for trip boats, time was money and, passing closely, they sent *Lily* rocking. The boat in front hesitated at a bridge and I knocked *Lily* into reverse to slow her. He had plenty of time to get through before the approaching trip boat but had decided to stop and let it through

Lily in the night convoy through central Berlin

first. Now we were too close together and, with no room to manoeuvre, we both had to go through the bridge together as a second trip boat loomed out of the darkness towards us.

"Hang on, Buzz." I pushed the throttle down. Roger walked into the wheelhouse in time to see the boat in front make it clear of the bridge, its powerful engine propelling the craft at double the speed of *Lily*.

"Beeeeep." The trip boat let out a warning blast but there was nowhere for me to go. I had to keep going; behind, another trip boat was looming. We were about to become a *Lily* sandwich.

"Beeeeep, beeeeep," came the trip boat's horn again. The next time, its skipper left his hand on it; the noise blasted long and far into the night. There was room for the trip boat to move but it was out to prove a point. I had moved *Lily* over as much as I dared. Roger was hanging over the side.

"Enough, that's enough!" he shouted. Buster barked and jumped on the spot in his bed, aiming his bark at the trip boat.

"What does he expect me to do?"

"Hold your ground; there's enough room for us both. Don't come over any more," Roger was yelling above the music coming from the boat.

"Shall I stop and let him pass?"

"No, keep going. If you stop, his wash will push us into the side."

At the eleventh hour, the trip boat moved and we passed with a few inches to spare on either side of the bridge pillars. The trip boat behind overtook without problem beneath the next bridge, proving the awkwardness of the previous skipper. With the drama of a near miss in pitch blackness behind us, we approached Museum Island and with it came a sense of calm. The choppy wash had subsided, the buildings lit in white lights looked both eerie and beautiful. Passing the Bode Museum and the Berlin Cathedral, out of the darkness came the haunting sound of a choir singing. It filled the air, adding an evocative feeling to the already Gothic scene.

Catching up with the commercial barge at Mühlendamm Lock, we were called in to penn through together. With a sigh of relief, we eased in and tied off. The night-time convoy had been short but full of drama. Seeing Berlin from that angle and at that time of night was very special. After locking through, a mooring was needed and they were limited. Roger eased *Lily* into Spreekanal. It was like entering another world; all was quiet and dark, very dark. I went to the bow with a powerful, handheld spotlight and shone it on the two bridges ahead as

I needed to check headroom. They had low, arched spans. *Lily* made it through with no problem. At the moorings, there were two boats secured either end, leaving us a small space to squeeze into. It was late and we were tired. Even Buster had dozed off but we managed to ease *Lily* in.

"Are you from England?" came a voice out of the darkness. The man was off the cruiser moored at the front.

"Yes, we are," I answered, trying to battle with ropes in the dark.

"Shall I move up; it's no problem?"

"No, we're in and that's all that matters this time of night. You're fine, but thanks all the same."

"Good." Turning to walk away, he called out, "Nice boat."

The Wassersportzentrum Berlin at Köpenick, where we overwintered from October to March, was an ice-free marina, achieved by compressed air being pumped through pipes on the river bed. When the temperatures plummeted below freezing, the system automatically switched on. This was not a necessary requirement for *Lily*, her thick steel hull capable of withstanding the hardest of winters, but it meant we could run the engine regularly and access the river to cruise throughout the coldest and darkest days of winter. The downside was the constant noise on the hull, although, over time, I became used to it.

Expecting a cold, harsh winter based on central European waterways, we decided I should move on board full-time. This way, *Lily* could be looked after properly, heating on and pumping through the system preventing frozen pipes or damage to the engine. By November, temperatures had dropped to -5°C. The easterly wind made it feel colder and conjured up waves on the Müggelspree, the waterway connecting Berlin's largest lake to the River Spree. These splashed against *Lily*'s hull, leaving a fringe of long, icy fingers dangling from her stern. At the end of November, on our twelfth wedding anniversary, we took Buster to the Christmas market and funfair at Alexanderplatz. Whilst sipping steaming *Glühwein* from thick glass mugs, Buster lapped up free samples of smoked sausage, attention from passersby and watching skaters on the ice rink. It was bright and colourful with stalls of German delicacies, hand-painted Russian Matryoshka dolls, Christmas decorations and sumptuous confectionery.

My time in Köpenick with Buster was special; we were reliving the full-time boating life we had had in England. I would wrap Buster in his fleece coat, take him on short walks in bitter temperatures, returning to spend snug, cosy nights in front of the wood burner. At weekends, when Roger arrived, we exchanged gas bottles, purchased solid fuel for the week and headed out onto the water, where, apart from the odd coal barge or water police vessel, *Lily* was the only craft on the move. She became a familiar sight; the locals grew to know us and we felt at home.

Despite the cold, Buster still craved to be in the wheelhouse and not below decks in the warmth. With his fleece coat on, he snuggled into his bed and watched as Roger and I guided *Lily* out of the marina. The riverside houses decorated in Christmas attire looked full of life but the moorings at the foot of the gardens stood empty and forlorn; even the boat clubs looked abandoned. Approaching the Müggelsee, *Lily*'s engine died. I was at the helm and quickly pushed the throttle forwards but *Lily* had nothing to give. My stomach lurched at the sound of silence and a wave of panic rose.

"What's up?" Roger called from below decks.

"She just died on me. I'll turn her over." With the engine in neutral, I turned the key and the engine fired but almost immediately died. "Nothing; you'd better come up and see." I turned the steering into the gentle breeze, hoping *Lily* would stay put. Being in a no-anchoring zone, she would have to drift until the problem was sorted.

In the engine room, Roger checked everything he could think of but found nothing. The breeze was increasing and the great expanse of the lake was visible in front. There were no moorings along the river; one side was shallow with low grassy banks, the other lined with industrial buildings. Our only hope was to try and reach the deserted moorings of a small boat club. The little flow on the river was pushing *Lily* in the general direction but the breeze was holding her off.

"I think I'll have to swim for it." Roger stared into the cold, grey depths of the freezing water.

"I knew we should have left the dinghy on the boat." I was cross with myself for taking it off. Roger stripped off to his underwear and T-shirt. With a long rope, he walked to the front of the boat and prepared to jump into the water. It was going to take him a while to pluck up courage. Waiting at the helm, I looked down at the controls, dreading the outcome, and noticed the depth. Quickly stepping out of the wheelhouse, I yelled, "Don't dive in for goodness' sake; it's only five feet deep." He gazed back at me and as our eyes met, we both realised it was shallow enough to pole *Lily* into the moorings. Holding *Lily* on the bow thruster, Roger quickly dressed and was soon on the rear deck, poling her through the waters of the Mugglespree. We could both sigh with relief but it was not the end of our problems. Reaching the moorings, there was no way out to the street. *Lily* was safely secured but we were trapped.

I carried Buster below decks and he curled up on the sofa. Covered in a warm blanket, he snoozed contently. With *Lily* secure, Roger made a more thorough investigation in the engine room and eventually discovered the diesel pump had fractured. There was no spare on board: time to panic. Roger phoned everyone he could think of but to no avail, the marina owner, and his suggestions of nearby contacts, all away for the weekend. There was another option – call the German water police. The last thing I wanted to do was become involved with the law and face a hefty fee for the tow back.

With daylight fading and, with it, our options, there was only one thing left to do – punt *Lily* all the way back to the marina. By now, Buster had itchy feet and wanted to get off the boat for a wee. Roger was able to lift him onto a small patch of grass outside the boat club's door, where he soon lifted his leg, relieved himself and did not waste any time returning to the boat. For him, the day out had been a dull affair. Roger began punting us home, carefully feeling for the shallower river bed, hugging the bank and jetties as much as possible. The wind had dropped and, with hardly any flow on the river, going was slow but it was surprising how easy *Lily* could be propelled with a simple ash pole. As darkness fell and the cheerful sparkles of Christmas lights began to flicker in the houses, Roger began to sing the 'one Cornetto' ice cream song, 'O sole mio'. We could have easily been drifting along Venice's Grand Canal, my Venetian gondolier punting and joyfully serenading me through waters twinkling with reflections.

Almost back at the marina, we heard the deep throbbing of an engine and, out of the darkness, came a trip boat. We had been saving battery power but now had to dash below and get the lights on fast. Unable to reach the marina before the boat passed, we braced ourselves for a knock from its wash. It came and, as luck would have it, was enough to propel *Lily* into the end of her own jetty. Roger quickly fastened a rope onto a cleat and the wash pulled *Lily*'s stern around, enabling Roger to pull her into place. We were safe and sound.

Roger's hands were sore and blistered from the punting; his back and upper torso ached. He was totally exhausted but happy and relieved to have delivered boat and crew back to safe harbour. Fastening *Lily* into her berth, Buster sauntered up on deck and looked at us as if we were both mad.

With a new diesel pump fitted, it was time for a Christmas shake-down cruise. Beyond the town of Erkner, famed as the birthplace of Bakelite plastic, we drifted into a series of three interlinked lakes, which culminated in a dead end. It was bitterly cold and we had only been moored a short while when the snow began to fall. Inside, *Lily*'s stove radiated warmth throughout the boat.

The next morning, there was a thin coating of ice on the lake and a hard frost covering *Lily*; her large, plastic fenders were dusted in it and the wheelhouse windows were frozen solid. With the saloon door open, the heat from the stove soon permeated into the wheelhouse and melted the frozen windows. At midday, knowing temperatures would rise no higher, we made our move. Most of the ice had melted but, in the shady areas, it was hanging on. In the canal cuts linking the lakes, ice protested loudly as *Lily* ploughed through, reminding us of the Carnadoe Waters and friends many miles away.

Pusher tugs with dumb barges full of snow-dusted mounds of coal were the only other sign of life on the river. Snow had fallen overnight and *Lily* was coated with several inches. I slipped Buster's fleece coat over his body and opened the wheelhouse door. He looked out, looked back at me and smiled. Leaping onto the bank, he plunged his nose deep into the snow and brought it out covered in the stuff, shook it off and ran across the small park at Schmöckwitz on the River Dahme, with a rare spring in his step. I watched as he waded through the drifts, which were deep enough to reach his stomach; at times he had to fight to

lift his legs through it. Roger and I togged up and cleared the snow off *Lily's* deck. A few birds were waiting around, hoping a friendly

Snowy conditions on the River Dahme, Berlin, over the festive season

local might bring them some scraps of food. I took pity on them and found some crusts of bread. Afterwards, we warmed up in front of the stove, tucking into a full English breakfast.

On New Year's Eve, Roger treated us to a Chinese take-away. Buster sat and waited patiently, knowing full well where his master had gone. Great squeaks of joy filled the boat when Roger returned with a smelly carrier bag in his hands. In Buster's opinion, a bowl of egg-fried rice was a perfect start to the new year.

Chapter Twelve

MECKLENBURG REVISITED

Easter saw us braving snow showers as we retraced steps back towards the Mecklenburg Lakes. Along the way, we visited places missed previously such as the Ziegeleipark Mildenberg. Despite the cold and snow, we huddled beneath fleece blankets on a narrow-gauge railway and toured the brickworks with Buster wedged between our legs, seeking out warmth. Our female guide and train driver, unable to speak much English, went the extra mile, doing her utmost to help us understand the commentary, asking others on the tour to help.

Rheinsberg proved more difficult to reach. A holdup at the newly automated lock and a fallen tree across the cut tried their best to prevent *Lily* reaching the waterside castle. We settled in at the lock side, expecting a long wait, but, after an hour or so, everything sprang into life and *Lily* was soon passing through. The fallen tree was only small and there was enough room for *Lily* to carefully pass it.

Approaching Rechlin and Lake Müritz felt like coming home. *Lily* was the first boat to arrive at the marina that season and Steven was there to see us in. It was good to be back. Buster smiled and wasted no time in refamiliarising himself with the grounds. Having our old mooring back for a month enabled

The impressive palace at Rheinsberg

Lily to be prepared for the forthcoming sea voyage in a familiar and comfortable setting. The short icebreaking incident in Berlin had scraped a small section of paint off the hull. Venturing onto salt water without treating it was not wise so a lift-out was arranged at a boatyard on the Mirower Kanal.

Roger waved me off from the pontoon and was still standing there watching as I motored *Lily* out of sight. Buster squeaked as he disappeared.

"It's just us now, Buzzy. Daddy will meet us there." The snowy-white egrets complained as *Lily* disturbed them wading in the cool morning waters, hunting for frogs. It was chilly as I entered the canal, the wisps of swirling mist growing thicker. By the time I reached the small lake and had found the entrance markers, it was dense. Relying on the GPS, I slowly steered *Lily* across the lake. "This isn't very nice, Buzzy. I can't see the markers." When I finally spotted them, I had drifted slightly off to starboard. Keeping a straight course was difficult in normal conditions but, with mist, easy to become disorientated. Lining *Lily* up, I motored through the gateway. A little further on, I could make out the darkness of the banks and the entrance to the canal. It was now a straightforward run to the boatyard where Roger would meet us, having taken the car to act as Buster's base whilst *Lily* was inaccessible.

Buster watched proceedings carefully and then fell into a deep sleep on the quayside as the sun burnt off the mist. Roger and I worked on *Lily*'s hull. She was in surprisingly good condition, the only area in need of work the icebreaking line around the bow, which could be carried out with her still hanging from the crane. Roger also changed *Lily*'s anodes from magnesium to aluminium, which were more suited to salt water.

With repainting complete, we spent a day on the Bolder Kanal. The route was only navigable for a short distance by motor vessel, its first lock disused however, it was possible to paddle it all by canoe. Entering the confined waters from the expanse of Lake Müritz, Buster rushed up to the bow, immediately sensing the change in environment. Everything looked bare; spring was yet to arrive.

To reach Rechlin, we had passed Fürstenberg, where a sorrowful sculpture loomed over the lake. With no moorings to access land and intrigued to discover more, we returned by car. I was saddened to discover it was the site of a concentration camp but not the first we had come across

Roger watching an early spring sunset at Rechlin

on our travels. At Oranienburg, Roger had visited Sachsenhausen, one of the most notorious camps in Germany, and we had taken *Lily* into the former brickworks of Klinkerhafen, a forced labour camp used in the construction of the harbour. However, Ravensbrück at Fürstenberg was a women's camp, particularly poignant, and, for me, touched a raw nerve. How could a stunningly beautiful place be linked to such atrocities?

Chapter Thirteen

TO THE BALTIC WITH BUZZ

The Silver Ribbon glistened and sparkled in the morning light. We were on new waters, experiencing the familiar feeling of intrepidness that Buster and I had come to relish. Beagles have a built-in sense of wanderlust, always wanting to follow a scent, take a snuffle around the next corner and see what they can find. The breed and I were similar in the sense of having itchy feet, wanting to move on and explore always in the forefront of our minds and, when the sun shone, there was nothing better than following your nose.

Winding its way through a mixture of lakes and narrow cuttings, the Silver Ribbon – the River Elde – would eventually carry us towards the Elbe. Stops at the tourist towns of Plau-am-See and Malchow were followed by a diversion to the Hanseatic seat of Schwerin, although the series of long, straight canal cuts to reach it seemed never-ending.

By the time the Schweriner See was entered, storm clouds had gathered. Appearing out of nowhere, they were driven across the sky by a fierce wind that buffeted and rocked *Lily*. In the distance, Schwerin's fairy-tale castle glowed gold against the backdrop of an increasingly darkening sky.

"We'd better get a move on. I don't like the look of that." My eyes were fixed on the grey smudges of rain falling off the back of the approaching clouds.

Roger reached forwards, and pushed the throttle down and *Lily* gave us all she had. Cutting through the growing chop of the waves with her weighty bow, she raced the storm clouds across the lake.

As we neared the castle, the storm closed in. Roger and I fought with ropes, gathered *Lily* in and secured her to the only mooring available whilst the wind tried its best to push her off. Buster watched with concern, or perhaps it was amusement, as thunder roared, lightning flashed and the heavens opened. Halyards rattled in a mad frenzy, ropes creaked and boats jostled as the wind-driven waves violently hit their hulls. Above the rooftops of Schwerin, the clouds had begun to swirl into a great vortex. Travelling at speed, they looked intent on sucking in anything and everything in their path.

Busy securing *Lily,* we had not noticed a hire boat approaching. It was not until the last rope was fastened that we saw it. The lightweight glass-fibre boat bounced; it had no weight to help hold its position in the stormy waters. The German crew were all out on deck, wearing frightened expressions rather than life jackets. The skipper motored back and forth but did not seem to want to moor. Roger stepped onto *Lily* and walked to the bow.

Twisting storm clouds forming over the rooftops of Schwerin

"Would you like to tie onto us?" he shouted through cupped hands, hoping to be heard over the wind.

"Are these the public moorings?" the helmsman yelled back. One of the children on deck had begun to cry uncontrollably.

"No, these are for the restaurant. I'll take your rope; you can come alongside."

There was hesitation followed by discussion between the crew, too much time wasted in coming to a decision. A young lady hugged the crying child and pointed out Buster, which brought about a temporary let-up in the sobs, but the wind then dealt a punishing blow, pushing the boat violently sideways and they started up again.

"We can't afford to eat here," the helmsman shouted as he battled with the steering. Before Roger could offer to purchase them a cup of tea and a slice of cake, he had promptly turned the boat around. We watched in disbelief as they headed onto the open lake, the child's terrified cries swept up and carried away on the wind.

The wild weather held us captive in Schwerin for longer than planned. The manager of the restaurant was accommodating, having no problems with us staying on the cliental

Crew Lily moored opposite Schwerin Castle

moorings provided we ate one meal a day in the premises. Money was tight but, being frugal with choices, costs could be kept lower than previous moorings in other towns. By eating at lunchtime or early evening, we could eat outside, which meant Buster was able to accompany us.

A few days had passed before Roger and I discovered we had witnessed a tornado. It had skimmed Schwerin but hit Hamburg, with loss of life and structural damage sustained. Container ships in the port had broken lines and been swept free. Devastation and destruction loomed over parts of Northern Germany. At such times, contemplation took over. How lucky we had been to make safe harbour and to have been on the outer limits of the storm. As for the people in the hire boat, the public moorings they sought lay further up the lake on the outskirts of town. Roger, Buster and I spent an afternoon walking there and scanned the rows of moored boats in the harbour but never saw them. Being on a hire boat and having to keep to a schedule, it was likely they had left days before we found out about the circumstances which had briefly brought us together.

At Dömitz, we joined the River Elbe. With a reputation for low water levels and shifting shoals, the channel had to be followed closely. Skippers of craft over 49 feet (15m) in length required a special qualification or had to be accompanied by a pilot to navigate the Elbe. We did not and felt privileged to be let loose on one of Europe's major waterways. A late afternoon cruise downstream saw us arriving in Lauenberg as the sun slowly set.

The following morning, we turned *Lily*'s bow towards the coast. On leaving Ireland, we had hoped to cross the Irish Sea from Dublin to Liverpool but the weather had other ideas. This had played havoc with Roger, the Irish Sea becoming his nemesis. The only way to rectify this was to venture out onto salt water again and where better to head than the Baltic Sea, bringing *Lily* home to Denmark? Surely with Buster, the Admiral, alongside Roger at the helm, we could successfully take on the Baltic.

Leaving the Elbe, we joined the Lübeck Canal. This once formed part of the Salt Route, dealing with vast shipments of the commodity. Some of the former warehouses had been beautifully preserved in the city of Lübeck, which, due to its extensive Brick Gothic architecture, was a UNESCO World Heritage Site. It was also the birthplace of marzipan and everything edible seemed to be flavoured with it, from coffee to ice cream. We frequently overindulged, particularly with the delicious marzipan cake.

Lübeck sat alongside the tidal River Trave, which flowed into the Baltic at the seaside town and port of Travemunde. Roger had telephoned the fishermen's harbour and booked a berth for *Lily*. After a relaxing morning cruise downriver and the first view of the Baltic from the wheelhouse, we eased *Lily* into her overnight spot.

"No, not possible, you must go." A man had appeared out of the motorsailer moored in the next berth and was frantically waving his arms up and down. Roger and I looked at each other a little confused. "See here." Now he was pointing at a small, red square on the quay wall. "Go, please, back away."

The Baltic seaports operated a red/green card system for berths. It was a simple arrangement which required the permanent berth holder to turn their small, coloured square situated on the berth to green when leaving. This indicated to visiting boats the berth was free and could be taken up; if left red but empty, the boater could assume its resident would be returning that

Restored salt warehouses in Lübeck

evening. It was considered bad manners to moor in one displaying red, even if it was only for a few moments. The berth reserved for *Lily* was showing red but the harbour master had already told us over the phone not to take any notice. Obviously, this gentleman, not being personally informed, thought the ultimate crime had been committed.

Chapter Fourteen

DENMARK OR BUST

Roger had woken early and taken Buster for a walk along the promenade and was back on board by the time I awoke. Buster, happily fed and watered, watched Roger single the ropes and programme the GPS. The well-known British actor Timothy Spall and his author wife, Shane, were a day behind us on their seagoing barge, *Princess Matilda*. We had been hoping our paths would cross since joining the Mittelland Kanal but different time schedules, workload and their unforeseen mechanical problems had not allowed it. Sadly, we would miss them again but knew better than to squander a good weather window.

With *Lily* being relatively slow, a decision was taken to break the journey to Denmark at the port of Burgstaaken on the German island of Fehmarn. This would allow Buster time ashore, as well as giving ourselves a well-earned break. It also acted as a safety precaution. Neither of us was sure how *Lily* would handle the open sea so, if the voyage was uncomfortable, land and safe harbour would not be far away. Roger had liased with our insurance company, providing a full cruising itinerary to Denmark and asking if the third member of the crew could be dispensed with as no one was available at short notice. Given our previous experience, the insurance company agreed but still insisted on extra requirements, one of which was the provision of a spare bilge pump. Roger thought this hilarious and declared that, next time he saw David, he would tell him he was worth a spare bilge pump.

From the chart table, Buster watched the waves lapping the hull. During sunny spells, he stretched out and soaked up the warmth; when gusty winds and drizzle hit, he curled into his bed and slept. *Lily* handled the varying conditions adequately and some of Roger's confidence at being on the sea was restored. Motoring into Burgstaaken, the sun reappeared to reflect off an odd-looking metal capsule sitting on the waterfront: an old Soviet submarine, part of the U-Boat Museum's collection.

After refuelling and taking one of the best side-on moorings *Lily* had had in several weeks, it was not long before the harbour master appeared. Roger explained our plans and was promptly ushered to his office. I was concerned; perhaps we had done something wrong or needed to report to an authority overlooked when researching the journey. Thankfully, it was nothing like that. The harbour master printed an up-to-date weather forecast and advised Roger to leave straight away; a weather front was approaching, bringing a prolonged unsettled spell.

The U-boat Museum at Burgstaaken on the German island of Fehmarn

"We should go." Roger was waving the printout.

"Are you sure? It's a really good mooring." He thrust it into my hands. It was obvious if we did not move now we would be stuck on the island for days.

"I'll walk Buzz; we'll have a bite to eat then push off. Agreed?"

"Agreed." I went below and prepared a light lunch.

With the sun shining and the Baltic Sea gently rolling beneath *Lily*'s hull, hugging the coast of Fehmarn, passing Staberhuk lighthouse, German soil was left behind. Buster had been sitting in his bed on the wheelhouse floor, his head leaning out to catch the breeze, but the further away from land, the more pronounced the swell and he soon retreated below decks. The Baltic Sea had strange wind-created effects, which produced an odd sensation. As the wind gently pushed *Lily*'s stern in one direction, the swell pulled her in the opposite. It was not a battle to control her, more of a gentle persuasion.

Roger and I shared duties at the helm, each trying to catch forty winks with Buster on the sofa when the other took over. The huge Nysted and Rødsand wind farm boasting 162 turbines slowly became visible, backed by the distant smudge of Danish land.

"There's Denmark!" shouted Roger and we whooped for joy but there was still some way to go and a major shipping lane to cross.

By the time the shipping lane was reached, Roger was tacking *Lily* back and forth. The sea looked smooth but the underlying pull was uncomfortable. It was unusual to see a barge at sea; one constantly travelling back and forth adjacent to a major shipping lane even more so. Unsurprisingly, it was not long before the Danish coastguard vessel took an interest. *Lily* had gigantic seagoing vessels thundering along the shipping lane to port, the coastguard vessel patrolling and monitoring to starboard.

"We're going across on this tack." Roger increased *Lily*'s speed. If all went to plan, she would be lined up to cross safely between two ships, one no more than a speck in the distance. That one turned out to be travelling faster than we thought, however, and *Lily* did not make up enough ground. "We'll have to go again." Roger turned *Lily* away to try again and, at the second attempt, the timing was just right. Seeing *Lily* would make it across without hindering traffic, the coastguard vessel steamed off in the opposite direction.

"Thank goodness he's gone; he was making me nervous!" I put my arm around Roger's waist and planted a kiss on his cheek. "Well done."

The sun was fading fast behind the spinning wind turbines but, with the country's most southerly town and port of Gedser on the island of Falster in sight, we were on the last leg and jubilant. Buster had slept the whole afternoon, only now returning to the wheelhouse to see where *Lily* had carried him. Reaching the guest harbour at Gedser meant skirting a vast sandbank. Coming into port by ferry, it was very prominent but from *Lily*, sitting low in the water by comparison, this advantage was lost.

"It's getting shallow, isn't it?" Roger was already closely examining the paper chart. "Hmmm, there should be a black marker out there somewhere but I can't see it."

"Let me have a look." I stared at the chart, then out to sea, I could not see a marker either and we were rapidly losing the light. Baffled, we continued slowly on our heading but it was becoming shallower.

"Pass me the binoculars." Roger scanned the sea but could not see anything. I checked the chart again and realised that the icon we were looking at was not a marker but the icon for a shipwreck. We were heading straight for the sandbank.

"We need to get the hell out of here," I screamed in Roger's ear. *Lily's* depth sounder was reading four feet and falling. Rapidly, he turned her wheel and immediately found deeper water.

In fading light, we fell in behind the Rostock to Gedser ferry and followed the buoyed channel into the marina. The journey, a total of 66 miles (106km), more if calculating the tacking, had taken all day to complete. By the time we entered the safe confines of Gedser Marina, it was 10 p.m. Exhausted and in need of sleep, the port became home for the next seven days as, around us, the winds howled.

Chapter Fifteen

ISLAND HOPPING

To me, the idea of island hopping sounded romantic; it conjured up opportunities of brief encounters with interesting people in exciting places. However, the thought of island hopping around Denmark did not hold the same sense of adventure as somewhere such as the West Indies might. But I was wrong, as there were interesting people, excitement and adventure aplenty.

With the weather improving, we could finally move on and not before time. Buster and I had enjoyed Gedser but were itching to see new places. Following the sea voyage, *Lily* had been thoroughly checked over – fuel filters cleaned and tanks filled with new diesel – and she too seemed keen to get underway. Before leaving, there was one thing left to do – hoist *Lily's* new Women on Barges (WOB) burgee. I had joined the Facebook-based group some time previously but the flag had only just been designed and made. As the group's first barge on the Baltic, *Lily* flew it with pride.

The Guldborg Sound was a narrow stretch of water separating the islands of Falster and Lolland, too shallow for many craft but ideal for a barge. Our first hop was to Nykøbing, still on Falster, then across the water to Guldborg on Lolland, before reaching the wider and deeper waters of Smålands Farvandet

and the Masnedø Sound, where *Lily* carried us safely into the port of Vordingborg on our home island of Sjælland. Good reason to celebrate and ice creams were the order of the day. Buster greedily licked out the

Nykøbing and the Nordic Sugar plant on the Danish island of Falster

tub of vanilla, dipping the tips of his long ears in it, relishing every mouthful. He had us in fits of laughter. Afterwards, he rolled about on the grass and grumbled, trying to remove the sticky mess from his face with his front paws.

"Look at that crazy dog." Roger was laughing so much, he could hardly speak. "What's wrong with him?"

"Guess he must have doggy brain freeze."

There was plenty to do at Vordingborg and the castle and its grounds became a regular walk. School children would sometimes be taking part in medieval re-enactments; it was fun to watch them learning archery and battle manoeuvres. Taking a break on a bench in the sun, Buster sat at my feet watching their games. In the evenings, we walked along the former railway track converted into a cycleway and footpath that reminded me of our fun-filled days on the Witham. The hedgerows were full of wild roses and lilac, which released a sweet, intoxicating scent that mingled with the aroma from the more potently scented fields of rapeseed. Buster would be celebrating his twelfth birthday later that year; he had slowed up a lot, got breathless and tired but still enjoyed his walks and felt deprived if they were cut short. I carried a bottle of water everywhere. After a drink and the obligatory biscuit, Buster felt refreshed and able to tackle another twenty minutes.

Lily was moored below the Goose Tower, part of Vordingborg Castle built by King Valdemar the Great in 1175. She was out on a limb, alone on the hammerhead of a long jetty, allowing Buster to lounge outside without disturbing anyone. The berth offered fantastic views up to the castle or across the water towards the road bridges linking Sjælland to Falster via the tiny island of Farø but, when the weather once again took a turn for the worse, I was left wishing she had been moored further into the harbour.

It was 3 a.m. when I finally phoned Roger. Buster and I had been awake for hours enduring the storm, which was hitting us side-on, causing *Lily* to thud hard against her fenders and the jetty. The RIB had lost a rope and was full of water. Extra ropes were

The calm before the storm – yachts in Vordingborg Marina, Sjælland

needed but they were missing from the bow locker. I had searched everywhere but could not find them. I managed to reach the RIB with the boat hook and refasten it to *Lily*. The weather was still giving it a beating but there was no way I could move it alone in the wicked conditions. If I slipped and went into the water, there would be no way of getting out without help. I had scanned the marina for the nearest emergency ladder; it was a good swim away. Despite being a strong swimmer, it seemed unlikely I would have reached it. I could have put our own ladder over the side but it would have been instantly lost in the violent rising and falling of the waves. Buster watched from the wheelhouse as the sea foamed around the hull; despite the pitch black of night, the white frothiness could still be clearly seen. I willed Roger to quickly answer his phone.

It was growing light as Roger arrived, tired and concerned, but he quickly sprang into action and adjusted the badly worn bow rope. In the passing hours, the winds had not abated; the halyards rattled as the wind screeched through the rigging of the yachts, sounding as if a demented banshee were on the rampage. It was driving me mad; my teeth were on edge and I was sure my head would explode if the noise did not stop. Buster was so pleased to see Roger he let out a chorus of barks but, once he realised there was work to be done, backed off, allowing us to get on with the task.

"I've looked everywhere for the ropes; where the hell are they?" I screamed above the noise of the wind.

"Where they always are." Roger fought against the wind to reach the bow, lifted the locker lid and looked inside. "Where the hell are they?"

"That's what I just asked you!" The wind was fierce, carrying our voices away, ripping at our clothes, making it difficult to stand on the exposed jetty.

"Do you think they've been stolen?" Roger was quiet, thinking. Time was ticking by. We could not afford to waste it.

"Rog, we need to do something. This rope is almost through." A driving gust of wind hit *Lily* hard, forcing her against the wooden jetty, squashing the air from the fenders, then fell away violently. Buster, sitting patiently on the wheelhouse seat, had been at eye level. As *Lily* dropped, he disappeared, plummeting out of view only to return a few seconds later. I stared at him; he was wearing his sometimes-smile, enjoying the surging ride as if at the fairground.

Suddenly, Roger rushed by me, heading for the wheelhouse.

"I know where they are. I packed them away for the sea crossing." He jumped on board and headed for the engine room. Roger had packed the ropes neatly away, coiled into a large, heavy-duty rubber bucket. He had pushed them into the furthest corner of the engine room, concealed from view by his toolbox. I would never have found them; the toolbox was ridiculously heavy and there was no way I could have moved it. I could have damaged not only myself but also something vitally important in the engine room. This was a lesson for us both: always to let the other know when changes were made. To allow more 'give' in the mooring lines, Roger purchased two heavy-duty rubber snubbers, which acted as shock absorbers, and fitted them to new, thicker ropes. They proved a welcome addition throughout *Lily*'s time on the constantly moving sea.

Two weeks of high winds, combined with work commitments, held us in Vordingborg. When it was finally time to leave, the weather bestowed a beautifully calm afternoon upon us, the sort of day which made it a real pleasure to be on the sea. Under our watchful eyes, Buster roamed freely around the decks, something which, in recent weeks, had become a rarity, not due to his capabilities but because of being on the sea and the unpredictability that comes with it. He basked in the sunshine and calm conditions, lying against *Lily*'s warm steelwork.

I could not resist paying Bogø a visit. There were not too many places with the word 'bog' in their name but, as Bognor Regis was just a few miles from my family home, it had to be done. Bogø was an island, although causeways at each end connected it to the islands of Farø and Møn. To reach it from Vordingborg, we had to pass beneath the huge Storstrøm Bridge. On trips to visit *Lily* in Germany, we used to use this bridge to access the ferry port at Gedser, often stopping to look at the bridge and dreaming that *Lily* may one day pass beneath it. Now it was really happening; we had to pinch ourselves, it was so amazing.

Giving the salmon pens off Bogø a wide berth, we picked up the channel into port. The waters of the Grønsund flowing between Bogø and Stubbekøbing were plied by *Ida*, one of Denmark's few remaining wooden ferries. As we turned *Lily* into the channel, *Ida* was leaving port. She was a thing of beauty, covered the water quickly and was soon alongside, her captain throwing me a wave from the bridge.

I squeezed *Lily* into the port; she instantly dwarfed it, her length taking up the entire rear quayside. It was quiet, our arrival an intrusion, but I instantly took to the place and its peacefulness. The village of Bogø was an uphill walk from the waterfront, where I was keen to see the old navigation school. Due to the treacherous waters surrounding the local islands, pilots were once in great demand. By law, every second son born into a family residing on Bogø had been required to train as a pilot and the school had remained in operation into the 1960s. Nowadays, with marked channels and GPS systems, pilots were no longer required but this was once a fiercely competitive profession amongst islanders.

It was the harbour festival and *Lily* became a firm and secure mooring for the visiting yachts. Buster watched with curiosity as one by one the boats tied on until we resembled a wide, floating raft. We were enjoying a drink in the wheelhouse when a flustered man ran up to the window.

"There's an engine failure; a yacht needs towing off the rocks." He had been running, the words blurted out between deep gasps for air. "Please can you help?" Roger dropped everything and the two of them, much to Buster's disgust at being left out, were soon in the RIB and rushing to the aid of the floundering craft. Going to help other boaters filled me with dread; not that I was unwilling to help, of course, but because of the possible repercussions. We had heard of an awful accident some years ago when a boat had gone to the aid of another that had become stuck across a weir. A rope was fastened to the vessel in distress but, when the rescue boat pulled away, the cleat onto which the rope was fastened came away from the other boat and, flying through the air, it struck the rescuer on the head, killing him outright.

I was astonished that not one other craft in port had a dinghy. Happily, Roger made the rescue without problem. Later that evening, the rescue boat organised for the event arrived — a reassuring presence — and the crew from the stricken yacht sought us out to offer their thanks, along with some beers. A very nice, though completely unnecessary, gesture of gratitude.

The Around the Islands Race was a timed event in which the yachts at the festival sailed a course from Bogø around Farø and Møn. With good weather forecast for early morning, deteriorating as the day went on, we wanted to get underway. Trying to release ourselves from several yachts whose crew had been celebrating into the early hours was not the easiest of tasks but they took it well and eventually slipped their lines, allowing *Lily* to escape. I had been looking

forward to the twisting route through the small islands of Lilleø, Tærø and Langø but the weather was not on our side as a greyness descended and, with it, the wind. Glancing through the gap

The Queen Alexandrine's Bridge, Kalvehave

between Bogø and Farø, I saw the first of the yachts setting out for the race and felt sad for them. After the last few days of calm and warmth, race day was a featureless grey but perhaps conditions were more favourable for yachties; they did have the breeze, after all.

At Kalvehave, *Lily* motored beneath the impressive Queen Alexandrine's Bridge, reputedly the most beautiful bridge in Denmark. It linked Sjælland to Møn, replacing the ferry which once plied the waters; in its shadow was a marina offering impressive views of the structure. Motoring in through the choppy conditions, the sea resembled the coast off Bognor Regis in December rather than the Baltic in June.

Despite being large, there was no room for *Lily* in the marina as all side-on moorings had been taken by the yachties, spaces the size of a small house left between boats. As our journey on the sea continued, it became obvious some did not welcome our presence – to them, a barge on the sea was like finding a fly in their soup; it should not be there – and those already berthed in the marina beat a hasty retreat below decks when they saw Lily approaching. We circled around and around, coming alongside a couple of yachts and slowing hopefully. However, no one offered to move or make room for us so we headed back out into grey, stormy waters to seek shelter in nearby Stege.

Chapter Sixteen

THE ISLE OF INNER PEACE

The island of Nyord was the slice of Danish heaven I had been searching for. I felt an instant connection to the place, the sense of peace and isolation enveloping me and holding me close. It was a comforting place; I could have happily remained there forever.

Buster sat alongside me at the bow as Roger carefully guided *Lily* across Stege Bay. It was early in the season and, as the navigation markers had not yet been placed, we were relying on Roger's course plotting and my sharp eyesight. Fishing sticks with nets strewn between them littered the bay; we were constantly weaving our way around them. If one had tangled in *Lily*'s prop, we could have been stranded for hours, trying to free ourselves.

As the emerald green hump of Nyord grew closer, I could make out the tiny harbour entrance and a man standing alongside watching us approach. Lining up for the entrance, he gave us a huge sweeping wave. It was the harbour master, waiting to greet us and see *Lily* safely into the reserved space. Buster looked pleased with the choice of mooring, pointed his nose in the air and breathed in deeply. Roger took *Lily* right into the tiny harbour, carefully turned her and took up the mooring in front of the island's fishing boat. She had a side-on berth and an uninterrupted view across Stege Bay. It was ideal so I stayed a week.

Lily in the small harbour on my island paradise of Nyord

After seeing Roger off to work, Buster was eager to explore our new island paradise and soon became frustrated by how long I was taking to get going, grabbing at my socks as I tried to pull them on.

"Buzzy, if you do that it will take me even longer," I told him. He gave a little bark. "OK, I'm coming," I said and he raced into the saloon to shimmy on the rug in excitement. I picked up my camera, packed two bottles of water, a few dog biscuits and an apple. It was going to be a hot day.

Leaving behind the small harbour, I followed a grassy pathway around the perimeter of the island. My soul revelled in the Marguerite daisies, clouds of cow parsley and wild, magenta-coloured roses set against a backdrop of calm, turquoise sea, Buster running in and out of the long, wispy grasses with a grin stretching from floppy ear to floppy ear and in the continuous sound of birdsong.

Halfway around the island, Buster and I stumbled upon a couple sitting on a bench, beside them a dog, his tongue protruding so far it almost reached the ground. After greeting each other, I realised I had seen the couple before. It took a while for my mind to register but slowly it came to me; they had appeared in a book about the island that I had picked up. What followed was one of the most wonderful conversations I had had in a long time.

Bent and Yrsa's association with Nyord was a long one. Bent's family were true Norboers, having lived and worked on the island for generations. Bent had gone to sea at the age of fifteen, with the shipping company Maersk, and had twice sailed around the world by the time he was nineteen. He and Yrsa had lived in some amazing countries, including Africa and India. In Africa, they had established their own village and set up a company to bore wells that provided safe drinking water for local communities. Their daughter-in-law was an African princess and yet, after all of their adventures, it was Nyord they had chosen to return to. Yrsa told me she was looking forward to settling on the island instead of just returning for summer holidays. She found the place magical in the depths of winter, when the sky turned black with murmurations of starlings swooping over the extensive salt marshes, the electric cables bowing under the weight of swallows gathering in preparation of migration and the frosty-covered sea ice glistening in winter's watery sunshine. She found it upsetting how so many people she met on Nyord could not see its beauty, especially during the winter months. I could see and feel the beauty of Nyord; there was a touch of Ireland's callows about it, a way of getting beneath your skin. There was no need for Yrsa to sell Nyord to me – I was already sold on the place.

Buster and I found inner peace on Nyord, something which had been missing over the past few weeks. The buffeting of seas, endless planning and constantly windy weather had become tiresome but, on this little island, it was all soothed away.

I made a surprising discovery on Nyord – a connection to HMS *Beagle* and her captain, Robert FitzRoy. A weather-worn poster in Nyord Harbour recalled how FitzRoy had given the world many nautically related items, amongst them the first version of the weather forecast, but, before this, he conducted experiments with various pieces of equipment including the storm glass. Storm glasses had been around since about 1750; however, the first proper report of one being used on board a ship stemmed from the Darwin expedition of 1831–1836. Eventually one of these curious pieces of apparatus was placed in every British fishing port but were lost, broken or damaged over time.

Over 100 years later, in 1982, Dane Stig Larsen sailed his yacht, *Lundie*, across the North Sea to the Scottish Hebrides, where he discovered an original storm glass still intact. On returning home, he spent many months attempting to analyse the active liquid inside, which produced crystals of varying forms depending on the forthcoming weather conditions. He proceeded to design a new storm glass based on FitzRoy's original that a company in Copenhagen was now producing.

When Roger arrived on Friday after a long week at work, we had to do some juggling about with transport. I drove the car back across Møn to Kalvehave on Sjælland, where it would be left for a few days, and Roger came to collect me in the RIB. Buster and I arrived with time to spare and took a short walk before spotting Roger skimming across the bay. Buster loved the RIB, although, in recent months, disliked being up front alone so I had taken to sitting on the side to have him close to me. On the return journey, Buster snuggled up to me and unsuccessfully fought heavy eyelids as the humming of the engine lulled him to sleep. We sped across the bay in evening sunshine, the crystal-clear water revealing the rocks we skimmed over in such clarity that it made me shiver.

Back on Nyord, we headed to the barbecue area, where a small crowd had gathered – mostly German yachties – who took great delight in watching Buster in his chin-strap-woey pose. The atmosphere and stunning sunset of our last night on Nyord was a perfect end to our stay.

Bright sunshine streaming through the portholes woke me. It was early but already hot inside *Lily*. Buster was sprawled on the saloon floor, in no hurry to move, but, with the notorious Bøgestrøm to navigate and a spell of good weather forecast, there was no time to lose. I thought I would be sad waving farewell to my little island but it was not so bad; I had shared some of its secrets, been blessed to have the place to myself on a couple of evenings and met the real Norboers. Buster and I had spent quality time together, enjoying walks, impromptu picnics and stunning sunsets. Nyord had worked its magic and I was ready to take on the next leg of our journey.

Nyord was surrounded by tricky waters and, similar to Bogø, had a long history of pilotage. The former pilot's lookout, standing on the island's highest point, had been converted into Denmark's smallest museum, offering views of the shoals and sandbanks. The great golden mounds of sand piercing the turquoise sea, lying dormant as if slumbering sea creatures waiting to catch out the unwary boater, stretched on endlessly as far as the eye could see. The channel was marked through the Bøgestrøm but I still sat on the roof and scanned the sea for each set of markers or any fishing sticks. Buster stretched his legs on deck then settled on the floor by the wheelhouse door. He had taken to this position a lot recently, preferring it to being on the chart table. Perhaps in old age he felt more in control being on the floor; he did not have to wait for us to lift him. It was a little precarious – Roger and I had to watch our footing – but, on longer crossings in calm seas, it was a good place for him. He would rest his head on the wooden doorstep, his nose sticking out into the fresh air, whilst the rest of his body lay stretched out in the wheelhouse. He was still *Lily*'s Admiral but more of a part-time one now.

Præstø Fjord cut westwards into Sjælland, a long diversion from the main channel but, on paper, the shallow sheltered waters looked perfect for a barge. The harbour master had reserved a side-on berth for *Lily* and, as we neared the marina, he telephoned to direct us into the spot. We felt rather special when we found a sign had been placed on the berth with *Lily*'s name and length.

Approaching the harbour, Roger had noticed the tell-tale was not letting out its usual flow of cooling water; something was causing a blockage.

"Come and look at this." Roger lifted the filter basket out of the engine room. "You're never going to guess what's in here." It was not unusual to get a small fish in the basket so I assumed that was what it would be. I looked into the basket and, in amongst a few strands of sea grass, caught sight of what it was – a moon jellyfish, large enough to cover the bottom of the basket and stem the flow of water through the filter. Buster snuck up and attempted to stuff his nose into the basket. The smell of the jellyfish must have been unappealing as he quickly recoiled with a shake of his head and started reverse sneezing,

Brightly painted houses in the sunshine town of Præstø

sounding like a pig in full grunt. I placed a finger over his nostrils. 'Thanks, Mum,' his eyes said.

I christened Præstø the 'sunshine town' because of its bright and cheerfully painted buildings in shades of orange, yellow and red. It was delightful to carelessly wander its cobbled streets, where rambling roses and hollyhocks sprouted from the smallest cracks in the pavements and the skies were full of screeching swifts. With the car still at Kalvehave, we took to the bikes, carefully placing Buster into the doggyhut. It was a long, hot ride; several stops were needed. At one stage, we resorted to pushing the bikes, the steep hill which needed climbing breaking us both. At the top, we looked down to the Queen Alexandrine's Bridge and, with the wind in our hair – or ears in Buster's case – free-wheeled down to Kalvehave and enjoyed ice creams on the waterfront before collapsing into the car and returning to *Lily*.

The island hopping was over; the onward route to Copenhagen involved motoring *Lily* along the coast of Sjælland, Denmark's largest island. However, bitten by the bug, there were a couple of possible island diversions I hoped to fulfil later in the journey.

Chapter Seventeen

SPIN DRYER TO COPENHAGEN

Buster trotted along the cliff path. Red poppies pierced the dull green, swaying sea of unripened corn and, below, heard but unseen, waves gently lapped the pebbly shore. *Lily* was moored in the fishing port of Rødvig at the southern approach to Stevns Klint; we were on familiar territory. Ahead lay our goal – Copenhagen. Destinations beyond had not really been discussed or believed possible but, with Denmark's capital city in sight, we felt invincible.

The sea was a deep inky blue against the pale limestone cliffs. Despite Roger plotting a course some distance from shore, it was still possible to spot landmarks along Stevns Klint, the church at Højerup perched precariously on the cliff edge, which, according to legend, each Christmas Eve moved inland the length of a cockerel's jump to prevent it toppling into the sea. There was the lighthouse I had climbed with June some years previously and, below it, the small radio station, first to record the end of the Cuban Missile Crisis.

The waves were strong but *Lily* rode them well; now and then, one splashed hard against her bow, sending glistening droplets of spray into the air like scattered diamonds. Everything was going well but, as *Lily* rounded the headland and Køge Bay was revealed, she left one room and entered another. The wind was instantly stronger and the swell and current it created were a problem.

Buster had grown used to rough patches during cruising and took no notice, snoring obliviously whilst poor *Lily* was pushed and pulled as swell and current fought with her. The bay was living up to its reputation of being a spin dryer.

Passing Stevns Klint and heading towards Køge Bay the sea became rough

The current in Køge Bay was caused by the sea being forced through the narrows of the Øresund, the straits separating Denmark and Sweden. Once the sea exited the narrows, it swirled at force into the bay, circling, causing a rotation of current. Pulling and tugging, it was one of the most uncomfortable voyages I had endured. Ahead, marking the so-called 'back door' into Copenhagen, the huge silver buildings of the power station reflected the sun's rays towards us. Roger had plotted a course directly for it but *Lily* struggled to get there.

Hours passed and Roger tacked *Lily* back and forth until, finally, she made headway but the visit to the laundry room was not over. As the sea began to shallow on approach to the channel, conditions worsened. Roger made a final tack to enter the channel, giving *Lily* a side-on swell for a mile or so and nowhere to run. We ploughed on until the land slowly began to rise, forming a more river-like environment that offered shelter.

Only craft with less than 10 feet (3.0m) of headroom could access Copenhagen via the 'back door', which saved a lengthy cruise through the strong currents of the Øresund and, after witnessing the outfall of it into Køge Bay, I was thankful that *Lily* was within this limit. There was one lock on our route; constructed to reduce the fast-flowing currents through the city, it was only opened at set times and we arrived with ten minutes to spare. I gave Buster a short walk; he trotted along beautifully, his tail sweeping rhythmically. He was happy but it was hard to tell why. Perhaps the city smells had reached his nose; hundreds of fast-food outlets, bars, restaurants and cafés sending his imagination spinning into a Køge Bay of gourmet delicacies.

The first time we had visited Copenhagen, Roger and I had light-heartedly spoken of mooring *Lily* at Amaliehaven; it was another pipe dream. That evening, it became a reality. I was exhausted from the spin-dryer cycle, running on adrenalin. Directly opposite *Lily*, the lights of the impressive Opera House shone in the night. It was beautiful. I refused to surrender to sleep.

"This is becoming a bit of a habit."

"What is?" Roger answered, without taking his gaze off the cityscape.

"Making dreams come true."

The mooring we had so desired had problems: an uncomfortable wash from water buses and accessing dry land was troublesome. Reaching the high quay wall from *Lily* was tricky, impossible for Buster without help. When the harbour master arrived, he recognised Buster's needs and suggested a different mooring to suit him better. With his detailed instructions, we made our way northwards, where he promised easy access to shore, no wash or swell, peace and quiet, and only a short walk from the city. It sounded too good to be true.

American Quay or Basin 7 was hidden between the Norwegian Ferry terminal and the famous Little Mermaid statue. It delivered everything we were promised and more. Being on floating pontoon moorings after struggling with fixed jetties on the moving sea was heaven-sent and Buster was able to come and go as he pleased. From here, we celebrated the summer solstice. Buster had a succulent pig's ear and, as he bit into it, crispy splinters flew across the rug, where he later snuffled, collecting the fallout. We sipped champagne and revelled in our good fortune. *Lily* had carried us safely to Copenhagen; we had come a long way together, not just on this journey, but in life. A great achievement all round.

Looking for free, dog-friendly entertainment was challenging so, when I saw a poster advertising an open-air concert by the Home Guard Music Corps, we went along. It was held in the grounds of Kastellet, a fortress built in the shape of a five-pointed star. Seating had been neatly arranged on a parade ground and the band, looking smart in green uniforms, were busy tuning up. We sat in the second row and settled Buster between us. After a short speech, which neither of us understood, the band started. Everyone became caught up in the spirit of the entertainment, clapping and foot-tapping, but, despite the light-hearted music, the atmosphere was tense as, above, storm clouds gathered.

When the first number was over, everyone cheered and clapped. Buster had been silent but, with the sudden applause, threw back his head and howled long and deep. People seated in the front row turned and looked at him; members of the band necked to see him, some placed down their instruments and rose to their feet to catch a glimpse of the howling hound. Everyone burst into fits of laughter as our old boy showed his appreciation for the brass band. Then it poured with rain.

Getting around Copenhagen was easy. Taking the waterbus one way, on which Buster travelled freely, and walking back the other, days out were not a problem and Buster could take them in his stride. The city's green spaces allowed opportunities for him to take a break and, with plenty to see, he was never bored. Days were filled with finding new places we could all experience together, no matter how odd they were.

The free-state of Christiania nestled in a cannabis-induced, hazy shroud. It was established in the early seventies by a group of hippies on a disused military camp and was one of those places which had to be experienced, whatever your views on it. No photography was allowed in the state: a shame as the unusual environment created some amazing images. Buster could not get enough of the place; he walked close to my legs but kept his constantly twitching nose high in the air. He was warmly greeted by some strange-looking people with long, twisted dreadlocks, wearing bright, psychedelic waistcoats, and he seemed genuinely sad as we left through the rustic wooden gate.

With Roger returning to work, Buster and I had the days to ourselves. Most of the time, we stayed close to *Lily* but, one day, headed slightly further. Kongens Have was Copenhagen's oldest park and surrounded the beautiful Rosenborg Slot, one of the city's many palaces. The park was busy with workers taking breaks and holidaymakers on sightseeing tours. Buster and I walked through the grounds and settled on a bench with a fine view of the palace. Lying at my feet, Buster fell asleep in the sun. I watched his chest rise and fall. His fur had grown whiter, his sandy shades were being washed away, surf coating sand on a beach. My boy had drifted into old age without me realising; he really was my Aged P. When Roger returned that evening, he enquired about our day.

"Do you realise, that dog has pooed on the doorsteps of some of the finest palaces in Northern Europe?" It was true, he had, but we had always been responsible and scooped the poop.

One evening, we bundled into the RIB to explore Copenhagen's smaller canals and find

Rosenborg Slot, Copenhagen

somewhere to eat. We chugged along the Christianshavn Kanal, beneath the newly installed bridge, which resembled ship's sails, and moored outside Noma, Copenhagen's most talked-about restaurant.

"They won't let us in here," whispered Roger.

"I don't want to go in. I want a photo of us outside so it looks like we have." We climbed out, keeping lifejackets on in the expectation of a swift eviction. To my surprise, the doorman was easily talked into photographing us outside what was then the best restaurant in the world, where even the rich and famous, let alone us with a dog in tow, found it impossible to get a table without booking several months in advance. Instead, we popped across the main thoroughfare into Nyhavn, with its brightly coloured façades, bars, cafés and historical ships.

The Italian restaurant we chose oozed atmosphere; it was busy, the food and wine delectable. Buster was provided with a huge bowl of water and sat contentedly, watching people promenading along the waterfront before he drifted off to sleep. At the end of the meal, Roger ordered coffee and asked for the bill. When the waiter

Outside of Noma, Copenhagen's famed restaurant, known for its New Nordic Cuisine

returned, Buster leapt to his feet and barked at him. I was not sure why; perhaps he just gave him a fright. The waiter jumped, taken aback, then calmed himself. I paid the bill and gave him a tip, something Roger and I regularly disagreed about. When the transaction was complete he asked, "How old is your dog?"

"He's almost twelve; an old boy now." I was pleased he was showing an interest after Buster had frightened him.

"I can smell death on him; he has two or three months, certainly no more than a year." He spoke quietly, making hurtful words sound pleasant in his Italian accent. I laughed lightly, not sure how else to react, but, beneath, he had plunged a knife into my heart. Roger laughed too but caught my gaze and held it. He watched my eyes fill with tears as I fought to keep my composure.

"Come on, let's go," he said. We walked away in silence with Buster happily trotting alongside. A few yards along Nyhavn, Roger wrapped his arm around my waist and pulled me close. "I told you not to give him a tip."

Colourful Nyhavn, Copenhagen's
17th century waterfront and canal

The words had hurt but it was true: Buster was getting old; sooner or later he would not be there to pull me out of the darkness which

still occasionally threatened to smother me. What would I do without him; how would I ever cope without the dog who had saved my life and given me reason to live? It was simply too painful to contemplate.

A week of city living was enough for me but, before leaving Copenhagen in its entirety, there was somewhere unusual I wanted to visit and, to reach it, *Lily* was needed. As we left the city, Buster sat on deck and gazed up at the tiny cabin windows of the docked cruise ships. When the waves began to build, he made his way inside and dozed in the wheelhouse, his head on the step catching the coolness of the Øresund's afternoon breeze. We were heading some five nautical miles out to the isolated Flakfortet, one of the city's island fortresses, open to the public.

Lily passed wind farms and another of Copenhagen's fortresses, providing tantalising glimpses of what could be expected at Flakfortet. She rolled unladylike in the swell and wash from shipping. I hoped the detour would be worth the discomfort. Ahead, the high mound of the island was visible, towering above the water with steep, grassy sides, encompassed by a great, grey wall. This was going to rate as one of the strangest moorings we had ever visited.

Motoring into the harbour, people stopped and stared, surprised to see a barge on the sea, perhaps even more surprised to see one in such an odd location. Inside the outer walls of the fort, the sea was calm, boats were moored to the outer wall and around the inner island housing the main fortress buildings. Fishing boat *Amigo* was docked near the restaurant; her owners were soon at our door, eager for information about *Lily* and her travels. Buster sat and listened patiently but soon demanded attention. We headed off to investigate the fortress, leaving Roger to look around *Amigo*.

Buster and I climbed to the highest point; it was a struggle for him ascending the wooden steps but determination drove him on. Slowly and carefully, we made it to the top and marvelled at the view of the Øresund and the bridge crossing it, linking Denmark and Sweden. Buster stuck his head in every hole he could find in the fortress gun turrets, relishing such excitement in each discovery I had a job to control him.

At the restaurant, bowls of breaded shrimp and glasses of deep ruby-red wine were the perfect accompaniment to the setting sun as it became lost behind a hazy weather front. As day-trippers prepared to leave, the hum of engines and departing fond wishes filled the air. We were one of only a handful of boats opting to stay the night in the unusual location. When it was time for *Amigo* to depart, we were bid farewell by their owners and the day-trippers on board.

"See you again on the Øresund, beautiful *Lily*," bellowed their skipper as he turned on the navigation lights and steamed out of the fortress, homeward bound. Their drink-jolly party waved as if their lives depended on it. Buster watched them fade into the distance.

The morning dawned in monochromatic dullness; it was not the kind of day which filled me with enthusiasm but Buster had an important date to keep. With his annual check-up and inoculations due, I had booked *Lily* in for a stay at Skovshoved Marina, north of Copenhagen, from where it was only a matter of crossing the road to reach his veterinarian's clinic. Our hound was going to see the doctor by boat.

Claus was away for his annual, month-long summer vacation so an appointment had been booked with a colleague, someone Buster knew, but, when we checked in, she was nowhere in sight. Instead, there was a young girl, a vet neither Roger nor I had seen before. Buster instantly disliked her, shuffled beneath the chairs, curled his top lip and growled. It was not like him; he was usually good at the vet's but the out-of-character behaviour continued in the consultation room. Despite my reassurances, Buster refused to be touched by the vet; even Roger was unsuccessful at calming him. The only way she could do her job was to muzzle Buster. It made me feel sad and scared for him but it was either that or a sedative.

With the inoculations successfully administered, a conversation about Buster's age and health followed. We were told he was in good condition, although advised to consider adding supplements to his diet and perhaps booking in for a blood test in the near future. On the way back to the marina, Roger and I discussed the consultation and decided that, once Claus had returned from holidays and *Lily* was settled in calmer waters, we would indeed book a further check-up for Buster.

Chapter Eighteen

A SWEDISH DIVERSION

Buster snuggled into my side and I put my arm around him. Despite being July, there was a chill to the early-morning air filtering through the open windows. Everywhere was blue, the sky was cloudless and the sea without a ripple; one shade dominated the view in every direction. We were heading to Sweden and had picked a perfect day to do so.

With our courtesy flag matching the colours of the day, we steamed into the tiny port of Kirkebakken on the Swedish island of Venn as the majority of overnighters were leaving. There was, however, little room for *Lily*, the few side-on moorings taken by lightweight yachts which did not need them. Bow to quay was the favoured way of mooring around the remainder of the harbour, resulting in an interesting half hour.

Roger turned *Lily*'s bow into the quay wall but, with no rear anchor to hold her, roping in was a struggle. Using *Lily*'s longest ropes, Roger fed them from the back bollards partway along the gunnels, through deck drainage holes and back to the quay, then lowered an old mud weight over the stern to hold her. It was not pretty and it certainly was not secure but, as no one had any intention of moving, it was the only option.

It was hot and, with midday only an hour away, temperatures were set to rise. There was only one thing for it – find a shady spot in a restaurant and linger over a nice meal. A small restaurant right on the quay looked inviting and shady. We headed in, winding our way through the busy tables until a waiter appeared at the door. He glared down at Buster and pointed, letting out a loud, "Errrrr."

At this point I wanted to say, "It's a dog, haven't you seen one before?" but, instead, the words came out as, "Is there a problem with the dog?"

Before he could answer, Roger noticed we were not with him and swiftly retraced his steps to ask, "Is it alright if we sit at that table over there?" He pointed to a table tucked into a corner, shady and quiet – it would have been ideal.

"Well, it's the dog."

"OK, don't worry, I'll get him to sit on the floor. The chairs look a bit too hard for him anyway." He laughed but was the only one. I sensed people turning to look. Buster sat down, raised his eyes to look at me and seemed to be saying, 'Oh dear, not another one of Dad's awful dog jokes; how embarrassing.'

"You can sit at that table but, if someone comes in with an allergy or dislike for dogs, I shall have to ask you to leave." The waiter ignored Roger's attempt at light comedy.

"Even if we've ordered food?" Before the waiter could answer me, Roger waved his hand dismissively and walked out of the place. When I caught up with him on the quayside, I squatted down beside Buster and gave him a hug. He nestled his chin on my shoulder.

"Never mind, old chap," I whispered into his ear. "We didn't really like the look of the place anyway."

We walked on in the growing heat and found another restaurant close by. What a difference! We were shown to a table partly shaded by a huge umbrella, where we ordered a chilled bottle of white wine and prawn smørrebrød. The owner of the restaurant, a lovely elderly lady, was busy passing the time of day with her clientele, quietly going from table to table, having short conversations. Spotting Buster, her eyes lit up, she clasped her wrinkled hands together in front of her chest and immediately came over.

"Lovely." She gazed down at Buster. "Would your dog like a drink? Please can I get it for him?" She returned with a champagne ice bucket filled to the brim with cold water, half a dozen ice cubes floating in it. "There," she said, placing it between Buster's front legs. "For you." And she gently stroked him.

"Thank you very much," I replied. "He needed that."

"It's very hot today and he is old, yes?"

"Yes, he's almost twelve; it's his birthday next month."

"Oh, how nice, he is wonderful, a good and wise dog, I can see this." She looked down as Buster messily slurped his water and crunched on the ice cubes.

"You enjoy," she said to Buster and, with a nod of the head, left to talk to her other customers. The meal was expensive, especially the wine, but I was more than happy to pay the price; the food had been extremely good and being able to have Buster with us worth every single penny or Swedish krona. How could two restaurants within fifty yards of each other have such different outlooks?

Later that afternoon, a couple in a flashy little Sunseeker powerboat asked if they could moor alongside, bow to the quay, rear ropes to *Lily*'s bollards. Our new neighbours were friendly, offered advice on guest harbours and told us about their circumnavigation of Sjælland undertaken the previous year. With them was a small dog with a wild array of hair which Buster took a shine to. He sat on the side of the boat, the young fluff ball on the back of his, looking as if they were deep in conversation.

"Do you realise your dog looks like Gizmo from the *Gremlins* film?" Roger asked. I felt my stomach sink; it was not the sort of thing you said to the owner of a Sunseeker. However, much to my surprise, the lady laughed and said, "That's his name and that's exactly why he has it." Gizmo was a Chinese Crested, although, to look at him, I would never have known. I had never seen one of these dogs with hair before but, apparently, one was quite often born in a litter of otherwise bald ones. This sweet little dog was adorable, much more attractive with his furry coat than without.

By early evening, the temperature was cooling. We climbed to the cliff top and, from the white-washed church, looked down on *Lily*, a tiny speck in the busy harbour below. A slight breeze had blown in and a haze had started to develop but the coastline of Denmark was still visible. Walking back through fuzzy barley fields the colour of ripening limes, Buster caught a scent and began scurrying back and forth. He had seen a huge hare lolloping along in the ruts of the field. At a picnic table, we sat and gulped cold mineral water from bottles whilst Buster continued searching for the hare. Occasionally, he stood on his back legs, trying to see over the top of the frothy sea of barley heads, where midnight blue coloured swallows skilfully skimmed and swerved, feasting on bugs.

"Well, Buzzy boy, you've been to Sweden," I whispered as he tucked himself under my arm later that evening in the wheelhouse. He lifted his head and

Across Venn's barley fields the mainland of Sweden was clearly visible

looked at me; his eyes twinkled and he wore his sometimes-smile. The sun was setting and coating the harbour in a rosy glow as light and delicate as a watercolour wash, candles were being lit and the atmosphere was magical; glasses clinked and the soft tones of laughter and conversation drifted across the packed harbour. It was not noisy or unpleasant, just a soft background murmur, as if crews were being respectful of the peaceful setting and no one wanted to break the spell. Boats were up to six abreast; row upon row of Danish and Swedish ensigns hung limply from sterns, between them only one British ensign – ours. As the last of the sun disappeared, the harbour master walked to the flag pole and reeled in the huge Swedish flag, ending our day on Swedish soil.

Buster poked his head around the wheelhouse door to see what all the noise was about. Once he realised what was going on, he watched in utter disgust for a few moments, snorted, then went below decks. It was another scorching day but haziness kept it from being as bright as the day before. Roger had motored

Lily along the coast of Venn and dropped anchor off low, sandy cliffs to go swimming. The water was cool and refreshing on my skin. I swam around *Lily* as she

The harbour master at Kirkebakken reeling in the blue-and-yellow Swedish flag as the sun sets

bobbed at anchor, enabling a good view of the tiny white barnacles on her hull; they had not wasted any time taking hold but it made a change from freshwater zebra mussels. This was our first swim since Lake Müritz almost a year previously and a real joy. Roger had fastened a rope to *Lily* as well as steps and was busy doing an aquatic Tarzan routine. Was it any wonder Buster had retreated?

After swimming, we took Buster ashore in the RIB to nearby Norreborg Harbour. At one time, there was a brick factory there and, on the shore, were the remains of hundreds of bricks, some completely intact, others shattered and water-worn nestling amongst the pebbles. Refreshed from swimming and the cooling breeze from the speeding RIB, it was time to bring our Swedish diversion to a close. As Venn was only small, we circumnavigated it in *Lily* before heading back to the Danish coast, changing the courtesy flag en route.

Chapter Nineteen

AUTHORS AND BARDS

The modern marina at Rungsted was characterless. A large, impersonal place with high-priced, on-site shops and restaurants, it was full of stick-thin women wearing oversized sunglasses, carrying designer handbags into which tiny, yappy dogs were tucked. It was also a gathering place for middle-aged men desperately trying to hang onto youth but failing miserably, their tanned and wrinkled skin imparting the appearance of an old wooden boat which had seen some weather. If you had a Tupperware boat, or what most would refer to as a 'gin palace', it was the place to be seen; if you had a barge, it was the kind of place to avoid …

Roger had been unable to secure a side-on berth so finding somewhere suitable for *Lily* was in the hands of the gods. Steaming into the marina at the end of a glorious summer day, the place was teeming with weekenders hanging on, squeezing every last ounce out of the day. Unlike many marinas in this part of the world, Rungsted had a visitor's pontoon but there was not a hope in hell of fitting onto it. A huge, flybridge cruiser had taken up pride of place. The crew, hiding behind sunglasses, sipped bubbly and stared down on us with an expression of disdain. Buster glared back at them and gave them his best Paddington Bear penetrating stare. It took a while but, eventually, smiles

The author Karen Blixen was born at Rungstedlund in 1885 and lived there for most of her life.

began to curve upwards from their stern faces; hands waved, cameras appeared and, as the snapping began, Buster shuffled around in his bed to turn his back on them.

'No paparazzi,' his demeanour said.

Roger spotted a berth displaying a green card – it was a box mooring. With *Lily* being high at the bow, trying to get off her front was almost impossible and certainly dangerous. Roger was quite agile for his age, whereas I was less sure-footed, refusing to jump off anything much more than a foot above the ground. There was always a lot of cursing and swearing when tackling something like this and it certainly was not a pretty sight. The only way to get Buster off was to put him in his life jacket and dangle him precariously over the bow like a handbag whilst someone else grabbed hold of him. As usual, Buster took it all in his stride and, once on firm land, was trotting about, eager to discover where his water-going time machine had transported him.

In complete comparison to the modern marina, opposite stood a beautiful, white-washed farmhouse known as Rungstedlund. A haven of peace and calm, this had once been the home of Karen Blixen, author of the famed novel *Out of Africa*. The grounds were free to wander and, as dogs were permitted on leads, a lot of time was spent exploring the mixture of formal planting, pastures and woodland. Beneath the shady boughs of a great beech tree, we came across Karen Blixen's final resting place, a simple, stone-topped grave.

Being closer to home was fortunate. It would have proved impossible to remain on *Lily* alone with Buster; not only were there difficulties boarding but also the weather conditions caused her to rock and roll in the box. The wind raged and roared; everyone we spoke to was getting fed up with the weather. It had been a hindrance for *Lily* and I would be glad to enter more sheltered waters.

Back in our rented house in Denmark, Buster bounded about in the garden as if he were a puppy; it was lovely for him to have the freedom of roaming in familiar territory. Most of the garden was laid to lawn; along one side was a low bank from where Buster could sit and survey the grounds. It was simple but perfect for an Aged P.

"I'm going to cut the grass." Roger had come in from work and almost immediately rushed back out the door again with Buster hard on his heels. A few minutes later, the lawnmower fired up. Out of the window, I saw Roger pushing it along the top of the bank. Buster followed slowly behind, drinking in the scent of freshly cut grass. Roger reached the end of the garden, turned the lawn mower and came face to face with Buster, now blocking the way. Roger tried to steer the lawnmower around him but lost his footing on the edge of the bank. Despite the stumble, he kept hold of the lawnmower, which careered down the bank, pulling Roger with it, where they landed in a heap. Buster stared at the scene in disbelief and I could not help but chuckle. The engine stalled and all was quiet. Roger attempted to stand but his foot gave way and he went down again with a bump.

"Bloody hell, Buster, that was your fault." Buster sauntered down the bank and sat down beside him.

"Are you alright?" I called from the house as Roger made another attempt to get up.

"Yeah, I'm alright. Take this dog inside, will you?" Buster gave Roger a frown but, before I could go and fetch him, he had retreated to his camping chair and nestled his chin into the arm. He remained there, watching Roger limp around the garden with the lawnmower until it was time for dinner.

Kronborg Slot at Helsingør dominated the low-lying headland. Despite being Shakespeare's Castle of Elsinore in *Hamlet*, there was apparently no evidence of him ever visiting the place. It had a commanding view overlooking the narrowest stretch of the Øresund, the mainland of Sweden only a stone's throw away. This was also one of the busiest shipping lanes in the world and we were about to tackle it in a Dutch barge.

Lily did not have the speed to avoid fast-moving ferries and commercial shipping; it was a case of carefully choosing the right moment and ploughing ahead. Approaching the pinch point, the narrows between Helsingør and Helsingborg, the ferries left port in both countries then crossed each other mid-channel and, by the time *Lily* entered their designated lane, were already moored and disembarking

Kronborg Slot overlooks one of the busiest shipping lanes in the world

passengers. With them out of the way, there was no cross-channel traffic to worry about. A large container ship had chosen to hug the Swedish coast and the yachts following were too far back to worry about. *Lily* was about halfway across when the ferries left port.

"Blimey, they didn't hang about. Come on, old girl," Roger urged. I gave *Lily* an encouraging pat on her varnished interior.

"Come on, you can do it, *Lily*, old girl," I added, tipping Buster a wink at the same time. He sensed the Admiral was needed on duty and scanned the view, checking for other shipping. The yachts behind realised they would not make it and turned, circling to await their next opportunity. *Lily* gave us her all and slowly and surely carried us away, leaving the route clear for the ferries to pass each other. *Lily* had made it. I sighed with relief and Roger eased the throttle back. Then the waves hit.

From nowhere came large, rolling breakers; a continuous wall of bright turquoise water slammed into *Lily*'s hull; bang, bang, bang, the colour so beautifully intense I could hardly draw my eyes away from it. *Lily* was receiving the full force of the open sea as it fought to enter the narrows and she rode it as if a galloping horse. When I finally glanced up, I could see the turrets of Kronborg Slot bouncing up and down as *Lily* rose and plummeted each wave. My mind thought *The Tempest* rather than *Hamlet*.

To enter Helsingør Marina meant turning *Lily* broadside into the already-uncomfortable conditions; it was not far but it was not going to be an easy ride.

"Are you ready?" Roger prepared to turn her. I reached forwards and put my arms around Buster, holding him tightly. He looked me in the eyes and grinned, more surprised at receiving an unexpected hug at the helm than the unsettling conditions we were facing.

"Yes." I could clearly hear the nervousness in my voice. Roger let *Lily* ride the next wave and turned her wheel hard. I closed my eyes. The whole boat slopped downwards and began to roll as Roger fought to get *Lily* into the marina entrance. Another roller hit and *Lily* surged sideways then downwards. I buried my head into Buster's warm body and prayed it would be over quickly. It only lasted a few minutes, though it felt much longer; the waves were so big and powerful that each one knocked *Lily* sideways and off course, her length causing her to wallow as she fell down into each trough and righted herself before the next one hit. Roger pushed *Lily* on and suddenly it all stopped. I opened my eyes to find the waters had calmed and *Lily* was motoring unhindered into the peaceful, clear waters of the marina.

Buster was on the roof. I had placed him there whilst I took photographs and he had unexpectedly settled down to sun himself and watch yachts come and go. On the Øresund, the breakers were still in abundance, the masts of yachts appearing and disappearing behind the harbour wall as they fought through them. In the distance, Kronborg Slot's turrets glistened and shone in the July sun; in the sheltered marina all was peaceful and calm. We relaxed, chatted to a boat owner interested in travelling the inland waterways of Germany and gave him a handful of maps we no longer needed, soaked up the magnificent view and decided to walk into town, paying for the mooring at the automatic machine on the way.

The cobbled streets of the town bustled with people; it seemed as if the world and his wife were on holiday but we managed to find a table in a restaurant. Buster lay beneath the table in the shade, taking the lunchtime outing in his stride. I wish the same could have been said for his attitude to the cheese shop. He could smell it way back down the street; his nose had started twitching and sniffing uncontrollably and he started to pull. When Buster pulled, it was reminiscent of a movie scene set in the deep south of America, an escaped convict being tracked by lurching blood hounds, the handler fighting to keep control of them. Imagine that scene in a crowded town centre on a weekend in July and you will get the picture – complete and utter chaos. Finally reaching the shop, he collapsed at the foot of the entrance steps and looked longingly up, his eyes begging and pleading for us to go and buy his favourite treat.

A few minutes later, Roger returned with a bag of cheese, which I am sure people across the straits in Sweden could have caught a whiff of. Buster snuffled at the bag, licked his lips and trotted alongside Roger back to *Lily* without pulling once. At the boat, he had a small cube of rich, mature cheddar, a wicked indulgence for a Beagle.

Chapter Twenty

THE SPITEFUL KITTYCAT

Buster did not relish the thought of venturing onto the Kattegat Sea; it sounded too much like 'kitty cat' to him. He considered the creatures unpredictable, temperamental and not to be trusted; one minute they were friendly, the next they would turn and, with claws outstretched, hiss and spit for no reason. In this, Buster's comparison was correct; what began as a pleasant trip along the northern coast of Sjælland on the Kattegat Sea suddenly turned into one of the worst voyages we had ever undertaken.

The first section from Helsingør to Gilleleje was pleasant enough. The day started overcast but was brightened by the sighting of dolphins off *Lily's* bow.

"There!" Roger pointed into the grey water. I looked but there was nothing. I had been longing to see a dolphin since we entered the sea but had almost given up hope. I waited, my eyes fixed on the water. Effortlessly rising to break the water's surface was a fin and I squealed in excitement at seeing my first wild dolphin. "Actually, they could be harbour porpoises." Roger pointed further out to where another couple were. I did not care; to me they were the same as dolphins and seeing them made my day.

Gilleleje was the northernmost town on Sjælland and also a busy port, a friendly place where fishing boats and leisure craft rubbed fenders. On the cliffs above stood a squat lighthouse. Built in 1772, it had a coal-fuelled light, one of only a handful in the world still operating this way. Leaving at 6 a.m., the day looked full of promise; the sun was already shining through grey clouds and the sea reasonably calm. This was going to be a long journey and we both wanted it out of the way; with the coastline being exposed to the full brunt of the temperamental Kattegat Sea, there was nowhere to seek shelter should the weather change. *Lily*'s slow pace meant a period of calm was needed; the forecast for the morning was favourable, although the wind was due to rise late in the day. If all went to plan, by the time that happened we would be safely entering the fjords, home waters and a more sheltered environment. But, as we knew only too well, when dealing with the sea, things rarely went as planned …

Buster was relaxed and snoozed contentedly in his usual spot. The underlying swell was still present but Roger managed to hold *Lily* on course for the first few hours. I had made up a thermos flask of boiled water before leaving – safer for preparing hot drinks than boiling a kettle on the move – and we had just finished a coffee when the sky began to grow unsettlingly dark. Squalls were closing in.

The first hit hard; the wind rushed in, sending an unnerving shudder through the wheelhouse. The waves increased in size and *Lily* found herself in a fight. Spray splashed over the bow as she climbed the waves; water landed on the side decks and ran down them to be drawn out of the drainage holes as she slammed back down. Rain began to fall, marring the view and creating a misty haze. As Roger began to tack, I made a mental note of a landmark – a telegraph pole high on the cliffs. An hour later, we were still in the same place.

When the squall had passed, *Lily* was finally able to make headway but the swell was reluctant to relinquish its grasp. It seemed as if invisible hands had hold of *Lily*'s hull and were pulling her, kicking and screaming, from safety. With nowhere to seek shelter, we had to keep *Lily* ploughing on or retrace our steps. Over halfway into the journey, the only way was forward.

When the next squall hit, it was too rough to hold course. Roger tried the tacking trick again, zigzagging *Lily* along the north coast, but, with each tack, our headway reduced.

"This is useless." I had almost had enough and could feel my voice breaking. My body ached from fighting to stay upright and we still had miles to go.

"Go below for a while. I've got to tack again so it will be lumpy. I'm alright with Buzz." Buster was smiling at me, seeming to say, 'It's alright. Go take a break. I'll keep tabs on things here.' Roger turned *Lily* and again headed into the unrelenting Kattegat, the swell drawing us further and further out to sea. There were hundreds of miles of open water ahead; the wind had no obstacles to slow it. On the inside of us, yachts were taking a closer line to shore, leaving us way behind to battle the waves whilst they seemed to skim over them. Hour after hour passed; Buster stayed by Roger's side, the Admiral refusing to leave his command. I took over from time to time to relieve Roger but battling with the steering was exhausting. I tried to snooze below decks for a while but the thumping on *Lily*'s hull was too loud to allow any fruitful sleep. Awake, it was impossible to stay below decks, the feeling of seasickness taking over, so it was back up into the wheelhouse.

Finally, Hundested hove into view, its familiar cliffs topped by wind-distorted trees, and Arctic explorer Knud Rasmussen's house was a welcoming sight. Right on cue, the clouds dispersed and the sun made an appearance. The swell continued to make *Lily* roll precariously but it did not matter any longer. We had safely made it to our home waters. As Roger throttled back, we entered the harbour. Buster looked at us, a contented sometimes-smile on his face. He had taken on the sea with the personality of a cat and won. He was a very smug dog indeed.

The northern coast of Sjælland viewed from the buoyed channel into Hundested and the fjords

Chapter Twenty-One

LILY MEETS THE VIKINGS

Over the horizon, a large orange-and-yellow striped sail came into view. Billowing in the breeze, it grew larger to reveal, beneath the great square of cloth, a long, thin hull with a sharply raked bow and stern. It looked threatening.

"Quick, make haste," Roger shouted as he guided *Lily* around the treacherous Lyænas Sands. Buster whimpered and gazed around. "The Vikings are coming; we'll be plundered if we don't escape!" The ship, *Sea Stallion,* was, at the time, the largest replica Viking longboat and a star, having appeared in numerous film and television dramas. It had also made an incredible journey under its own steam – well, a team of rowers, to be more precise – from Roskilde Fjord, where it had been constructed, to Dublin. We had escaped the Vikings on this occasion but would have further encounters with them.

As *Lily* entered Roskilde Fjord, she was greeted by harbour porpoises and smacks of moon jellyfish so dense I thought they would bar her way. It was clear, blue and beautiful, a perfect summer's day to enter the shallower depths of home waters. As familiar landmarks came into view, my emotions stirred; the constant concern for Buster's health, the months of planning, juggling of day jobs

*Lily on Roskilde Fjord,
our home waters*

and boating, battling weather and sea conditions had taken their toll. All the hard work would now pay off. I was exhausted and looking forward to welcoming a period of calm into our lives.

"This is it," I said to Roger. "I can't believe we've made it home."

"I know," he replied, "Little old *Lily* from Nottingham on Roskilde Fjord: totally unbelievable." Yet there on Roskilde Fjord we were, all of us together; how it should be. The Admiral had seen us safely home.

At Roskilde, crowds flocked around *Lily*. We had become used to receptions such as these and, at first, they had been fun. Over time, though, the novelty had worn off and even Buster managed to develop a thoroughly disinterested look in a vain attempt to stall questions.

"I wish I had a recording of all the answers; then I wouldn't have to keep saying the same thing," sighed Roger, after going through the standard list for the umpteenth time.

"I think I'll scream if someone else asks, 'Is this a traditional British narrow boat?'"

Motorbikes and vintage cars arrived for a weekly gathering, bringing with them many enthusiasts, amongst them a couple of local characters with beer cans in hand. Buster took to them and they stayed for the evening, chatting about life in general. We were visited by some of Roger's work colleagues, keen to see the strange-looking boat which had made it to Denmark. Pushing through the crowds came a fresh-faced, blonde-haired man, full of questions but not the usual ones. He wanted to know how *Lily* handled at sea, her weight, more about her hull and build design; it made a refreshing change to the Danes' favourite, "How much would a boat like this cost?" His name was Ture and he was one of the Roskilde Viking Ship Museum's chief boat builders and restorers; no wonder he had been interested in *Lily*'s design. He invited Roger to spend a day with him, working on the Gislinge Project, established to reconstruct a small Viking ship from the twelfth century. Roger eagerly accepted and joined Ture and his team working with 180-year-old oak. Using traditional methods, each piece of wood in the clinker-style hull had to be painstakingly *The Roskilde Viking Ship Museum*

measured, hand-cut or cleaved then fitted using nails produced on site to form the body of the boat. At the end of the day, the ground was littered in oak off-cuts and shards, which we were permitted to collect; they would come in handy over the winter, fuelling *Lily*'s stove.

Slap, step. Slap, step. Slap, step. I heard Roger coming along the quay. I did not have to turn around.

"Your foot is getting worse. You'll have to go to the doctors."

"It really hurts today." He let himself into the boat, fumbled around taking his sock off and gave his foot a rub. Buster thought Roger was preparing for a game and snatched at it. "Ouch, Buzzy, that was my toe."

"He didn't mean it. He wants a game. Go on, play the sock game with him." Roger went below decks, knelt on the floor and began whirling the sock around his body. Buster chased after it as if it were a rabbit.

After weeks of doctors' appointments, seeing specialists, numerous x-rays and scans, a hairline fracture was found in Roger's foot. In the same place as the break all those years previously, it had caused a condition known as 'drop foot'. There was no plaster cast; instead, a leg brace and pair of clogs which needed to be worn for the next year.

"I'm not wearing clogs."

"Pity we're not still in the Netherlands; you wouldn't have felt so silly," I laughed but Roger did not think it was funny. Both the leg brace and the clogs would hamper our boating. Thank goodness we had made it home. "How do you think you broke it?"

"I don't know, unless it was when I dodged Buster with the lawnmower."

Buster silently slunk off.

At Jyllinge, we enquired about a winter berth. Buster loved the surroundings and he could ride in the wheelbarrows provided for crews to transport their baggage around the marina. He had a soft spot for the rides after Dad introduced him to them from an early age at animal farm. If it was decided to overwinter in Denmark, Jyllinge would be ideal, especially with Buster in mind, and not just because of the wheelbarrows. I could see he would be happy here. There was a short, circular walk, ideal for colder days, and I knew it would be inspirational for me too. The views across the fjord to the small islands of Eskilsø and Lilleø, the well-kept grounds, good restaurant and take-away on site, shops a ten-minute walk away all contributed to this being the perfect place for *Lily* to spend winter.

Most of the summer was spent on Roskilde Fjord. We harbour-hopped our way around, took trips on the RIB and spent nights at anchor. *Lily* became quite a Viking herself, attracting as much attention as the longboats. At Frederickssund, we walked with Buster along the water's edge, where the large blue discs of the wild chicory flowers danced in the breeze, to the Viking village and open-air theatre, sometimes watching Nordic sagas being acted out. Frederikssund was the closest port to our house; it made a pleasant change having *Lily* nearby.

Frederiksværk was known as the City of Steel. It sat close to the entrance of the fjord, allowing large freighters to enter the factory site and transport steel plates by water. The fishmongers situated in Frederiksværk Harbour was always busy, displaying a massive selection of both smoked and wet fish. Herrings were plentiful and cheap; they became a delicious lunchtime treat, fried gently in olive oil until the skins crisped, eaten with great hunks of freshly baked bread spread thickly with butter. Seafood platters of smoked salmon steaks with prawns, crab and lobster became a succulent extravagance. Roger was always keen to try the more unusual produce on display, although he drew the line at weaver fish fillets, despite the fishmonger singing its praises. Somehow something that sported poisonous spines in its fins did not come across as being particularly appetising, either with or without them. On one occasion, he chose smoked lamprey, which I found totally disgusting and even Roger had to admit was not one of his best choices. Buster, however, thought differently, tucking into the unexpected treat with great gusto.

Buster excitedly tore open his birthday present containing a fluffy, pink, squeaky elephant and a bag of tasty pigs' ears. After all the excitement, he stepped onto the jetty to lie in the warmth, happy and content. A few hours later, we drove to his favourite beach and walked along the sands, paddling and throwing stones. Buster followed Roger into the depths.

"Best put his lead on; I think he wants a swim," I suggested.

"I doubt it; he hasn't been swimming since he fell in the Soar all those years ago." But Roger leant down and fastened Buster's extending lead onto his collar. Buster swam all the way around Roger's knees before emerging on shore to shake himself, covering me in a fine spray of cool salt water.

Later in the day, we returned home and lit the barbecue, ensuring there was an extra sausage on the grill for our boy's special day.

"Twelve years old. Who would have thought it?" Roger ruffled the back of Buster's neck. "Perhaps he will make thirteen now?" I hardly dared hope that he would. There had been a time when I did not think Buster would make double figures but he had proved me wrong on many occasions. Roger seemed convinced Buster was going to live forever, or at least a few more years, but something deep inside told me not to build hopes, to enjoy each

day I had left with him. Perhaps it was because I had grown up with animals, seen plenty of them grow old, or maybe I was more in tune with Buster. After all, almost every minute of my day was spent with him. But as the days passed, I was tricked; that little glimmer of hope began to edge in and I too began to think Buster would make his next birthday.

Buster waits patiently for
a barbecued sausage on
his twelfth birthday

Chapter Twenty-Two

THE ANCHORAGE

There was no room for *Lily* in the small harbour on the island of Orø. It was growing late and somewhere needed to be found before darkness fell. Venturing into the neighbouring Isefjord late in the day, and on a weekend, had proved a stupid move; we should have known better. The only option was to anchor overnight.

As the sun slowly began to sink behind a rise of lush meadows and golden wheat fields, I eased *Lily* into a beautiful anchorage, weaved her through a handful of gently bobbing yachts, picked my spot and called to Roger, standing at the bow, "Let's stop here." He gave me the thumbs up and released *Lily*'s anchor. It rattled away for a few moments as it plunged into the depths, the sound clearly audible over the engine.

"Back up," shouted Roger. I followed his instructions until he was happy *Lily* could swing safely and securely. Buster gave me a squeak; I lifted him down from the chart table and removed his life jacket. He trotted out of the wheelhouse door and dropped down on his side. Grumbling under his breath, he began shimmying his way around the boat; Buster back buffer working its magic, making *Lily*'s cream-coloured bodywork shine in the setting sun.

Roger set up the barbecue. I had recently purchased a new metal support to hold disposable ones that bolted onto *Lily*'s hand rails and I was eager to try it out. Buster watched in quiet anticipation as sausages sizzled and cooked, sending flavourful smoke curling up into the darkening sky.

The next morning dawned bright and warm; the sun streamed through the windows, creating flickering reflections on the ceiling. It was the perfect day for doing not much at all and that was the plan: a relaxing day, doing odd jobs, taking in the views and catching up on some reading. Days such as these were rare.

We ferried Buster back and forth in the RIB when a walk or toilet break was required. A tiny fishing harbour on the mainland

The boys enjoy a paddle and a quiet moment together on the pebble beach at Ejby on the Isefjord

provided shore access for Buster, who seemed to relish the trips, standing at the bow, his paws on the tubes and ears flapping uncontrollably in the speed-induced breeze. Walks along the waterfront, pretty cottages with rambling roses, paddling in the pebbly bay, watching yachts on the fjord dodging the Holbæk to Orø ferry: all snippets of a happy day.

The clean washing fluttered lightly in the breeze as *Lily* rocked gently at anchor. Buster revelled in having deck freedom and lounged all over *Lily*, only moving into the wheelhouse when the midday sun became too hot. He snored contentedly from wherever he lay as I became engrossed in a book and Roger varnished the rear cabin portholes.

The gentle hum of an approaching outboard motor caused me to look up to see an elderly man in a small, open fishing boat. He pulled alongside *Lily* and spoke to Roger about fishing on the fjord. Later that afternoon, he returned, bringing some small flat fish from his day's catch, gutted and prepared, ready for cooking. When the journalist Kate Adie published her autobiography, she entitled it *The Kindness of Strangers*. Over the years, the actions of waterway folk had given me reason to think of that title on many occasions and I was reminded of it yet again by the old gentleman of the sea. That evening, Roger cut the fish into small strips: dipped in batter and shallow fried to make goujons, they were served with a side salad and Danish remoulade. It was divine and Buster – who, of course, had a little taster – thought so too.

Something had woken me from a deep sleep although it was still and silent, eerily so. I went into the wheelhouse and the sight which met me took my breath away. The darkness of the night sky had been shamefully banished into the background, drowned out by hundreds, thousands, millions of stars. I had seen spectacular night skies before but this was like no other; it was as if a jar of glitter had been carelessly strewn across the black velvet backdrop. I opened the door and stepped onto the cool deck; high above *Lily*, a shooting star sped through the sky in a relentless plummet. I was spellbound; the beauty of the night had me captivated. I recalled the words of my late nan, "When you see a shooting star, turn around three times and make a wish." A bit dangerous on deck but, nevertheless, I did it anyway and never told a living soul what I wished for on that special night.

Some hours later, I was woken again; this time it was evident what had caused the disruption; the wind was howling and the anchor chain thumped as *Lily* took a hit from a powerful gust. I rose and peered out the nearest porthole. The beautiful, star-strewn sky had been replaced by low cloud; had it all been a dream? *Lily* was holding so I slipped back into bed but did not sleep well, getting up a further three times throughout the night to check.

I felt Roger jump out of bed in a panic and opened my eyes to find it was daylight. The wind was still howling but had subsided a little.

"She's alright. I've been up several times to check," I told him.

"I don't recognise where we are." Roger was gazing through the porthole and sounded confused. "Shit, we're in trouble," he yelled, rushing towards the wheelhouse. Buster groaned and rolled over on the bed until diagonally across it, taking up as much room as possible, pushing me out in the process.

"It's alright, Buzz, you can have the bed. I'm getting up to see what all the fuss is about." Roger was right: the anchor must have slipped and the wind was pushing *Lily* broadside towards the shore. Was that why the Admiral had given me a push?

By the time I reached the helm, Roger was out on deck preparing the RIB in case it was needed to tow *Lily*. I turned on the instrument panel. We had not set the anchor slip alarm the night before but there was no time for recrimination as the depth sounder showed we were in just three feet of water. *Lily* was alright but fast action was needed; the wind was continuing to push her into shallower water. Through the howling wind, I shouted, "I can drive her out; there's enough depth."

"Start her up but don't put her in gear. I'll try to haul her with the anchor winch first; we need to get the bow round." Buster appeared and squeaked; he wanted to go ashore and do his business.

"Buzz, I'm afraid you'll have to wait. We're in big trouble. Be a good boy." I lifted him up and placed him on the seat behind me, from where he could see what was going on, hoping that would be enough to take his mind off things.

Roger winched away for what seemed an eternity. When he shouted to move *Lily* forwards, I gently knocked her into gear, the brass accelerator handle cool beneath my sweaty palm. She edged forwards a short distance. I heard a clonk and she stalled. I took her out of gear and yelled over the wind to Roger, who was yelling at me to keep going. I tried again and the same thing happened. *Lily* was not aground; it had to be something around the prop. Roger continued winching – back and forth in long, wide movements – and, very slowly, *Lily* inched forwards. Buster was becoming desperate, his squeaking growing louder. I felt dreadful for him but there was nothing I could do.

"Turn the wheel right round to port as far as it goes and try again," Roger yelled. I reluctantly fired up the engine, afraid of doing more damage, and went through the same routine. This time *Lily* kept running but, from the way the steering felt, I knew something was wrong. As the bow began to straighten, I watched the depth sounder flashing up increasing numbers and began to feel better; soon it was reading double figures.

"Stop her there." Roger looked exhausted and windswept but again began pumping the winch, winding *Lily* in. With the anchor finally up and Roger back in the wheelhouse, I quickly explained there was something wrong. He took the helm and gave the wheel a jiggle, "You must have freed it; she seems alright now." Buster whined, a long pitiful cry, and we both looked at him with deep concern. "Right, Buzzy, your turn now." Roger gave him a gentle ear tug, then rushed below decks to get some clothes on!

I motored *Lily* towards the tiny harbour to make Roger's trip in the RIB as short as possible and, at the same time, got Buster into his life jacket. A few minutes later, the boys were heading off at speed, jumping the choppy waves and heading for dry land, whilst I made a couple of turns of the bay. I was not worried by being alone at the helm but conditions were not good and, despite Roger's assurance that all was well, I was not convinced. Turning *Lily* to port, her steering stiffened. I fought to get her round and, when I eventually did, she seemed sluggish.

Buster was in full cry as Roger brought the RIB in against *Lily*'s side. With toilet issues out of the way, he wanted his breakfast.

"He's got the wind up his tail today, hasn't he?" I tried to help Buster on board. He dismissed my help, jumped by himself, pushing past me and heading for the galley.

395

"You're telling me! He was like a mad thing on shore, darting about like something possessed." Roger hauled himself out of the RIB. Once secure on tow, Roger took the helm and I went to feed the hungry hound, who was barking in outrage at discovering his breakfast had not been served.

We had only been underway for five minutes when *Lily*'s engine stalled. I immediately rushed into the wheelhouse, where Roger was now convinced something was around the prop. Outside, conditions had worsened; not only was *Lily* drifting; she was uncontrollably bouncing around in open water.

"I'll have to drop anchor and take a look." The wind fought with *Lily* but the anchor held firm. I stayed at the helm as Roger began a lengthy clearance of the propeller. *Lily* had become entangled with a mooring buoy; its rope, floating buoy and metal pole with flag indicator were wound tightly around the propeller shaft, its weight dragging somewhere out of sight below her hull. How on earth *Lily* had managed to move, let alone pull, the whole contraption along for a few miles beggared belief.

A couple of hours later, *Lily* glided into the harbour on the island of Orø. It was Monday; the weekend boaters had vanished, leaving it empty. Buster with his full breakfast tummy had slept on the sofa, oblivious to the clearing of the prop, waking only at the drop of revs from *Lily*'s engine as I turned to moor her against the quay.

Buster had taken up his newly found comfort spot in the wheelhouse and, with the door open, dozed, watching the Holbæk ferry arrive and depart at regular intervals throughout the day. We had been on Orø a few days, blessed with fine weather, but, watching gathering storm clouds from the shelter of the wheelhouse, could see that was about to change.

It grew darker and rain began to fall — slow, large, heavy droplets, releasing the evocative smell of petrichor. I expected Buster to move but he remained still and sleepy in his bed as the odd raindrop fell on his head. Suddenly, a flash of lightning and a great roar of thunder triggered a violent downpour. I rushed below decks to shut windows whilst Roger hurried outside to pack away the fold-up bicycle used to reach the local supermarket earlier that morning. Returning to the wheelhouse, Buster was in the same spot, still sound asleep.

I reached past him to close the door. He opened his eyes and gave me a look which seemed to say, 'What on earth are you doing, shutting the door?' Gently, I stroked his head. "Are you alright, Buzzy boy?" He was soaking wet but I do not think he had realised, so deep had been his sleep.

Back on Roskilde Fjord, rough, windswept weather drove us into Lynæs harbour. Despite tucking *Lily* behind larger vessels, she was still bouncing about.

"This is awful." I was trying to prepare our evening meal but, without a view of the horizon, was beginning to feel queasy.

"Tell you what," said Roger. "Let's take the train home tomorrow and collect the car. Then we can please ourselves, Buzz can have time in the garden and we'll check back on *Lily* in the evening."

Early the next morning, we walked into Hundested to catch the train. Buster had not been on one since visiting the Christmas market in Germany so when I sang out, "Choo choo, come on, Buzzy, come on, Buzzy, choo choo," he was beside himself. He lifted his nose off the ground, held his tail high and swished it from side to side in great sweeps as he trotted along. As the train trundled into the station, Buster's eyes shone with excitement; he was eager to get on and have a snuffle around the compartment before settling down to watch the countryside flash by.

Chapter Twenty-Three

ADRIFT

With my parents due to make their first visit to Denmark, I wanted to take them on the small ferry that crossed Roskilde Fjord. On the way back to the house, we decided to give it a dummy run. Buster was no stranger to ferry travel. He walked around the deck and sat with his nose facing into the wind, letting it gently lift his large, floppy ears and breathing in deeply, feeling through scent the world around him.

"Will you take a photo of me with Buzz?" I pushed my camera into Roger's hand. He was not a keen photographer and I always had to coax him into it. Buster snuggled between my legs for the shot, his body beautifully warm against my skin.

Disembarking in Kulhuse, Roger pulled the car over. "Come on, let's take Buzzy for a quick paddle." It was an unexpected stop, one which had Buster quivering and squeaking as I tried to unfasten his car harness. He ran back and forth on the beach, stuck his nose into the warm water rock pools and paddled out as far as his extended lead would allow. Up to his tummy in the water, he stopped and looked back at us both. It was a deep look; he tilted his head and his eyes twinkled but he held the gaze. It seemed he was taking in every last detail about us. Roger and I waited, watching him, laughing, then I reached into

my pocket, pulled out a treat and the moment was broken as he rushed towards me, sending sea water splashing.

On the car ferry, MF Columbus crossing Roskilde Fjord from Sølager to Kulhuse

When we turned to head back along the beach, I thought Buster looked tired but he walked happily alongside Roger, still wading in and out, enjoying the coolness of the water.

A lovely evening followed; we barbecued whilst Buster sat in his camping chair, relaxing into his chin-strap-woey position and eagerly awaiting his own chargrilled sausage. At the end of the meal, we toasted marshmallows and, as an extra-special treat, Buster had his own, which he greedily licked off the plate, its long, sticky tendrils catching on his muzzle, tickling and sticking to his face. It was late by the time we returned to *Lily* but, with little planned for the following day, I put a film on to watch. Buster curled up around the back of my legs on the sofa; at home, warm and snug, he was soon fast asleep.

We were woken by a loud moan and jumped out of bed to find Buster sprawled on the floor. I knew he was in trouble: his tongue hung out one side of his mouth, his gums were extremely pale and the light in his eyes was fading, bodily systems shutting down. He had been sick and had defecated. I stroked his face and gently spoke to him, told him it would be alright. Roger rushed about cleaning up and helped me gently swing Buster away from the mess on the rug.

"We need to get him to Charlotte," Roger shouted, rushing down the harbour for the car as fast as he could with a broken foot.

Inside *Lily*, a strange kind of hush descended. I dressed quickly and spoke in whispers to Buster, trying to keep him calm. I heard the car reversing furiously along the harbour wall. Buster heard it too and made a slight movement.

"Daddy's coming." Buster lifted his head towards me and gave me one of his sometime-smiles.

A few moments later, Roger was descending the stairs. "It's alright, puppy," he said. On hearing him, Buster lifted his head right around as if he was desperate to catch a glimpse of his dad. For a moment, I thought he was going to try and get up; instead, he attempted to wag his tail but could only lift it slightly off the floor. Roger leant down, stroked Buster gently then scooped him up in his arms and, with him held tightly against his body, began to climb the steps into the wheelhouse. Looking over Roger's shoulder, Buster met my gaze then took one last look around and relaxed, safe in his daddy's arms.

I made a swift grab for Buster's faithful old bed before following them. Roger had left the car directly outside the wheelhouse and I bundled into the back seat and flung open the opposite door. Roger leant in and gently laid Buster into his bed next to me. He sank deeply into it, looking snug and secure. He was breathing very slowly. Wrapping my arms around him, I bent down and whispered in his ear, "I wonder what adventures await the puppy today." Then we were off in a mad rush, weaving and dodging lobster pots and bundles of fishing nets strewn along the quayside. Roger called Charlotte as we raced along the empty, early-morning roads. Buster was fighting for breath; we were five minutes into the journey and I knew we would not make it.

The golden sun was beginning to rise over the newly harvested wheat fields; low-lying mists swirled and eddied and I thought, what a beautiful day to die. As I talked quietly to Buster, hugging and stroking him, he took a few more gasps then, as far as I could tell, was gone. I waited. Roger drove on. I thought Buster moved so I waited a little longer but realised it was the movement of the car. I leant down; Buster's fur brushed my cheek but I could not feel him breathing. We needed to stop.

"You need to say goodbye, Rogie. He's gone," I whispered and the tears started to fall and the hurt began to rip at my heart. Roger turned the car onto country lanes shrouded in golden light and pulled over. What followed were precious, private moments; we tried not to be sad because, if there was such a thing, Buster's death was a good one, yet we found ourselves drowning in uncontrollable grief, set adrift on a raging sea of emotions.

I thought of Charlotte, waiting anxiously. She would be growing concerned over the time we were taking to reach her.

"We need to get to the vet's," I whispered. Reluctantly, we drove on in silence, knowing there was nothing she could do for our beloved boy.

I could not bear to stay in Lynæs any longer. I hated the place; it was full of bad memories. *Lily* was not the same without the patter of Buster's paws on her deck and it was time to move on; time for *Lily* to undertake her first voyage without her Admiral. We were not going far – to the next harbour of Frederiksværk – where Buster had celebrated his twelfth birthday just ten days before he died.

In the days and weeks which followed, inconsolable in grief, all our boating plans faded into oblivion. Messages and cards flooded in from all over the world and it was only then I realised Buster had touched many more hearts than just Roger's and mine. Much-appreciated support was received from family, friends, groups and associations, in particular the WOBs, my fellow lady boaters, who were phenomenal.

I was unaware of the Norse legend about the Rainbow Bridge and, when it was sent to me by a WOB, shortly after Buster's death, it immediately became an important part of his story. In Norse mythology, the Rainbow Bridge connected this world to the next; when a faithful pet died, he went to lush green meadows at the foot of the bridge. There he was cured of any illness or disease that may have blighted his life and could enjoy warm, sunny days, plenty of food and water and play with other animals. Until, one day, whilst running through the fields, something caused him to stop and sniff the air; a familiar smell had come to mind. Glancing around, he saw his owner and ran towards him. Reunited forever, they crossed the Rainbow Bridge together.

I have taken comfort in the legend and know other dog owners who have done the same. Rainbows have become known as Buzzy-bows and, whenever one is seen, I am reminded of my constant companion: not only the Admiral of our ship but the dog who saved my life and gave me reason to live.

A few days later, we awoke early and sat in the wheelhouse with our morning mugs of tea. There was not a lot to say; the sky was threatening and a smudge of a rainbow was rising out of the Jægerspris shore. The distant rumble of thunder began to grow closer and then the rain, unable to contain itself any longer, spilled forth to join the tears running down my

Rainbow over Roskilde Fjord

face. The rainbow grew, stretched across the waters of Roskilde Fjord to arc over the barge and join the shore at Fredericksværk. The thunder was now deafening. Roger and I looked at each other and smiled through the tears.

"Do you know what I think?" I managed to blurt out through my sobs.

"Yes, I know." Roger nodded his head.

"Buster has his new legs and is galloping towards the Rainbow Bridge."

We listened to our boy thunder across the meadows and knew in our hearts that he was alright.

Epilogue

SOME MONTHS LATER

I awake, having dreamt or imagined the warmth of Buster against my arm. It only takes the briefest of moments for reality to kick in and immediately the tears begin to fall. The last few months have been filled with every emotion possible. Sadness and loneliness have taken over the place which Buster used to fill; my constant companions are darkness and guilt. Guilt that perhaps I could have done more for Buster, that boating was too much for him in his later years, but then, in amongst the very darkness of these feelings, I recall the final moments of his life. Buster was not sad to be leaving; his job was complete. Now it is up to me to show him I can cope. He taught me so much – to look forward, not be afraid of adventure and that it is alright to just follow your instincts, no matter what others think.

There it is again: that familiar feeling of warmth, followed by a nuzzle. My fingers are being prised apart by a warm, wet tongue and a cold nose. Then there is a muffled yap and a minuscule growl.

"Maksimillian, what are you doing?" I question in a sing-song tone and a plump Beagle puppy jumps onto my tummy, licking my salty tears away and nibbling my chin.

"Oh, Maksi, don't do that." Squirming and laughing, I prise the wriggling bundle away. Holding him above my body, I look deep into his brown eyes and say, "I wonder what adventures await the puppy today," then hug him to my chest.

From the galley, Roger calls, "It's about time you two were awake. I've got a brew on and the weather's looking good."

On the chart table alongside Buster's tatty old bed, lined with a soft blanket especially for *Lily*'s new crew member, lies a plotted course for Sweden. It will be hard to finally cruise out of Roskilde Fjord but I cannot help wondering if Maksimillian will have what it takes to rise through the ranks of seadog to become an Admiral. I guess only time will tell …

*Lily's newest crew member –
Sweet Courage Maksimillian,
courtesy of Per Hergott Petersen*

Barge Art

It is believed that narrowboat crews of old painted their craft in bright colours to add cheer to the mundane work of the British Victorian era and to provide a means of escape from the industrial age. Romantic scenes of far-away places featuring castles, churches and lighthouses standing alongside winding waterways were interspersed with everyday sights, in particular: wild flowers, such as roses, daises, forget-me-nots and pansies. Over time, this unique form of British folk art became more commonly known as 'Roses and Castles.'

Whilst the true origins of barge art have been lost in the mists of time, it does bear a resemblance to Eastern European and Scandinavian folk art. Others, however, believe it stems from the Romany gypsy, who decorated their horse-drawn caravans in a similar style.

The decorative barge art in this book is a nod to those narrowboat crews of the past and to the artists keeping the tradition alive today and is for all those who dare to dream of far-away places.

Contact The Author

If you enjoyed reading this book, the best way to show the author your appreciation is by please leaving a review on Amazon.

I hope you will join my mailing list http://eepurl.com/di6xC5 so you can be amongst the first to hear about my future books. I would also love to hear your feedback about the book or to answer any questions you may have. Do please get in touch with me by:

Website: www.alisonalderton.com
Facebook: www.facebook.com/lilyandthebargebeagles
Instagram: www.instagram.com/lilyandthebargebeagles
Email: alison.alderton@mail.com

If you enjoy memoirs, I recommend you visit the Facebook group We Love Memoirs to chat with me and other authors there:

www.facebook.com/groups/welovememoirs

I look forward to hearing from you.

Alison Alderton

Beagle Welfare

Thank you for purchasing this book; a donation will be made to Beagle Welfare for every copy sold.

The Beagle Welfare Scheme

Registered Charity in England and Wales No 328633
Registered address: Coulters Hill Cottage, Pipey Lane,
Newborough, Staffordshire DE13 8SJ
Tel +44 (0) 1283 575175
www.beaglewelfare.org.uk

About Beagle Welfare

The Beagle Welfare Scheme was founded in 1979 as an initiative by the committee of the Beagle Association. At the time, many breeders were concerned about the problem of pedigree dogs flooding general rescue organisations. It made sense for breed clubs to take the lead – after all, who better to deal with pedigree dogs than those who spend their lives with them?

Beagle Welfare developed as an autonomous organisation with supporters all over the country and a budget of several thousand pounds. It continued to maintain close links with the breed clubs and, in 1990, became a registered charity. Not only is charitable status beneficial to Beagle Welfare but it also provides safeguards for the people who generously donate money to help the hounds.

The main aims of Beagle Welfare are:

- The prevention of maltreatment and cruelty to Beagles and to encourage responsible ownership of Beagles throughout Great Britain
- To rehome Beagles whose owners are unable to do so
- To provide advice and guidance to Beagle owners
- To encourage responsible practices in the breeding of Beagles throughout Great Britain.

Today, nearly four decades since its foundation, Beagle Welfare has an extensive network of dedicated supporters and volunteers, including a board of trustees, area officers, fosterers, home checkers and the always-essential fundraisers. With their help, the charity rehomes around 300 Beagles a year – a figure that can only increase in line with the growing popularity of the breed.

The Beagle Welfare Rehoming Centre

In the spring of 2011, Beagle Welfare signed the lease on a two-acre property in the Staffordshire countryside. The centre cares for unwanted Beagles until suitable new homes are found and, as a single-breed rescue centre, the specific needs of the Beagles can be met.

Most of the hounds live sociably together in log cabins; they benefit from living with, and learning from, each other. Dogs that live this way adjust more quickly than those housed in individual kennels. Troubled souls gain confidence and the naughty ones learn how to behave!

Thanks to generous fundraising, donations, legacies and grants, the centre has a fully equipped washroom where the hounds can be spruced up and given any veterinary treatment required. Outside they have a paddock with toys, equipment and an obstacle course to keep them amused and for bad weather there is an indoor play area. In addition, the centre boasts a reception cabin where potential adopters can meet Beagles in a relaxed, homely atmosphere and watch the Beagle Welfare DVD *Taking Your Beagle Home*.

Adopting from Beagle Welfare

Beagle Welfare is meticulous in ensuring all Beagles in its care go to suitable homes. Potential new owners have to complete an 'application to adopt' form and must be prepared for a home-check visit. There is full information on the adoption process on the website.

The website is full of information about Beagles and Beagle Welfare and also features the rehoming list, giving brief details of all the hounds that are waiting for new homes.

Visit: www.beaglewelfare.org.uk

Jackie Williamson
Trustee, The Beagle Welfare Scheme

Jackie Williamson and her Beagle Harry

Acknowledgements

There are many people who have helped shape our story to whom I owe thanks.

Firstly, to my dear Buster, the Admiral who gave me a reason to wake up each morning, filled my life with love and smiles on even the darkest of days. I miss you each and every day.

Doug and Wendy Hall of Cliffmere Beagles for entrusting Roger and me with Buster in the first place, for staying in touch over the years and remaining approachable, helpful and interested in our life with their puppy. Also to Wendy for being one of my foreword authors.

Brian Cassells, for his encouragement, kind words and taking the time to write a foreword.

Mum and Dad, for allowing me the freedom to live my life differently from others and travel extensively.

Keith Woodcock, for waiting patiently and making dreams come true.

Hilary Harris and her family, for the Halcyon Days, for love, laughter, friendship and some of my fondest memories of Buster.

The encouragers, supporters and readers of early drafts including Mark Boyter, Carole Erdmond Grant, Jackie Parry and Steve Wait.

My editor, for always remaining approachable and supportive, helping to manipulate Buster's story into shape whilst always remaining totally aware and respectful of fragile emotions along the way. Your dedication and professionalism to this project are much appreciated.

Wendy Dalton, for giving Buster his 'sometimes-smile'.

Erik Thomassen, for initial help with the artwork and ongoing web support at www.alisonalderton.com.

Edith Gelin, talented illustrator and friend, for allowing her artwork to be reproduced.

Jackie Williamson and the team at Beagle Welfare, totally devoted to Beagles and working tirelessly to provide better lives for those hounds in need.

The words from the Beagle Standard, "The man with the lead in his hand and no dog in sight owns a Beagle," remain the copyright of The Kennel Club Limited and are reproduced with their kind permission.

The boating associations, clubs and organisations who have made life afloat such a wonderful experience. The publications featuring our extensive travels and all the people we have met along the way – you have all helped shape Buster's story and our lives.

There were many vets over the years, in many countries, but special thanks must go to those in Denmark: to Charlotte for her ongoing care and referral to Claus, who without doubt gave us two extra years with Buster. Always on our wavelength, honest and caring even after Buster's passing, how can Roger and I ever thank you?

Everyone who took the time to send us comforting messages following Buster's death. We had no idea he had touched so many hearts.

To Per and Karen from Sweet Courage Beagles, who unknowingly helped us to rebuild our broken hearts.

Roger, thank you for everything, for being supportive and trusting in me, encouraging and always striving to put back my lost confidence, belief and self-worth. Without you, there would have been no Buster, no *Lily*, no travels. I owe you everything and you are my everything.

Dutch Barge *Lily*, for carrying us safely along rivers, canals, lakes and across seas. For being our safe haven, home afloat and provider of adventures extraordinaire.

And finally, little Maksimillian, for showing both Roger and me the way through heart-crushing loss.

Glossary

Accommodation bridge	bridge providing access to land either side of the canal
Aegir	tidal bore that flows upriver on a strong, incoming tide
Anode	sacrificial metal used to protect submersed steel parts of a boat from corrosion
Boat Safety Certificate	inspection certificate for boats that comply to British safety regulations
Bow	front of a boat
Bow thruster	propeller in a tube mounted across the bow below water level to aid sideways manoeuvering
Burgee	small flag
BWB	British Waterways Board
Cill	raised portion of the floor of a lock chamber, forming a stop against which the lock gates bear when they are shut
Comastic	coal tar pitch vinyl resin thixotropic coating with anti-corrosive and water-repellent properties used for painting onto steel hulls
Crannóg	artificial island built in a lake. They are some of the oldest dwelling places, dating from prehistoric times
Cratch	soft cover over the forward cockpit of a narrowboat,

	based on a solid or glazed triangular cratch-board which is supported from the cabin-top by a top plank
Cut	another name for a canalised section of waterway
Depth sounder	digital device which reads the depth of water beneath the hull
Dumb barge	barge without means of self-propulsion
Ensign	flag flown on the stern of a boat indicating the country of registry
ETA	Estimated time of arrival
Fast-cat	high-speed, twin-hulled ferry
Fly boats	see packet boats
Flybridge	open deck on a cruiser, located on the cabin roof and usually having a duplicate set of control equipment
Fresh	excess flood water above the normal river level
GOBA	Great Ouse Boating Association
Gongoozler	person who watches boats and boaters
Gunnels	top edge of side deck
Halyard	rope for raising or lowering a sail or flag
Helm	steering position of a boat
Hull	lower body of the boat generally from the gunnels down to the keel
ICC	International Certificate of Competence is an internationally recognised boating qualification accepted in many, but not all, countries
IWA	Inland Waterways Association is an association protecting the interests of navigable inland waterways in Great Britain
IWAI	Inland Waterways Association of Ireland is an association protecting the interests of navigable inland waterways in Ireland
Keel	lowest member of a boat, similar to a spine
Lock	chamber with upper and lower gates capable of raising boats up and down to overcome a significant change in water level
Lock key	also known as a windlass; device for opening the paddles of a lock

Packet boats	fast, passenger-carrying vessels, also known as fly boats
Paddle-wheel effect	sideways motion imparted to the boat by the rotation of the propeller blades when forward motion is retarded. Sometimes called 'prop walk', which is an accurate description of the action
Painter	rope attached to the bow of a tender or dinghy
Péniche	French steel motorised river barge of 350 tons
Penn	to pass through a lock
Pound	section of canal between locks
Puddling	clay and sand mixed with water and used as a watertight lining for canals
RIB	rigid-inflatable boat
Staunch	gated pass in a weir through which, historically, boats were usually winched
Stern	rear of a boat
SSR	Small Ships Register is a listing for small boats from the UK
Tabernacle	partly open socket or double post on a boat's deck into which a mast is fixed, with a pivot so the mast can be lowered to pass under bridges
Tack	to change course by turning the bow into and through the wind, bringing the wind to the opposite side
Tell-tale	fine jet of water expelled through an outlet in the hull of the boat indicating water is flowing freely through the cooling system
Tjalk	type of Dutch barge with a curved bluff bow
Towpath	walkway alongside a waterway, derived from the days when boats were either man-hauled or towed by horse
Tupperware boat	derogatory term for a glass-fibre boat
Wind	to turn a boat around to face opposite direction, often wind-assisted, hence 'wind'
Windlass	see lock key